D1607645

STRATEGIC USES OF PUBLIC POLICY

Business and Government in the Progressive Era

Donna J. Wood
Graduate School of Business
University of Pittsburgh

Pitman Publishing Inc.

A Longman Inc. Company

Pitman Publishing Inc.
1020 Plain Street
Marshfield, Ma. 02050

A Longman Inc. Company
95 Church St.
White Plains, NY 10601

Associated Companies
Longman Group Ltd., London
Copp Clark Pitman, Toronto
Longman Cheshire Pty., Melbourne
Longman Paul Pty., Auckland

© **1986 Donna J. Wood**

Library of Congress Cataloging-in-Publication Data

Wood, Donna, 1949–
    Strategic uses of public policy.

    Bibliography: p.
    Includes index.
    1. Food law and legislation — United States — History. 2. Drugs
— Law and legislation — United States — History. 3. Food industry
and trade — Government policy — United States — History. 4.
Drug trade — Government policy — United States — History.
I. Title.
KF3869.W65   1985   344.73′0423   85-16996
ISBN 0-273-02439-6   347.304423

Manufactured in the United States of America
10   9   8   7   6   5   4   3   2   1

PITMAN SERIES IN BUSINESS AND PUBLIC POLICY

CONSULTING EDITOR
EDWIN M. EPSTEIN
University of California, Berkeley

CURRENT BOOKS IN THE SERIES:

Table of Contents

Contents

List of Tables

List of Figures

Preface

Making strategic use of public policy — businesses' attempts to secure competitive advantage through the powers of government — has
a surprisingly long and distinguished history in the U.S. For almost
a century, businesses have sought to use their local, state, and federal
governments to gain competitive advantage in the marketplace. This
book explores some of the antecedents of strategic business–government relations, through a case study of the interests, issues, and actors involved in the passage of the 1906 Pure Food Act.

This book applies the theory of strategic uses of regulation to a
case that is seen almost universally as a measure exclusively for consumer protection. Wasn't the Pure Food and Drug Act intended to
put an end to the widespread adulteration of foods and medicines at
the turn of the century? Wasn't it intended to protect the health and
pocketbooks of unsuspecting consumers who had no other way of
being assured that they had full access to relevant product information? Wasn't it designed to deal with rats ground up into potted meat,
with ketchup made from pumpkin and saccharin, with artificial colorings, flavorings, and preservatives in manufactured foods? Wasn't
it supposed to eliminate the possibility of unwitting narcotic or alcohol addiction among the consumers of patent medicines? The answer
to these questions is a qualified "yes," but·it is the nature of the qual-

ifications that has been lost to our understanding of this portion of American business history.

Reputable food and drug manufacturers wanted some controls placed on the unsavory practices of their price-cutting, poor-quality competitors. How could manufacturers compete effectively against those offering cheap goods to eager consumers, who had no idea that the products they purchased were unwholesome or of poor value? How could producers introduce any rationality into their manufacturing and distribution processes, when the growth of interstate commerce made it necessary to comply with different packaging, labeling, and content laws in every state?

Beyond these completely understandable problems of reputable food and drug companies, however, there were other strategic business issues at stake. In the late 1800s there was no "food industry" or "drug industry"; instead there were more than 30 separate industries engaged in rather loosely defined but nonetheless fierce competition. Trade wars emerged in several of these industries, and the more forward-looking executives soon learned that law and regulation could serve as a powerful weapon against their competitors. In some cases the firms that employed the most up-to-date manufacturing and distribution technologies or sold the products of modern chemistry emerged as the winners; in other cases, makers of "traditional" products used public policy to gain valuable time to implement new technologies and structural patterns.

The consumer protection laws that emerged at the turn of the century, far from creating onerous burdens for reputable corporations, served as tools for the strategic growth of many businesses, and as ways of reshaping industries. To be sure, such laws offered consumers some satisfying symbolic assurances that their interests were protected, but they also provided businesses with opportunities to take full advantage of new technologies, to grow, to establish new markets, and to thwart the interests of their competitors. Many of the patterns established during the Progressive Era can be seen in modern business–government relations, and many of the structural changes introduced then into the food and drug industries can be seen to foreshadow the shape of our modern industries.

A surprising number of food and drug businesses at the turn of the century were quick to seize the advantages offered them by shifts

in power from the states to the federal government. Using public
policy to serve business interests began to take some subtle twists as
business leaders observed during this time that consumer protection
laws could effectively serve interests much broader than those of
consumers.

Producing a book like this is not an individual effort. Many people and their organizations have supported this research, and I want
to thank them all for their efforts. Faculty and administrative colleagues in the Graduate School of Business at the University of Pittsburgh generously acknowledged the potential of this project by supporting it through a grant from the Project on Corporate Social
Responsibility of the Business, Government, and Society Research
Institute, which provided materials, supplies, and research assistance, and through two Faculty Research Grants, which provided
large chunks of concentrated time to invest in research and writing.
This support, of course, was critical to the completion of the project.
Historical research, rewarding as it is, has its pitfalls. Robert Ay-
itey Stephens, Marcy Stryker, Mary Mallott, Christine Moorman,
and David Witt covered themselves in dust numerous times, tracing
down obscure references and leafing through aged documents to find
many of the materials used in the book. Most of them had the good
grace to get excited when they found a new source, an interesting
quotation, or a buried and long-forgotten document. The manuscript
was typed, retyped, edited, and revised (endlessly, it seemed) by
Cheryl Day, Kevin Duffy, Dorena Moore, two Macintosh computers,
and me.
Barry M. Mitnick did his best to keep me on the right theoretical
track and cheered me on unerringly at the very points where such
cheering was critical to moving to the project's next step. Samuel P.
Hays offered a great deal of guidance and encouragement in my efforts to move into one of his favorite territories — the Progressive
Era. R. Edward Freeman employed his considerable talents in helping me to simplify the argument in the book. William C. Frederick,
Robert Perloff, Lee E. Preston, Jim Weber, and James A. Wilson
offered critical comments, relevant items they came across in their
own research, and many valuable suggestions during various phases
of the project. With colleagues like these, the work was much easier

and less lonely. Their contributions to this book represent the operation of the scholarly community at its best.

Edwin M. Epstein, Consulting Editor of the Pitman Series in
Business and Public Policy, and William M. Roberts, President of
Pitman Publishing, through their enthusiastic support, gave me the
incentive to look the manuscript over "one more time," resulting in
a substantial rewrite and a much tighter argument. Michael Weinstein of Pitman produced the book from a jumble of words, tables,
figures, and tidbits sent in the mail. Barbara Kellam-Scott's copy ed-
iting greatly improved the manuscript.

My family, finally, kept telling me to get on with it, and I had
little choice but to heed their advice. G. Daniel Bednarz, my hus-
band and chief critic, has a talent for spotting the central idea in a
morass of evidence and helped enormously in this regard. My son,
Jacob Wood–Bednarz, thinks he may have to learn to read after all to
keep up with what his mother is doing. To my parents, James I. Wood
and Donna Gibbs Wood, who set me on this track long ago when
they miraculously provided a set of the World Book Encyclopedia,
this book is dedicated.

one

Strategic Uses of Public Policy

IT HAS BECOME COMMONPLACE FOR BUSINESS LEADERS TO COM-
plain about the burdens of government regulation — high costs, delays in implementing business strategy, endless haggles over definitions and details, voluminous paperwork, and onerous reporting requirements. Yet almost in the next breath one can hear the same
speakers for businesses and industries demanding an "industrial policy," suggesting that consumers are best served by heavily regulating
certain industries (e.g., telecommunications), or pleading for a uniform federal rule on some health or safety issue, to protect them from
charges of negligence and to serve as an industry norm (or minimum
standard of performance).

As examples of the business community's frequent desire for regulatory protection, consider the following news items, all from *The
Wall Street Journal* within the past few years:

> *The Idaho Potato People Tell Us This Is an Extremely Serious Mat-
> ter:* Some people will do anything to sell a potato. But, the Idaho
> Potato Commission says, when they label as Idaho potatoes those
> grown elsewhere, that's carrying things too far. Lawyers at the Boise

firm of Moffatt, Thomas, Barret & Blanton, representing the commission, have busied themselves in recent weeks sending cease-and-desist letters to potato packers and others who have allegedly misused the trademark Idaho potato. . . . [A] letter is going out to the Idaho Potato Co., which ships potatoes in bags prominently labeled with the company name. The company has two offices. One of them is in Warehouse Point, Ct. The other is in Montreal, Quebec (Moffitt, 1982).

Fake Food: To Dairymen's Dismay Imitation Cheeses Win Growing Market Share: On May 14, agents of the Wisconsin Department of Agriculture, Trade and Consumer Protection swooped down on Tom and Ken's Shoprite supermarket in Milwaukee, citing the store for breaking state law and confiscated alleged contraband shipped across the border from Chicago. The agents' haul: a 175-pound cache of imitation cheese. Wisconsin, where dairying is a $3-billion-a-year business and the state's largest industry, regards imitation cheese in much the same way as the federal government looks upon counterfeit money (Buss, 1981).

U.S. Plans to Deregulate Alcohol Industry, But Suppliers and Retailers Oppose Move: The Reagan administration plans to deregulate the alcoholic beverage industry, but the move is arousing concern and opposition from the industry itself. Assistant Treasury Secretary John Walker told reporters that the department plans to cut its staff enforcing the Federal Alcohol Administration Act to about 100 persons from the current 400. He said the regulation of dealings between manufacturers and wholesalers and their retailers "would be reduced or eliminated." . . . Mr. Walker said yesterday that the administration believes that many of the prohibited practices enhance competition in the industry. But Abraham Tuck, Washington counsel of the Wine and Spirit Wholesalers of America, said he would "absolutely" oppose any move to reduce the regulation (Taylor, 1982).

Few people would argue that government regulations are *not* costly and burdensome; the evidence concerning the costs of regulation is fairly substantial (see, e.g., De Fina, 1977; Weidenbaum, 1977; Leone, 1979; Bevirt, 1978). The argument that government regulation *on balance* is more costly than it is beneficial, however, has yet to be justified. Most such arguments address the costs and

benefits of "social" regulation — that is, regulations designed to offer
diffuse benefits to a large segment of the population or to protect "the
public welfare" (see Wilson, 1974) — but when most of the public
discussion seems to focus on regulatory costs and burdens, it is easy
to overlook that businesses often find it in their best interests to *request* regulation, and that the government (in its various organizational manifestations, including Congress and the regulatory agencies) often finds it beneficial to "the public interest" to grant these
requests. This study offers historical evidence that businesses can
have substantial interests in securing legislation and regulations that
typically would be categorized as "social" in nature and intent.

The intervention of businesses in American public policy processes is not a new development, although it may seem so because
businesses have not exhibited consistent, visible political participation. The roots of businesses' political activities are embedded deep
in the American social structure, however quiescent business leaders
may seem to be at any given time. After a relatively long period of
apparent quiescence (or, perhaps, relative invisibility) in political affairs, U.S. business leaders have recently displayed great interest in
once again overtly entering the political arena, and in defending
there the legitimacy of their intentions and actions. Tremendous
growth in political action committees, public policy committees of
corporate boards, Washington offices and corporate lobbyists, and
public affairs management provides convincing evidence of the trend
toward dramatically increased political participation by business representatives.

Much scholarly attention has been paid to the political activities
of businesses in recent years, and a great many perspectives have
been applied. The academic literature has focused for the most part
on theoretical and prescriptive work in the areas of business–government relations, the political economy of regulation, agenda-building
and the development of public policy issues, corporate social responsibility and responsiveness in political affairs, and the ability of businesses to use regulation and public policy as tools for achieving their
strategic objectives.

There are many reasons, of course, for the burgeoning interest
in business's political roles. These include the ascendance of the Re-
publican party, with its unapologetic enthusiasm for unbridled cor-

porate capitalism in almost any form; the abuse — deserved and un-
deserved — heaped upon big businesses in the 1960s and early 1970s;
the recessions and economic uncertainties of the late 1970s and
1980s; the growth of the federal budget and budget deficits; the increasingly difficult and turbulent competitive environment of international business; and, perhaps, the academic and consulting community's tendency to move away from the concept of corporate social
responsibility (stressing business's legal and ethical obligations to
stakeholders and society) toward corporate *responsiveness* (stressing
demand-pushed actions in response to changing environmental conditions and the expressed interests of stakeholder groups).

The existence of continuing concern about the *legitimacy* of business's political participation, however, suggests that some basic questions remain unanswered. How far can business leaders afford to go
in using their influence with legislators, regulators, and others in government? How can they afford *not* to be involved in public policy
matters that will affect their operating and strategic policies, their
market positions and product offerings, and their profits? What op-
tions do they have for political involvement that will help them to
move in advantageous strategic directions and at the same time help
them to balance the competing needs, interests, and demands of their
stakeholders? Is it desirable — or possibly inevitable — for businesses to attempt to use the powers of government to further their
"private" interests?

Readers who are familiar with these events, trends, scholarly approaches, and questions of legitimacy will not be surprised that businesses have responded to an increasingly uncertain and threatening
environment in part by seeking to use political processes for their
own ends. It is *not* a tenet of common wisdom, however, that the
strategic use of regulation and public policy by businesses has a long
and distinguished history in America. The strategic use of public policy by corporations is not a new idea, nor has it "reemerged." In
general, business leaders have always guarded and exercised their
political roles; they have been aware for a century and longer that
public policy affects the allocation of society's resources and thus affects the ability of businesses to fulfill their goals and objectives. In
some eras business leaders have simply exercised these roles more
quietly than in others.

In this book, the Progressive Era antecedents of modern business–government relations — particularly the strategic uses of public policy by businesses — are examined through a study of the actors and interests involved in the passage of the 1906 Pure Food Act, often considered to be one of the earliest pieces of federal consumer protection (or "social") legislation. The book's central thesis is that the nature and extent of businesses' political participation is a function of the existence of social structural and ideological supports for corporate political activities, the objective and subjective conditions of competition for particular businesses and industries, and the perceptions of business leaders as to how public policy choices will affect resource allocation.

The data for this study are drawn for the most part from primary documents — Progressive Era books, periodicals, and newspapers; records of Congressional hearings and floor debates; autobiographies of principal actors; and publications of the federal and state governments, industry and trade associations, and individual businesses. Secondary sources, including biographies, histories, statistical compilations, and government and industry analyses, were used to supplement primary data where necessary. Although innumerable primary materials are available, their quality, when judged by current standards of research, is less than satisfactory. Nevertheless, enough information is available to make some preliminary suggestions about commercial and manufacturing interests in the first federal food and drug law and thereby to underscore the idea that the strategic use of public policy by business interests carries the weight of a long-standing and legitimate, if perhaps not entirely respectable, tradition.

In the next section of this chapter, the historical and theoretical significance of the Pure Food and Drug Act is explored, justifying it as an appropriate context in which to investigate the ways in which businesses choose to make strategic use of public policy and regulation. The remainder of the chapter outlines the book's theoretical framework, beginning with a consideration of several models of business–government relations, continuing with an examination of theories of regulatory origin and their relationships with the concept of the "public interest," and concluding with a discussion of the strategic uses of regulation to satisfy private interests. A brief summary of the issues at stake in the pure food and drug controversy is presented at the end of the chapter.

THE "PUBLIC OUTRAGE" HYPOTHESIS: THE SIGNIFICANCE OF THE PURE FOOD AND DRUG ACT

When Upton Sinclair published *The Jungle* in 1905, the American people were shocked and sickened and insisted that something be done. It was not Sinclair's socialist theme or the terrible fate of his protagonist (who was cheated, robbed, beaten, made ill, and stripped of his family by the realities of capitalism) that caused such a public uproar; it was instead his brief description of filth, disease, and squalor in the practices of the meatpacking industry — Rats ground up into sausages? Tubercular cattle and hogs turned into beef jerky and canned hams? Sawdust, animal droppings, entrails, insects, and blood as the chief components of potted meats?

The publishers, seeking to avoid a libel suit, had sent investigators to Chicago to verify the accuracy of Sinclair's allegations. President Theodore Roosevelt, not to be outdone, sent his own blue-ribbon investigatory team to confirm Sinclair's fictional account, and the Meat Inspection Act raced through Congress and was signed by the President on June 30, 1906. Unfortunately, the Pure Food Act also became law on that day.

The joint signing was not a coincidence, but it was unfortunate because it lent credence to the assumption, which is common in the current pharmaceutical regulation literature, that Sinclair's novel and related health scandals were critical causal factors in the passage of both the Meat Inspection Act and the Pure Food Act. More broadly, common wisdom often asserts that Congress typically passes "laws in the public interest" only when it is forced to do so by the weight of public opinion, which peaks during or after some major crisis or scandal. This assertion then becomes the assumption upon which the critics of regulation can argue that "public interest" legislation (or "social" legislation) is typically the outcome of ill-considered Congressional response to public outrage, and thus is poorly thought out, impractical, and unnecessarily costly.

This "public outrage" assumption and the antiregulatory arguments based upon it have been very strongly held and defended by critics of pharmaceutical regulation (see, e.g., Peltzman, 1974; Grabowski, 1976; Temin, 1980; Grabowski and Vernon, 1983). The 1906 Pure Food Act represented the first broad-based federal entry into the domain of regulating the content and labeling of medicinal products, and it is often mentioned in a trilogy of significant statutory changes that includes the 1938 Food, Drugs, and Cosmetics Act and the 1962 Amendments to that act. Each of these laws was pushed by outraged public demand after a major scandal, so the argument goes, and overall, because they were so hastily drafted and passed, they have proved to be more cumbersome and costly than beneficial.

One can understand this assertion in the case of the 1962 Amendments, which were passed after public disclosure of the thalidomide tragedy in Europe. Because their mothers took this drug in early pregnancy, an estimated 10,000 babies worldwide were born with the severe physical deformities described by the term "phocomelia." (See Harris, 1964, for an account of the entire set of issues surrounding this law, and Insight Team, 1979, for a full discussion of the origin and consequences of thalidomide.) For the 1937–38 episode when a poisonous patent medicine killed more than 100 Americans, the public outrage hypothesis is also plausible, though it is by no means certain that sulfanilimide deaths *caused* passage of the law that replaced the 1906 act (see Cavers, 1939). In the case of the 1906 Pure Food Act, however, *there was no major public health crisis.* Concerns about public health and about the safety of foods and medicines were certainly evident, but they were not the sole, or even the most important impetus to passage of the law.

The public outrage or crisis generation assumption has some valuable functions when writers who are intent upon other analytical or political purposes must make an obligatory nod to history. It can serve as the foundation for a tidy (though perhaps mythical) stream of historical continuity, from which it can be argued that when Congress acts to satisfy public outrage, it acts incautiously and without due regard for the long-range consequences of law and public policy. ("They did it in 1906, 1938, 1962 — are they going to do it again?") The assumption can then serve as the basis for decrying social legislation and regulation and for constructing a negative cost–benefit ratio to show convincingly that it is consumers, as well as businesses, who are hurt by such ill-conceived acts of Congress and the regulatory agencies. In the case of food and drugs, however, the assumption and its resulting arguments are far more convenient than they are accurate.

It is true that the three major food and drug laws — 1906, 1938, and 1962 — were all passed within a year of shocking public disclosures. (In the case of the 1906 act, however, the most significant "shocking disclosures" had more to do with the Meat Inspection Act than with the Pure Food Act.) On the other hand, all three laws evolved over long periods of time, they were the subjects of intense public and private scrutiny and debate, and they served interests and purposes beyond those of consumers or "the public."

The 1962 Amendments to the Food, Drugs, and Cosmetics Act originated in 1957 in Senator Estes Kefauver's Subcommittee on Antitrust and Monopoly, although the issues the Amendments sought to address emerged much earlier, in 1951, with Federal Trade Commission investigations into drug pricing. The Amendments were initially directed at preventing certain "anticompetitive tendencies" in the pharmaceutical industry, including alleged price-fixing, reciprocal licensing, and "excessive" profits. Consumer protection elements were present but less significant in early versions of the proposed law. After disclosure of the thalidomide tragedy, however, industry representatives and members of Congress agreed to retain some consumer protection aspects (such as the requirement for premarket testing of drug efficacy) in exchange for dropping all antitrust provisions (Harris, 1964).

The 1938 Food, Drug and Cosmetics Act, which replaced the 1906 act, was passed shortly after disclosure of over one hundred deaths from a poisonous proprietary elixir. In addition to the provision that drugs be tested for safety before being marketed, the act corrected some enforcement deficiencies of the 1906 Pure Food Act and added requirements for accurate labeling, factory inspections, and standards for the identity and quality of food and drug components. The 1938 act was strongly supported by the Food and Drug Administration, consumer advocates, and many food and drug manufacturers (Cavers, 1939; "Food legislation," 1963).

The genesis of the original federal legislation governing interstate commerce in foods and drugs — the 1906 Pure Food Act — is no less complex and lengthy, but it is considerably less well known. Far from being a kneejerk reaction to an immediate crisis, the Pure Food Act was the outcome of a 25-year struggle among numerous constituencies (Wiley, 1929; Anderson, 1958; Bailey, 1930). Table 1.1 is an indicator of the pure food issue's longevity; between 1890 and 1906, the House and Senate considered no less than 56 pure food bills.

It is now well established for some regulatory laws (e.g., the Interstate Commerce Act of 1887) that businesses actively promote federal legislation and regulation when it is apparently in their interests to do so (Hilton, 1966; Kolko, 1965; Harbeson, 1967; Purcell, 1967). Recent demands by chemical manufacturers for federal rules on warning labels for toxic chemicals in the workplace, and the cooperation of over-the-counter drug manufacturers in developing standards for tamper-proof packages (in the wake of the 1983 Tylenol murders) are more current examples. In the case of major food and drug legislation, however, few analysts seem aware that businesses had *any* vested interests at the turn of the century in securing passage of a federal law.

In examining the public and private issues surrounding the passage of the 1906 Pure Food Act, this book is not intended to be a chronological account of events (see Bailey, 1930, and Anderson, 1958, for such accounts), but an analysis of themes, concerns, and threads of collective consciousness and actions. This historically based analysis allows greater understanding of the functions of government and the uses to which it can be put by various interest groups. Further, the study emphasizes that business was not then, any more than it is now, a unified entity able to speak with a single voice on public policy issues. Competition among businesses and industries, the cornerstone of capitalism, is also a key factor in understanding business–government relations.

THE "ADVERSARIAL" AND "PARTNERSHIP" HYPOTHESES: THE SECTORAL APPROACH TO BUSINESS–GOVERNMENT RELATIONS

Business, government, and the public are often spoken of as if they were distinctly separable entities — with some functional overlaps and interdependencies, to be sure, but with markedly different interests and memberships. When business leaders serve in high governmental positions, and when former politicians become corporate

TABLE 1.1

Pure Food Bills Introduced in Congress 1890–1906

Legislation regarding interstate commerce in foods has been constantly
before the Congress of the United States for about eighteen years. Senate
Bill No. 3991, introduced June 3, 1890, by Mr. Paddock, passed the
Senate about fourteen years ago. Since then the following pure food bills
have been introduced in the Senate and the House:

SENATE BILLS

No.	Date	Introduced by
3391	June 3, 1890	Mr. Paddock
1	Dec. 10, 1891	Do.
1488	Jan. 11, 1892	Mr. Hiscock
2984	Apr. 22, 1892	Mr. Wilson
3796	Jan. 30, 1893	Mr. Faulkner
471	Mar. 18, 1897	Mr. Gallinger
4015	Mar. 2, 1898	Mr. Faulkner
4144	Mar. 16, 1898	Do.
5375	Jan. 27, 1899	Mr. Thurston
2048	Jan. 3, 1900	Mr. Allen
2049	— do —	Do.
2050	— do —	Do.
2222	Jan. 8, 1900	Mr. Hansbrough
3618	Mar. 15, 1900	Mr. Proctor
3796	Mar. 26, 1900	Mr. Jones
4047	Apr. 6, 1900	Mr. Foster
2426	Jan. 15, 1900	Mr. Mason
5262	Dec. 18, 1900	Do.
1347	Dec. 9, 1901	Do.
3015	Jan. 20, 1902	Do.
2987	— do —	Mr. Cullom
3240	Jan. 27, 1902	Mr. Depew
3342	Jan. 29, 1902	Mr. Hansbrough
6303	June 28, 1902	Mr. McCumber
198	Nov. 11, 1903	Do.
88	Dec. 6, 1905	Mr. Heyburn
3623	Jan. 24, 1906	Mr. Hopkins

TABLE 1.1

Continued

HOUSE BILLS		
No.	Date	Introduced by
283	Dec. 18, 1889	Mr. Conger
11297	July 8, 1890	Mr. Turner, of Kansas
109	Jan. 5, 1892	Mr. Holman
4438	Jan. 21, 1892	Mr. Smith, of Illinois
8603	May 6, 1892	Mr. Meredith
4618	Dec. 18, 1899	Mr. Babcock
6442	Jan. 16, 1900	Mr. Glynn
7667	Jan. 30, 1900	Mr. Sherman
5441	Dec. 18, 1897	Mr. Brosius
9154	Mar. 15, 1898	Do.
2561	Dec. 7, 1899	Do.
6246	Jan. 15, 1900	Do.
9677	Mar. 16, 1900	Do.
12973	Dec. 19, 1900	Do.
276	Dec. 2, 1901	Mr. Sherman
3109	Dec. 6, 1901	Mr. Hepburn
4342	Dec. 10, 1901	Mr. Kahn
9351	Jan. 18, 1902	Mr. Warner
9960	Jan. 23, 1902	Mr. Sherman
12348	Mar. 10, 1902	Mr. Corliss
5077	Nov. 27, 1903	Mr. Hepburn
6295	Dec. 8, 1903	Do.
6295	Jan. 21, 1904	Do.
4527	Dec. 6, 1905	Do.
7018	Dec. 13, 1905	Mr. Davidson
12071	Jan. 16, 1906	Mr. Lorimer
13859	Feb. 2, 1906	Mr. Rodenberg

SOURCE: House Report No. 2118, "Pure Food." Washington, D.C.: U.S. Government Printing Office, 1906.

executives, lobbyists, and consultants, there are murmurs (and sometimes shouts) of conflict of interest. When environmental or consumer protection groups win legislative or regulatory victories, rum-
blings are heard about the antibusiness intentions of these "public
interest" groups. This way of thinking about social institutions can be
called a *sector* approach to social structure.

In distinct sector approaches (see Figure 1.1), the social system
is divided like a pie, where each slice represents a sector with a dis-
tinguishing characteristic or set of features. In overlapping sector approaches, a Venn diagram can be used to illustrate the notion that
sectors have distinctive functions but may to some degree have overlapping memberships. For example, the traditional structural-func-
tionalist way of delineating basic social institutions — the family, religion, education, government (or the polity), the economy — is a
sector-like division of the social system. Each institutional sector is
distinct from all others; it is responsible for performing certain tasks
so that the society's work can be accomplished through a specialized
division of labor (even though individual people hold overlapping sector "memberships" in their activities and interests).

This way of categorizing social institutions and their primary
tasks, although primitive, is at work whenever one hears statements
to the effect that business and government depend on each other (are
partners) or have incompatible mandates (are adversaries). Such
statements, and the sectoral view of the social system that undergirds
them, represent two common hypotheses about the nature of business–government relations — the adversarial hypothesis and the
partnership or community of interest hypothesis.

Federal and state governments play two direct, formal, institutional roles for businesses. First, they *guarantee* the rights and privileges that are essential for the proper functioning of capitalistic enterprise. Second, they *police* or *enforce* the fulfillment of those
obligations to the society or portions of the society that restrict business activities. When government is viewed, as it often is, as an agent
of social control, it is clear that these two functions represent government's double-sided efforts to make sure that the institutional bargain
or social contract is fulfilled by all societal sectors.

Guaranteed rights and privileges include the right to own, alter,
and dispose of private property as one sees fit and the right to enter
into contracts and expect them to be enforced. In terms of the right

FIGURE 1.1

The Sector View of Business–Government Relations

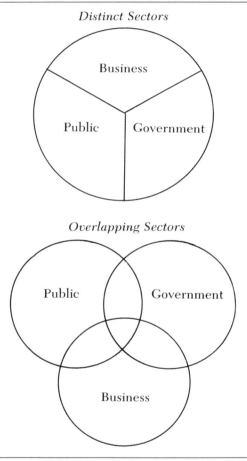

Distinct Sectors

Overlapping Sectors

to private property, restrictive obligations include the duty to use one's own property in a manner that does not harm the interests of others, as well as the responsibility to avoid interfering with the property of others without their permission. A person's right to own property means that the person is obliged to forfeit any claim to the property of others, except as such a claim can be upheld by law and in the courts. Contracts are equally subject to the requirement of reciprocity. The right to enter into contracts is meaningless if the contractors cannot be expected to abide by the terms of the contract (see Anderson, 1981, for an extended discussion of these issues).

That the rights–obligations relationship is reciprocal is sometimes overlooked by analysts who pose models of the business–government relationship based only on one of the governmental roles defined above. For those who are inclined to see the government as a police officer, checking to make sure that businesses fulfill their obligations — demanding, for example, that labels be accurate and that companies refrain from engaging in anticompetitive behaviors — the *adversarial* model of business–government relations seems most appropriate. For those who tend to focus on government's role as the guarantor of rights and privileges — guarding, for example, the individual's right to privacy or the organization's right to have contracts enforced in court — the *partnership* or community of interest model seems to be a more adequate description of the business–government relationship.

The adversarial model pits business and government against each other as virtual enemies, and suggests that the mandates and principal interests of these two major societal sectors are not only dramatically different, but are often diametrically opposed. Business's search for profits may be seen as necessarily conflicting with government's mandate to protect the public welfare; or the antagonism may lie instead in the argument that businesses must strive to use resources in efficient and effective ways, but that government organizations have few or no market pressures on them to serve as incentives for efficiency or effectiveness. Government in the adversarial view can be seen as a hostile or punishing parent, an implacable bureaucratic antagonist, or, at best, a deeply resented irritant to businesses.

The partnership or community of interest model views business and government as two intertwining and complementary units of the social system, striving for the same ultimate goals, with each unit benefitting substantially from the activities of the other. The jointly held ultimate goals can be as specific as increasing productivity and gross national product or as global as securing the survival of "the American way of life." Government in the partnership model is seen as a working marriage partner, a supportive friend, a reliable party to an informal contract of reciprocal benefit with businesses, or, in the more cynical view, a corrupt and compliant bedfellow of big business.

Both positions can lay claim to considerable evidence. The adversarial model's supporters can point to a national psychology of personal freedom and the notion that the best government is the least government, along with the ideology of free enterprise and laissez-faire economics. They can claim, with substantial justification, that the federal government's regulatory efforts in the past two decades have been extremely costly and even punitive. They can point to numerous issues on which business and government representatives disagree sharply (e.g., tax policy, budget deficits, allocation of governmental resources, regulatory requirements). Supporters of the partnership model, on the other hand, can draw upon the functionalist analysis of systemic division of labor (that is, complex systems require specialized institutions) for theoretical and ideological support, and they observe that the tasks of business and government are inextricably intertwined — one could not survive without the other. With respect to regulation, partnership advocates point to the many examples of industry-sought regulatory activities, along with the benefits that businesses may reap from regulation. Table 1.2 shows some of the mutual benefits reaped in the business–government relationship (Anderson, 1981; Davis and Frederick, 1984).

Because both models seem to fit reality and both have such clear evidence to support them, it is apparent that neither model is truly descriptive of the relationship between businesses and government, either as institutions or as organizations. Both the partnership and the adversarial models assume that all business organizations and all government organizations, respectively, are enough like each other, expressing similar or identical interests, to be grouped together into categories called "Business" and "Government" without further distinctions being made among them.

Clearly this simple typological view of the social system is inadequate if one truly wishes to understand how business organizations influence and are affected by public policy, and how government organizations influence and are affected by corporate policy and activities. Businesses are of many different types: They are small, large, or medium in size; they employ many people or only a few; they are labor-intensive or capital-intensive; they are privately or publicly

TABLE 1.2

Mutual Benefits in the Business–Government Relationship

Benefits Provided by Business to Government:	Benefits Provided by Government to Business:
Performs society's necessary economic functions.	Provides legal protection: right to private property, contract enforcement, policing, charters.
Pays taxes.	
Employs citizens.	Provides infrastructure supports: monetary system, weather service, zoning, traffic control, roads, airports, harbors, uniform standards, system of weights and measures.
Generates income for those who pay taxes.	
Collects taxes as an agent of the government.	
Provides technical expertise.	
Produces and disseminates knowledge.	Subsidizes some business activities, through land grants, low postal rates, strategic materials stockpiling, etc.
Provides the products and services that government needs for its own operations.	
	Protects markets: import–export restrictions and promotions, fair trade laws, loan guarantees, direct financial support.
	Purchases much of business's output.

owned; they are single-business enterprises or conglomerates; they design, manufacture, advertise, transport, sell, finance, install, maintain, alter, or destroy things; they rely on domestic or on foreign markets or on some mix of both; they are profitable or not; they are located in major cities or in farmlands. Given the great diversity among business organizations, it is difficult to argue that *all* businesses, or perhaps even a majority of businesses, could be in agreement on most public policy issues. The history of federal and state regulation shows clearly that businesses have rarely spoken with a unified voice on matters of public policy (see, e.g., Magaziner and Reich, 1982).

Consulting, engineering, and some manufacturing firms have been the financial beneficiaries of the pollution-control regulations that have been costly for many other businesses. Small businesses, appreciative of special tax credits and low-interest loans given to them by the government, may resent and resist any proposal that similar benefits should be provided to their larger competitors. Profitable firms may lobby against federal bailouts of failing companies like Chrysler or Continental Illinois, arguing that the incentive to succeed is diminished if failure is to be so well cushioned. Given the great diversity of interests, competitive conditions, resource needs, and "clout" within the American business community, is it reasonable to talk about "business" as though these substantial differences did not exist among the organizations making up the economic sector of society?

The same argument can be applied to the monolithic use of the concept of "government." State and local governments do not have precisely the same interests, abilities, or structures as the federal government. The legislature, the courts, and the executive agencies cannot be expected to be in agreement on all public policy questions. Even two agencies under the direction of one administration may act against each other's interests. This is perhaps most vividly illustrated by the contradiction between the Surgeon General's report on the health effects of cigarette smoking and the imposition of labeling and advertising restrictions on tobacco products, on the one hand, and the continuation of federal market orders and price supports for the tobacco industry, on the other (see Miles, 1982).

The sectoral approach to a social system has some appeal when the task is to make rough distinctions among social institutions at the most abstract level. Applying such an approach to real-world questions, however, is clearly inappropriate and inaccurate. Of what use is it to anyone or any group to say, "Business wants X, Government wants Y, Consumers want Z," if those "institutions" are each composed of organizations, groups, and individuals with widely varying interests and objectives?

INTEREST GROUPS AND "THE PUBLIC INTEREST"

Both of the sector-based hypotheses about the nature of the business–government relationship depend to some extent on the conceptual distinction between "the public interest" (the official domain of the government) and "private interests" (the purview of businesses and other nongovernment organizations and persons). In the sectoral view, the reason the two sectors are distinct (whether the relation is adversarial or partner-like) is that their interests are fundamentally different, the governmental sector serving the interests of the abstract whole, and the business sector serving the individual interests of people and groups.

Which of the sector hypotheses is to be favored may depend upon one's view of the relationship between self-interest and the public interest; these fundamentally different interests may or may not be seen as compatible. If the utilitarian or laissez-faire position is taken, that the cumulative effect of independent, self-interested acts is to provide the maximum social benefit, then the partnership model of business–government relations is likely to be favored, because the interests of business and government are seen as being compatible, although different. If one contends, however, that self-interest and the public interest are necessarily contradictory at times — that a virtual prisoner's dilemma exists in the relations between two major societal sectors — then the adversarial model of business and government interaction will seem more accurate.

The "public interest," however, is a peculiar concept. The "interests" so described can refer to diverse elements of the population — for example, to voiceless or powerless citizens, groups who are said or believed to uphold "the American way of life" (such as family farmers), or to imperfectly informed consumers — and even to nonexistent elements, such as future unborn generations. The term can refer to values, ideals, concepts, hopes, material objects, money, or the health or lives of persons themselves. The public interest can be articulated diffusely or specifically, abstractly or concretely. Indeed, in political action terms, "the public interest" is a very useful concept for defending and justifying almost any action or decision; it expresses a deeply held if poorly defined value in American culture. It can be an almost irrefutable justification — no one could be against the public interest, just as no one could be for total pollution of the earth.

However, the reason that "the public interest" is generally set in quotation marks is that no one has been able to define it precisely. Indeed, it takes on an incredible array of meanings in use. The term must therefore be used with great caution by social and organizational analysts and scholars. The distinction between "the public interest" and "private interests" has been particularly troublesome. It could be argued, on the one hand, that "public" and "private" interests had become blurred but are now reemerging as distinct, identifiable sets of objectives. To support this view, evidence could be produced to show that the onslaught of legislation and regulations designed to implement socially desired goals (such as environmental protection and equal employment opportunity) is creating a context in which public and private interests are clearly at war and some "hard choices" have to be made.

It could also be argued that public and private interests, far from becoming more distinct, are blurring and overlapping more than ever before. For evidence, one could point to the "revolving door" between businesses and government agencies for high-level personnel, the national defense implications of certain key industries, and the arguments of scholars such as Schultze (1977) and Lindblom (1978) that government *must* serve the interests of businesses in order to secure "the public interest."

I must agree with R. Edward Freeman (personal communication, 1984) that "the public interest" is little more than a bad-faith concept, both analytically and in practice. Although the concept can be taken to mean that public policy processes should (or do) have generally beneficial outcomes, the truth of this definition is open to question on many fronts. Democratic voting procedures (e.g., majority rule, the electoral college, representative legislatures) deny the possibility of rule by a dictatorship; that is, it is not possible that one person's preferences are always (or even usually) implemented. However, the same processes of democracy also deny any "general public interest" outcomes — democratic procedures make it highly unlikely that public policy outcomes can be seen as beneficial to all or perhaps even most segments of "the public." That which the majority agrees upon may benefit or serve the interests of only a very small portion of the society and, of course, it may harm the interests of some societal segments.

"The public interest" is not at all useful as an analytic or theoretical concept. As a condensation symbol, however, (see Edelman, 1964, 1971) — a concept that connotes a rich muddle of political and emotional meaning — it has been extremely useful to various interest groups and policy-making bodies. The concept of "the public interest" is important to this study for two reasons. First, it is often linked

to so-called social legislation and to regulations, of which the Pure
Food and Drug Act of 1906 is said to be an early and classic example.
Second, as used during the Progressive Era, "the public interest" was
not a phrase that necessarily expressed interests contrary to those of
businesses. In this study, then, "the public interest" is *not* used as an
analytical concept. Rather, the study examines how various Progressive Era interest groups made use of the concept of "the public interest" in their own political pursuits.

"Social" regulation is defined as regulation that seeks to implement noneconomic goals and values. Commonly cited examples are
the "Big Four" regulatory agencies of the 1970s: the Consumer Product Safety Commission, the Equal Employment Opportunity Commission, the Environmental Protection Agency, and the Occupational
Safety and Health Administration. The Food and Drug Administration is also typically included in the category of "social" regulatory
agencies.

"Special interest groups" are often held responsible for the origin, growth, and extreme costliness of these regulatory agencies.
These groups, allegedly representing "the public interest," are often
accused by critics of the agencies of acting in fact *against* the public
interest by creating an environment in which American businesses
cannot operate efficiently or effectively and, thus, where businesses
cannot compete well in either domestic or international markets. Social regulations have been blamed for the downturns and poor competitive showings of the steel and auto industries, among others; for
high unemployment rates; for excessive costs to consumers; for a decline in product innovation; and for a host of other economic and
social ills.

Consumer protection groups, environmentalists, and other interest groups have long sought to use the power of government to
accomplish their aims and to achieve their interests. The interests of
these groups have often been articulated in terms of "the public interest," and have been accepted by some lawmakers in that light.
Parents of children with rare diseases have lobbied the government
for more federal funding for research and medical care costs; it is in
"the public interest" that the physical well-being of persons be valued
highly. Highway safety advocates have pushed for mandatory seat
belt use and for built-in safety equipment in automobiles; it is in "the

public interest" that lives not be lost needlessly in auto accidents. Diabetics lobbied intensively for the Food and Drug Administration to abandon its proposed ban on saccharin; it was in "the public interest" that the rights of this minority to purchase desired products be protected in a democratic system. Innumerable other interest groups have acted to obtain desired outcomes from various governmental units, often couching their desires in terms of "the public interest."

The idea that business is also an interest group surfaces as well whenever we hear or read about "the business community's views" on some proposed or enacted public policy. And business's "position" on public policy issues can also be phrased in terms of "the public interest." As we have seen in the last section, this monolithic view of business as a sector is not very useful for understanding either business–government relations or the development of public policy. Individual businesses can constitute independent interest groups, and they can combine with other businesses or with nonbusiness groups to form coalitions with the purpose of influencing legislation or regulation (and, of course, their interests may or may not reflect "the public interest").

All interest groups, including businesses, represent human and organizational actors who can have significant input into the development and resolution of public policy issues. One of the fascinating features of interest groups is not that they have interests in influencing the government to act one way or another, but that they may have very intricate interactions and arrangements among themselves that can influence the actions they choose to take and that can change independently of the government's actions. Interest groups may mobilize advocates who can provide material, interpersonal, symbolic, or moral resources; they may enter a public policy controversy at almost any point and in many different fashions; they may form coalitions with other interest groups, including those whose "fundamental" interests are radically different from their own; they may agree to disagree among themselves on issues that are tangential to the issue that brought them together, or they may simply pretend to ignore such peripheral issues; they may also cut separate deals with various coalition members and shift allegiance from one coalition to another. They can align with, backstab, support, cheat, work for, and fight against each other; they can change political positions and coalition memberships with lightning rapidity. There is nothing monolithic about interest-group politics, in theory or in practice.

In the last section we saw that both the partnership model and the adversarial model of business–government relations require a monolithic and therefore inaccurate typology of social institutions. It seems much more useful and desirable to accept the idea that businesses can be independent "interest groups," that they all do not have the same interests, and that they seek to have a voice in the affairs of government in much the same way that other interest groups do. That is, businesses will seek government assistance and intervention in the marketplace when it seems to be in their interests to do so and when they perceive that they have the capability to intervene. When businesses perceive government policies and practices as harmful to their interests, they will oppose such policies and practices. Clearly, this hypothesis does not suggest, as the sector hypotheses do, that businesses will act politically as a single unit.

This self-interest model of business–government relations allows for adversarial *and* partner-like interactions to occur. It admits a certain symbiosis in the relationship, but it does not demand that partners never fight viciously or exhibit radically different interests and behaviors. Most importantly, it does not assume — indeed, it denies the likelihood — that all businesses or all government units will act together as a coherent faction, will have the same interests, or will be ranged against representatives of the "opposite" institution on public policy matters. It permits pluralistic interest-group politics to operate *among* members of the business community (and among members of the government community as well).

It is this model of self-interested groups and organizations involved in a pluralistic system of identifying and deciding upon public policy issues that lies at the heart of the idea that businesses can and do use the powers of regulation and public policy strategically to further their own competitive goals and objectives. We shall turn shortly to this concept of the strategic uses of public policy. First it is necessary to explore two antecedent theoretical perspectives that posit industries as the beneficiaries of certain classes of legislation and regulatory activity.

THE "BENEFITS TO INDUSTRY" HYPOTHESES: CAPTURE AND ECONOMIC THEORIES OF REGULATION

The idea that industries at times have requested regulation by the federal or state governments has traditionally been associated with the theory of "economic" regulation, which emerged in part as a response to earlier "capture" theories of regulatory origin. A brief review of these two theoretical perspectives will be useful in setting the stage for more recent developments in the strategic uses of regulation (see Posner, 1974, for a thorough discussion).

The period under consideration in this study (1887–1906) represents what Marvur Bernstein (1955: 74) referred to as the "gestation phase" of the regulatory life cycle. In his analysis of the independent regulatory commissions, he noted that "frequently 20 years or more may be required to produce a regulatory statute" (p. 75). As can be seen from the synopsis that follows, Bernstein's analysis was attuned to the argument that regulation is imposed to correct some defect of the market or to protect "the public interest" in some other fashion.

The first stage of "slowly mounting distress over a problem," according to Bernstein, is followed by "recognition of acute distress," prompted by a scandal or an economic situation. Organized groups then swing more heavily into action, demanding a legislative solution to the problem and ultimately achieving this objective:

> The forces resisting regulation are powerful and ingenious, and are overcome only by the effective efforts of advocates of reform, sustained by a favorable public response to their demands and led by a strong president. These proponents lay their emphasis on securing the enactment of a law and obtaining public recognition of the claims of certain groups for protection against abusive business practices (p. 76).

Bernstein's organic metaphor of the regulatory cycle continues through adolescent, adult, and senile elderly phases. It is, of course, less a theory of agency origin and development than a set of observations on the ebb and flow of regulatory effectiveness. Note that in the quotation above Bernstein asserts that the problems perceived by the public and prompting the outcry for regulation are nothing more or less than "abusive business practices." By suggesting that "business" and "the public" are opposing forces in the development of regulatory legislation, Bernstein greatly oversimplified the policy-making process and laid the groundwork for "capture" theories of regulation.

Essentially, the "capture" argument suggests that Congress's apparent intent (to protect "the public interest") in passing a consumer protection law is easily and routinely thwarted during the implementation phase, when the law's language must be rewritten into detailed regulations and when enforcement procedures must be developed and applied. Inadequate technical expertise among agency personnel and the exchange of executives between the regulated industry and the regulating agency, among other factors, are said to enhance the ability of regulated industry representatives to gain concessions and delays, to assist in writing regulations, and to dictate rules and procedures to the agencies that supposedly oversee their activities (Mitnick, 1980b:14, 95–96).

Barry M. Mitnick (1980b:95) defines the "capture" perspective as follows: "The capture view holds the regulatory mechanism is basically workable and desirable but is somehow 'captured' by the regulated parties so that it serves their interests rather than the public interest." According to Mitnick (p. 95), "capture" can be accomplished in several ways: (1) The regulated industry can control the regulatory agency directly; (2) agency and industry activities can be coordinated to serve private interests; (3) the agency can be neutralized by making sure that its personnel are ineffective or that it lacks any true authority to impose sanctions on regulated businesses; (4) regulators can be coopted so that they view regulation from the industry's perspective; (5) a reward system can be established that leads inevitably to a partnership between business and government representatives.

The capture argument is of interest to this study because it provides a possible explanation for why industry representatives may be less than vigilant in opposing laws that are designed to restrict their activities. If business leaders perceive strong public opinion in favor of a regulatory law, if they see that their own opposition to such a law could damage their public image, and if they understand and are willing to use their power during the implementation phase to control the law's effect on them, then there is little incentive for business leaders to oppose publicly any law that is commonly seen as being "in the public interest," particularly if there is strong public sentiment, a great deal of media attention, or broad-based coalitions supporting the law. Instead, business leaders can express general, ambiguous support for consumer protection laws, or they can keep silent altogether and enter the public policy process during the implementation phase, when they can be much more effective in securing their private interests with little public opposition (or even awareness).

Such a situation may have existed during the long period of public debate over federal food and drug legislation in the Progressive Era. In fact, there were early and powerful allegations that food and drug manufacturers had succeeded in "capturing" the Bureau of Chemistry (the Food and Drug Administration's predecessor) after passage of the 1906 Pure Food Act. Long before the "regulatory capture" argument had been articulated by scholars, Harvey W. Wiley (Chief of the Bureau of Chemistry from 1883 to 1912 and probably the strongest single proponent of the 1906 act) had documented his charges that the "public interest" aspects of the Pure Food Act had been gutted entirely during the regulatory implementation process. Indeed, he entitled the first volume of his memoirs *The History of a Crime Against the Food Law* (Wiley, 1929).

Can the "capture" argument account for the development in the Progressive Era of public policy concerning food and drug adulterations? It is difficult to determine the degree to which businesses were quiescent or vaguely supportive of a federal food and drug law, but we do know that a number of businesses were actively engaged in the controversy. In any case, even if most affected businesses were quiescent, it would be impossible to determine the motives for such behavior. Recalling that most businesses had relatively little experience in dealing with regulatory agencies during this period, the "capture" motive, however appealing, is unlikely as an explanation of business behavior during the fight for legislation. The evidence to be presented in subsequent chapters further suggests that other factors, more favorable to the idea of economic regulation (though not entirely favorable), were likely to have had greater salience for the business leaders who became involved in the pure food battles.

The economic theory of regulation holds that the "capture" argument is misguided at best. This perspective maintains that industries (or portions of industries) actively seek to use the coercive powers of the government to guarantee protection and competitive advantage for themselves. In this view, "regulation . . . tends to be *sought* by industry for its own protection and subsequently serves this purpose" (Mitnick, 1980b:111; emphasis added). That is, there is no need for industry to wait until the implementation phase to have an impact on regulatory practices — no need to "capture" the agency while no one is looking — because much regulation was desired and requested by the regulated industry itself.

What could an industry possibly gain by being heavily regulated? George J. Stigler (1971:3), the originator of the economic perspective on regulation, identifies four categories of benefits that businesses can achieve through regulatory protection: "(1) direct subsidy, (2) control over entry, (3) powers affecting substitutes and complements, and (4) price-fixing." We shall see that in one way or another all of these benefits, but particularly the third, were at stake for the industries that would be regulated under a federal food and drug law.

Richard A. Posner (1974) has suggested that such benefits accrue to regulated industries indirectly as well as directly, because regulations establish the groundwork for "shared rules of behavior" among all members (or among the most powerful members) of an industry (Mitnick, 1980b:117). Shared rules may or may not allow an industry to function as an informal cartel, but in all cases such rules define the boundaries of permissible competitive practices and impose normative as well as legal limits on "free" competition. When "honest" business owners, for example, find themselves unable to compete with their less scrupulous counterparts, they may look to the government to define and enforce new rules of competitive behavior that will allow them to do business honestly and that will force all their competitors to do so as well.

The empirical evidence that has been marshalled in support of the economic theory of regulation includes Stigler's (1971) analyses of motor carrier regulation and occupational licensing, several studies of railroad companies' actions to secure passage of the Interstate Commerce Act (Benson, 1955; Kolko, 1965; Hilton, 1966; Harbeson, 1967), and Norman Nordhauser's (1973) study of federal oil regulation, among others. An interesting feature of this body of work is that there are two quite different normative assessments of the findings that regulatory agencies serve the interests of regulated businesses. One view, which seems to be common among older historical works, is that economic regulation and "captured" agencies are perversions, that the purpose of government is to serve the needs and interests of "the people" and not those of special interests such as businesses (see, e.g., Kolko, 1963). On the other hand, George J. Stigler (1971:17) calls this perspective "the idealistic view of public regulation," and says that "so many economists, for example, have denounced the ICC for its pro-railroad policies that this has become a cliche of the literature. This criticism seems to be exactly as appropriate as a criticism of the Great Atlantic and Pacific Tea Company for selling groceries." Why should businesses not seek to use the power of government to serve their own interests? Why should business interests be defined automatically as contrary to "the public interest"?

The economic theory of regulation has some distinct advantages as an explanatory theory. It does not depend on a narrow definition of "the public interest" as the interests of consumers or some other nonbusiness group. Industries or business coalitions may represent the public interest just as consumer or labor groups may. Unlike "capture" or "public interest" approaches to regulation, the economic theory treats the power of government as a resource that can be the object of negotiations and varied outcomes. As Victor J. Goldberg (1976) has noted, many economists, assuming that regulation is intended to correct marketplace abuses or misallocations of resources, may see outcomes such as barriers to entry or price-fixing as "failures of regulation." Is it unrealistic, though, to suggest that the businesses and industries receiving the benefits of reduced competition and greater environmental certainty would consider such regulatory outcomes to be a resounding success? Perhaps the economic theory's principal advantage is that it seems to be so well supported by historical as well as more recent research (although Posner, 1974, suggests that economic theories of regulation have the critical disadvantage of seeming to accommodate almost any set of data).

The economic perspective on regulation has traditionally been applied to agencies such as the Interstate Commerce Commission or the Civil Aeronautics Board — regulatory bodies that control single industries tightly and that have relatively weak consumer benefit justifications to offer. Can it serve as an adequate explanation for the initial development of food and drug legislation and regulation, where the consumer benefit aspects seem to be so strong?

Two problems exist. First, there was no "food and drug industry" during the Progressive Era: there were 30 or more separate industries that would be affected by federal legislation. How could firms within all these industries have acted together to seek regulations that would be mutually beneficial? Second, the 1906 Pure Food and Drug Act is commonly viewed as "social," not economic legislation. In fact, there are few examples of legislation that seem to stand as hallmarks of the relatively pure intent of Congress to protect consumers and "the public interest" against fraudulent or dangerous business practices. The 1906 Pure Food Act has remained one of these legislative hallmarks. How then can it also be claimed as "economic" legislation to benefit industry?

Modern historical researchers have discredited the earlier idea that most "social" legislation during the Progressive Era resulted from the efforts of reformers to protect consumers and workers from the ravaging horrors perpetrated by big business, and that such laws represented victories of "the people" over "the interests" (e.g., Hays, 1957; Wiebe, 1962; Weinstein, 1968). Thomas K. McCraw (1975:170), reviewing many of the major historical descriptions of American regulation of business, says that "taken as a whole, historical writing offers few clear patterns of regulatory behavior, except that it demonstrates the inadequacy of either 'capture,' the 'public interest,' or the two in tandem as satisfactory models."

Lee Benson (1955), in a study of railroad regulation and the founding of the Interstate Commerce Commission, says that "the central issue of the era emerges as the important, but hardly revolutionary, question of how the profits of the private-enterprise system were to be divided among various groups of entrepreneurs and how the system itself was to be best preserved." David Vogel (1981:164) has suggested that a true polarity of interest between business and other interest groups was not visible in American politics until the late 1960s. Comparing "social regulation" from an interest group perspective in the Progressive Era, the New Deal, and the 1970s, Vogel asserts:

> During all three periods the pattern of government intervention significantly influenced the distribution of political power among

various interest groups. In the Progressive Era, these shifts largely occurred within the business sector; the conflicts over antitrust policy, federal regulation of the railroad and banking industries, and tariff rates pitted particular segments of the business community against other profit-sector enterprises, both large and small.

The polarity or "class conflict" of which David Vogel writes in his analysis of business–government relations in the 1970s — a clear dichotomy of interest between businesses and the public — was *not*, contrary to common belief, a factor in the passage of the 1906 Pure Food Act. Instead, as we shall see in subsequent chapters, the interests of businesses, consumers, and other interested parties were often compatible and occasionally identical.

The businesses and industries involved in the pure food controversy were smaller, less heavily capitalized, more geographically dispersed, and less heavily concentrated than steel, banking, or railroads. Were they, however, any less politically active? Were they seeking legislation that would allow the development of food or drug cartels operating under shared rules and seeking the security of being a regulated industry? In part this may have been true. Was each organization and coalition seeking legislation that would benefit it more than its competitors? This perspective will also find support. In the main, the businesses involved in the pure food controversy did not fight in harmony against a government perceived as oppressive; they fought among themselves to seize comparative advantage through the power of regulatory legislation.

THE "STRATEGIC USES" HYPOTHESIS: PUBLIC POLICY AND BUSINESS INTERESTS

If it is too monolithic to view all businesses as a single sector with similar interests, it can also be inappropriate to view all businesses within a single industry as having similar approaches to environmental conditions, including regulation. Organizations operating in the same industry are not all alike. Each has distinctive competencies to exploit; each attempts to maximize the value to be obtained from their geographic location, their personnel, their experience, their interpersonal connections, their product or service characteristics, the demographics of their markets, and a multitude of other factors. Even their approaches to environmental conditions are different, as the reactive–responsive–proactive distinction illustrates.

Firms that are attuned to significant developments in the environment attempt, according to the strategic uses hypothesis, to use regulation to achieve comparative advantage — an edge over their competitors — by avoiding or minimizing the costs and obtaining the benefits of regulation. As Barry M. Mitnick points out, "expenditures that are perceived by some firms as costs are received by others as benefits" (1981:71). In an important sense, the strategic uses perspective views regulation as little more than one environmental condition among many. That is, organizations find it necessary, if they are to survive, to scan their environments continuously and to adapt to changing conditions. Like the weather, the state of customer demand, interest rate levels, or any other environmental condition, a single regulation or set of regulations can have very different strategic implications for individual firms within an industry.

The idea that companies can *benefit* from regulation is not a new idea; it has long been accepted by those who promote economic theories of regulation. These theoretical approaches concentrate, however, on regulatory benefits to an *industry* (or at least to the dominant firms within an industry). The strategic uses of regulation perspective, in contrast, proposes that regulation can be used by individual firms as a competitive tool, just like any other tool or distinctive quality. The firms attempting to use regulation and public policy to their own advantage need not be the industry leaders — indeed, they could have virtually any position in the industry, including the least profitable, the smallest, or the most likely to fail — and they need not be working together to achieve common benefits.

There is a distinct contrast between the economic perspective on regulation and the strategic uses perspective. As Mitnick (1981:74) observes on the nature of regulatory benefits to firms:

> Regulation can favor firms either through (1) direct market intervention that gives direct support to the industry in question or that protects it from new firms or competing technologies, [this is essentially the economic theory of regulation] or through (2) happening

to suit the particular advantages of certain firms. In the second case, regulation may provide competitive advantages to firms in particular positions.

What might be some of the strategic advantages that individual firms could seek through attempting to influence law and regulation? Competitive advantage, obviously, can take many forms. Mitnick points out, for example, that regulation may force innovation, "providing unforeseen opportunities for profit" (1981:72). Cost reductions and profitable ventures from projects such as energy conservation and materials recycling are examples of positive outcomes from environmental protection regulations. It is also plausible that regulation may benefit one or a few firms in an industry by requiring the use of a technology that these firms but not others in the industry have already mastered. In this case, the firms having the mandated technological expertise hold a substantial advantage over their competitors, who must purchase, install, and learn to use a new technology.

Robert A. Leone (1977) points out that regulation changes the cost structure of industries and thus can provide unexpected benefits to firms that are well positioned to take advantage of their competitors' financial difficulties or their own particular strengths. As an example he cites the pulp and paper industry's mandate to comply with water pollution regulations and points out that "almost 80 percent of the industry's capacity will incur essentially uniform cost increases, while some 20 percent of capacity will be very costly to clean up" (p. 65). Needless to say, the 20 percent of the industry that incurs "excessive" clean-up costs will be in some competitive difficulty, because price increases are likely to be more than the extra clean-up costs for the 80 percent, but less than the extra costs for the 20 percent (Leone, 1977:66).

Mitnick (1981:76) proposes that the strategic benefits of regulation will tend to be reaped by "larger firms, firms with particular technologies or locations, and firms with certain specialized expertise." He continues, "Firms with such comparative advantages may actually find it in their interest to support apparently restrictive regulation, not only for any possible net profits from treatment, but also for the advantages to be gained over less fortunate competitors" (p. 77).

Regulation may create new markets for enterprising companies that can provide products and services to help other companies conform to regulatory demands (Mitnick, 1981). It may provide the opportunity for firms to gain goodwill or other benefits from stakeholders by demonstrating their willing compliance with law and regulation. (On stakeholders, see Emshoff and Freeman, 1979; Sturdivant, 1979; Mendelow, 1981; Freeman, 1984.) Regulation may favor certain businesses because of their geographic location; for example, manufacturing plants located in relatively unpolluted areas with free-flowing winds may have an easier time meeting air pollution control standards than their competitors located in valleys or other areas where temperature inversions are common and other sources of pollution are significant. Certainly any firm with in-house expertise that is newly utilized to comply with regulation is in an advantageous position relative to firms who must contract with outside agents or search for and employ experts — both relatively costly processes — to gain the necessary expertise.

Several features distinguish the strategic uses perspective from that of economic theory of regulation. There is no requirement or presumption in the strategic uses approach that the firms in an industry act in concert to seek or to benefit from regulatory activities — within an industry, some firms are likely to seek regulations (although they may not seek the same regulations), some will oppose any regulation, and some will be quiescent, from ignorance or intent — nor is it necessary to show that regulation has been *sought* by businesses in order for them to benefit from it. Firms may choose to be inactive during the policy-making phase, or they may be unaware that regulatory changes are occurring, but they can still seek to obtain benefits from regulation after the law has been passed and the regulations written. Further, there is no "free rider" problem as there is with both the capture and the economic hypotheses (or at least the free rider problem is greatly reduced). The actions of one firm or a coalition of firms will not necessarily benefit all firms in the industry; indeed, the whole point of using regulation strategically is to *outwit* the competition, not to help them.

There already exists some historical evidence that businesses have recognized since before the turn of the century that regulation could serve strategic functions. Richard H. K. Vietor (1977) examined the events and conditions preceding passage of the Hepburn Act of 1906, which gave the ICC the power to set rates. Vietor concludes:

> The findings show that support for federal rate regulation came from shippers suffering competitive dislocations due to rate structures unsuited to changing market conditions. Opposition to greater federal control came from shippers and railroads that benefited from the existing ICC-enforced rate market configurations. This evidence explains Progressive Era politics as a response to the rapidly changing conditions of the market economy, rather than with the value-laden rhetoric of liberal reform or conservative triumph (p. 49).

Vietor's study is sometimes cited as support for the economic perspective on regulation, but what he actually shows is that rate regulation by the Interstate Commerce Commission was an outcome desired by only some members of the rail transport industry. It was, in fact, an attempt on the part of some companies to gain a competitive edge within the industry by obtaining strategic benefits from regulation.

The idea of strategic uses of regulation is a way of expanding the economic theory of regulation from strictly economic to social regulation. Richard A. Posner (1974:353) notes that "the 'consumerist' measures of the last few years — truth in lending and in packaging, automobile safety and emission controls, other pollution and safety regulations . . . — are not an obvious product of interest group pressures, and the proponents of the economic theory of regulation have thus far largely ignored such measures." Posner has proposed that regulation can serve as a "substitute" for the uncertainty-reduction features of an industry cartel, and that ". . . the demand for regulation (derived from its value in enhancing the profits of the regulated firms) is greater among industries for which private cartelization is an unfeasible or very costly alternative — industries that lack high concentration and other characteristics favorable to cartelizing" (p. 345). In the absence of conditions favoring the emergence of a cartel, firms will enter the political process to obtain favorable regulation, which can take many forms (e.g., subsidies, gifts, import–export controls, price-fixing, standard-setting). Any regulatory form, including those favorable to cartel-like operations, is likely to have differential effects on industry members "when there is significant asymmetry among the positions of industry members." Thus, each firm has an incentive to participate in a coalition because each wants to have its own best-suited regulatory form adopted. "This suggests that it may be cheaper for large-number industries to obtain public regulation than to cartelize privately" (Posner, 1974:346).

Mitnick (1981:80–81) proposes that a "theory of strategic use of regulation" would "relate the set of benefits achievable through change in the state of regulation (creation or removal of regulatory agents) to contingencies in the firm's position and environment and to available strategies." The evidence to be presented in this study provides considerable support for this perspective and contributes to the development of such a theory by showing how businesses sought to use law and regulation — whether or not they had actively sought those regulations — in their own interests and in particular to gain competitive advantage over others in their industry.

Robert A. Leone (1977:66) points out the desirability of recognizing that regulation is inevitable and that it is often useless for managers to pretend it does not exist or to assume that it will go away:

> One need not enthusiastically embrace government controls to recognize that regulations are a growing and permanent reality. Managers who respond to these controls as if their only impacts were measured in administrative red tape and higher production costs will continue to think of these regulations as a nuisance to be 'managed around' rather than as a reflection of fundamental changes in the economic environment.
>
> Thus the regulatory boom — like any other change in the economic environment — creates costs for some, opportunities for others, and challenges for all.

From a managerial perspective, the strategic use of regulation offers a practical, sensible, positive approach to business–government relations and to the government's regulatory functions. The evidence provided in this study shows that the strategic use of regulation to promote the competitive interests of individual businesses is by no means a new idea. To be sure, the current business environment is different from that existing at the turn of the century, but the notion that businesses can employ the powers of government to achieve comparative advantage is one that has a fairly well developed, if not very well known tradition.

CONCLUSION: ACTORS, INTERESTS, AND OUTCOMES IN THE PURE FOOD CONTROVERSY

Regulation is a fact of modern life, just as it had begun to be a fact of life in the Progressive Era. Explaining the behavior of firms in such an environment, however, has proved not to be a simple task.

Some perspectives on public policy, as we have seen, find their roots in a confrontational approach to political efficacy; in the idea that government is essentially unresponsive to the desires of constituencies and must be forced into action (e.g., Cobb and Elder, 1972). The "crisis generation" or "public outrage" hypothesis of the origin of social regulation discussed earlier in this chapter is so founded, and thus it cannot be relied upon to explain the development of wide-ranging, controversial issues that proceeded in a different manner. The economic perspective on regulation, on the other hand, is based on the idea that government and business tend to be mutually supportive, and particularly that government will be responsive to an industry's requests for protection and stability. The economic perspective has much to offer as an explanatory tool, but it cannot easily accommodate the different competitive interests of businesses *within* a regulated industry.

Where there are two clearly antagonistic camps of politically active groups and individuals focused on a single issue, the development of public policy is a relatively straightforward set of events that can be modeled neatly. In the case of the 1906 Pure Food Act, however, many issues arose, separately and in tandem with others; many parties entered the controversy (as well as the precontroversial stages of the issue's development) with a host of motives and interests that did not necessarily remain the same throughout the period before passage of the law. Many parties changed their positions, sometimes more than once, and the many issues that were involved became solidified as "the pure food issue" only in the very last stages of public and Congressional debate. A sampling of these issues and the "generic" issues into which they solidified are shown in Figure 1.2.

36

FIGURE 1.2

Dimensions of the Pure Food Issue

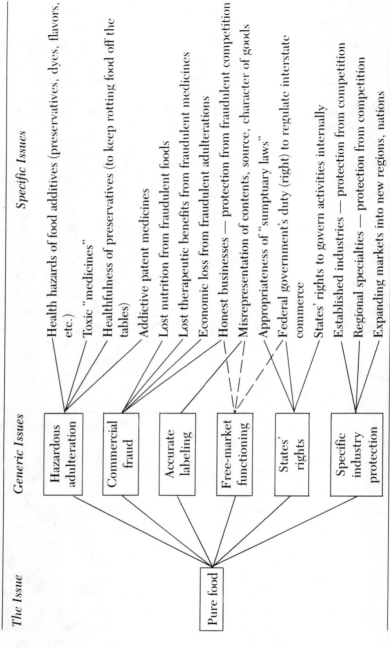

The Issue	Generic Issues	Specific Issues
Pure food	Hazardous adulteration	Health hazards of food additives (preservatives, dyes, flavors, etc.)
		Toxic "medicines"
		Healthfulness of preservatives (to keep rotting food off the tables)
		Addictive patent medicines
	Commercial fraud	Lost nutrition from fraudulent foods
		Lost therapeutic benefits from fraudulent medicines
		Economic loss from fraudulent adulterations
		Honest businesses — protection from fraudulent competition
	Accurate labeling	Misrepresentation of contents, source, character of goods
	Free-market functioning	Appropriateness of "sumptuary laws"
		Federal government's duty (right) to regulate interstate commerce
	States' rights	States' rights to govern activities internally
	Specific industry protection	Established industries — protection from competition
		Regional specialties — protection from competition
		Expanding markets into new regions, nations

The sort of complexity illustrated in Figure 1.2 is not uncommon to the development of public policy issues, and clearly it is still much too simple a depiction of the issues involved. Indeed, it might be reasonable to speak of an *issue set* rather than a single issue in many cases. Extrapolating directly from the concept of a role set, the idea of an issue set allows us to see that numerous conflicting or imperfectly compatible opinions can be expected on any given policy issue and that there is no a priori reason to deny legitimacy to any of these opinions. It is unproductive, theoretically and practically, to draw the battle lines so tightly into pro and con on a policy issue. Such solidification hinders the processes of negotiation, compromise, and reiteration that reflect political realities.

Given that so many issues were at stake in the development of the 1906 Pure Food Act, it should not be surprising that the outcome was not entirely satisfactory to any interest group. On the other hand, virtually all groups involved in the controversy achieved some of their objectives and were able to take some satisfaction from the outcome of their efforts. It would be remarkable if so many actors, with so many different interests and interactions among themselves, could achieve an outcome that would please all or even most of them (see Maitland, 1983).

In the chapters that follow, we shall see that the food and drug businesses of the Progressive Era exhibited a full range of behaviors with regard to the possibility of federal legislation governing their activities. Some firms fought the idea bitterly and continuously, some firms sought and welcomed the notion of federal control, and some firms were silent on the issue. Some firms changed positions several times; some entered the battle early, others were quite late. That they all chose their actions on the basis of some assessment of desirable outcomes can be inferred.

The strategic uses of regulation perspective, which provides the major theoretical framework for this study, does not depend on assumptions of combative or cooperative relations between businesses and government units. It does rely on the idea that the pursuit of self-interest can lead to many different types of relations between businesses and government organizations. It allows each organization to be perceived as an entity independent of all others; it recognizes that firms need to adapt to environmental conditions and to take advantage of opportunities that arise; and it respects the fact that organizations have objectives that often put them at odds with other organizations, particularly their competitors. The story of the 1906 Pure Food Act is essentially a story of competition and efforts to gain competitive advantage within the boundaries of law and public policy.

two

Business and Government in the Progressive Era

FROM THE HISTORIAN'S AERIE, THE PROGRESSIVE ERA SEEMS
marked by contradictions, as though a ruptured social order had not
yet reasserted itself, had not reconfigured into an orderly set of institutions, goals, and means. Although U.S. urban areas did not contain
a majority of the population until 1920, the dramatic trend toward
urbanization and the rapid pace of industrialization left their indelible
marks on a society that by the 1880s was agrarian only in the statistical
sense: ". . . it should be remembered that as early as 1870 about 47
percent of those gainfully employed west of the Mississippi were in
nonagricultural pursuits" (Clough and Marburg, 1968:91).

Two predominant themes of the period — at times antagonistic
and at times allied to one another — were to be found in the economic and organizational conditions surrounding industrialization, on
the one hand, and in the normative responses of people and groups
to industrialization, on the other (see Hays, 1957). Industrialization
was accompanied by a number of organizational and social structural
changes. Large workplaces — factories, mills, distribution centers —
became not only possible but desirable; they contributed to efficient
production by permitting economies of scale, and they reflected a

redirected focus in the economy from labor to capital. Workers became more replaceable than ever before, not only because successive waves of immigration brought enormous supplies of labor into the country, but also because the tasks of industrial factories were segmented and simple enough to allow a new worker to step into the place of a former worker with hardly any delay in the manufacturing process. The replaceability of workers in turn gave rise to the twin phenomena of labor solidarity and the growth of unions, on one hand, and the relative ease with which foremen could obtain "scabs" to operate the factories and mills during a strike, on the other hand (see, e.g., Weber, 1958). Family and individual mobility increased as it became clear (though for many, inaccurately so) that jobs, security, and the road to riches all lay in the cities. And as urban populations grew, so did the incidence of crime, drunkenness, divorce and abandonment, and other forms of "social pathology," requiring the official and charitable attention of the police, the local governments, and the more privileged classes.

The contradictions of this era could be seen both in the material conditions of life and in the ideological themes that moved the people. Socialism and Social Darwinism were both widely advocated; technological advancements in agriculture had not quite made obsolete the farmer's mule and plow. Utopian communities and inner-city squalor existed side by side; great fortunes were built amid conditions of the most wretched poverty. Hopes for the moral progress of humankind were closely linked to expectations of economic progress, yet rising concerns about social justice and consumer protection clashed publicly with desires to maximize the nation's real wealth. The concentration of wealth and power embodied in the "trusts" was widely recognized, but at the same time a strong belief in the individual's power to succeed through diligence, intelligence, and discipline remained prominent in the collective consciousness.

In the annals of business history, the Progressive Era is perhaps most notable as an age of expansion, growth, mergers, and intensely fierce competition. Industrialization proceeded at an undreamed-of pace, bringing with it a wealth of technological and organizational innovations. Mechanical inventions and their industrial applications provided a technological base for greater efficiency and productivity in manufacturing. Immigration and domestic migration to urban areas provided industry with cheap and easily replaceable labor, which in turn helped to hinder the budding development of labor organizations.

Samuel P. Hays (1957:9–12) notes that the expansion of transportation networks was crucial in helping to make possible rapid industrial development. Railroads, waterways, and Rural Free Delivery allowed for the first time the possibility of mass markets (and thus the profitability of mass production); they also permitted, for manufacturers, "a simpler distribution system, involving fewer middlemen and more direct buying and selling, replacing the innumerable traders formerly required" (Hays, 1957:12). In the words of two analysts of business history:

> Cheap transporation permitted the United States to conquer its greatest economic handicap — space. It made possible the bringing together of widely dispersed raw materials for processing. It allowed producers to sell their wares throughout the entire national market. It permitted the decentralization of industry as against centralization in congested areas. And it fostered a division of labor which is a condition for high production per worker, and hence of economic well-being (Clough and Marburg, 1968:112).

Furthermore, when combined with the popularity and number of regional and national magazines and newspapers, simplified distribution systems enhanced the value and the volume of advertising and allowed manufacturers to link firmly, in the public mind, product quality with brand name or region of origin. This phenomenon, of obvious benefit to manufacturers, generated problems as well. Fraudulent misrepresentation of brand names, regions of origin, and even generic names became a problem for many of those who manufactured and sold foods, beverages, drugs, and other consumer goods.

Transportation (especially railroads), steel and coal, utilities, and banking were the most closely watched industries of the time. The *Commercial and Financial Chronicle*, the principal weekly business publication, devoted most of its space to editorials, news items, and financial reports concerning these industries. These were also the industries of the "robber barons," those mid-19th-century geniuses of finance, expansion, and acquisition who built corporate empires, amassed considerable fortunes, and controlled a great portion of the national economy (see Josephson, 1935; Myers, 1936). The attention paid to these industries is understandable, for they formed the foundation of the nation's economic growth and the basis for its blossoming prosperity.

That prosperity, of course, was far from evenly distributed — certainly not in terms of per capita or family income, and not in terms of the business world, either. Earlier data are not available, but the *Historical Statistics of the United States* shows that in 1913 almost 15 percent of total national income was received by the top one percent of the population. This figure has gradually declined over the years; in 1948, for example, the top one percent of the population received 8.38 percent of total income (*Historical Statistics,* p. 302), and in 1981 15 percent of total income was received by the top five percent of the population (Statistical Abstract, 1981:438).

Figure 2.1 shows the distribution of a large sample of families into various income classes for 1901. This figure shows a very large proportion of families earning between 400 and 800 dollars per year: Seventy-five percent of the sample falls into these categories. As Table 2.1 shows, however, average annual individual earnings for 1900 were $483, suggesting that most families in the lower and middle income brackets had more than one worker contributing to total family income.

Statistics on the distribution of expenditures for the 11,156 families in the Census Bureau's 1901 sample are presented in Table 2.2. The poorest families, of course, spent over 50 percent of family income on food and were unable to save anything. The wealthiest families in the sample were able to save a considerable portion of their income, spent relatively less on food (although their actual food expenditures were 400 percent more than those of the poorest families), and had available a substantial amount for discretionary spending.

Table 2.3 provides data on labor force participation by sex and age of workers, and these data can be compared to total population figures, in Table 2.4. The top set of figures in Table 2.3 shows the actual number of workers in each age and sex category, in thousands. The total labor force in 1890 consisted of 21,833,000 workers, or 34.7 percent of the population. In 1900, 36.4 percent of the population was in the labor force. The bottom set of figures in Table 2.3 shows the labor force participation rate, which is the proportion of all members of a category who are in the labor force. Thus we see that in

FIGURE 2.1

Percent of Families in Various Income Classes, 1901

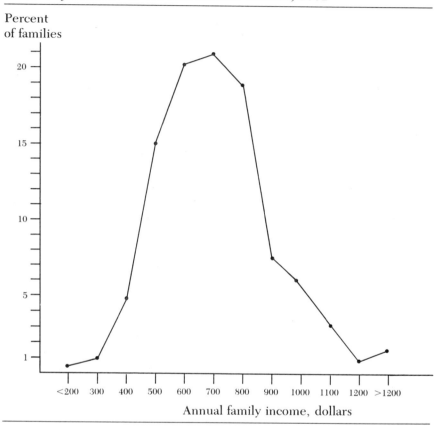

Percent
of families

Annual family income, dollars

SOURCE: Compiled from *Historical Statistics of the United
States*, Volume 1, page 321. The data were obtained from a sample
of 11,156 "normal families."

1890, 84.3 percent of all adult males were gainfully employed, as
were 18.2 percent of all adult females. The third set of figures shows
percent distribution, or the percent of the labor force comprised of
each sex and age category. In 1890, women were only 17 percent of
the total labor force. The figures have an unfortunate bias in that child
labor was not included in labor force statistics in this era. As we shall

TABLE 2.1

Average Annual Earnings of All Employees, 1870–1909

Year	Average Annual Earnings, in Dollars
1870	489
1880	386
1890	475
1900	483
1904	482
1909	545

SOURCE: *Historical Statistics of the United States*, Series D-722-727, D-735-738.

see later, child labor was considerable during the Progressive Era and was the focus of reform efforts.

Overall, the problem of locating the individual in a new social order was a poignant and difficult one. To many it seemed that millions suffered to enrich a few. Prisons and insane asylums tortured the wretched and ignorant, and the faint voice of structured inequality whispered that hard work and discipline would not guarantee an individual's success. Concentration of economic resources produced inequities that called for redress. Further, industrialization and mass marketing made scarce a necessary resource of the free market — accurate information — and seemed to create, along with the promise of security and success, a host of difficulties not easily defined or solved.

IDEOLOGICAL CONDITIONS

Samuel P. Hays reports that 68 utopian novels were published in the period 1865–1915. They provide a window of sorts to the troubles and hopes of the times:

> Popular utopian novels revealed . . . clearly the hope of Americans to find an easy solution to industrial problems. . . . The most widely read, Edward Bellamy's (1850–98) *Looking Backward* (1888), scored an immediate success — it sold almost 400,000 copies — and in-

TABLE 2.2

Consumption Expenditures, in Current Prices, of City Wage and Clerical-Worker Families of Two or More Persons, by Income Class, 1901

		NORMAL FAMILIES		INCOME CLASS (BEFORE TAXES)											
Series No.	Item	All Income Classes	Under $200	$200–$300	$300–$400	$400–$500	$500–$600	$600–$700	$700–$800	$800–$900	$900–$1,000	$1,000–$1,100	$1,100–$1,200	$1,200 and over
554	Number of families	11,156	32	115	545	1,676	2,264	2,336	2,094	806	684	340	96	168
555	Average family size, persons	4.0	3.2	3.4	3.8	3.8	3.9	3.9	4.0	4.2	4.1	4.3	4.0	3.8
556	Average income	$651												
557	Average expenditures for current consumption	$618	$196	$312	$389	$466	$540	$612	$693	$771	$816	$900	$973	$1,052
558	Food	266	100	148	187	218	249	266	287	319	326	349	367	384
559	Rent	112	33	56	73	87	100	113	126	132	144	158	161	183
560	Fuel	28	13	19	23	26	27	28	29	30	31	34	35	41
561	Light	7	2	4	4	5	6	7	8	8	9	10	11	12
562	Clothing	80	17	27	39	53	65	79	94	105	117	136	145	165
563	Sundries	124	31	59	63	77	93	119	150	177	189	213	254	267

SOURCE: *Historical Statistics of the United States*, Volume 1, p. 321.

TABLE 2.3

Labor Force by Age and Sex, 1890 to 1970

(Labor force in thousands of persons 16 years old and over, prior to 1947 14 years old and over. Annual estimates are averages of monthly figures. Includes Armed Forces overseas, except for decennial data. The introduction of data from the decennial censuses into the estimation procedure in 1953 and 1962 and the inclusion of Alaska and Hawaii beginning 1960 have resulted in three periods of noncomparability.

YEAR	TOTAL LABOR FORCE Total	MALE						FEMALE					
		Total	16 to 19 years[1]	20 to 24 years	25 to 44 years	45 to 64 years	65 and over	Total	16 to 19 years[1]	20 to 24 years	25 to 44 years	45 to 64 years	65 and over
Labor Force (thousands)													
Decennial census:													
1970 (April)	82,049	51,502	3,593	6,271	22,111	17,434	2,092	30,547	2,609	4,683	11,652	10,432	1,171
1960 (April)[2]	69,234	47,013	2,634	4,554	21,829	15,765	2,231	22,222	1,703	2,475	9,382	7,742	919
1950 (April)	59,223	42,779	2,204	4,537	20,389	13,275	2,373	16,443	1,331	2,521	7,666	4,416	509
1940 (April)	52,966	39,959	2,565	4,993	18,705	11,859	1,838	13,007	1,396	2,698	6,081	2,554	279
1930 (April)	47,404	37,008	2,795	4,747	17,498	10,173	1,795	10,396	1,591	2,316	4,404	1,842	243
1920 (Jan.)	40,282	32,053	2,947	4,080	15,353	8,290	1,383	8,229	1,640	1,785	3,314	1,310	180
1900 (June)	27,640	22,641	2,834	3,302	10,560	4,958	987	4,999	1,230	1,179	1,791	672	127
1890 (June)	21,833	18,129	1,997	2,836	8,513	3,937	846	3,704	984	938	1,216	476	90

Labor Force Participation Rate
(percent)

Decennial census:

Year													
1970 (April)	58.2	76.6	47.2	80.9	94.3	87.2	24.8	41.4	34.9	56.1	47.5	47.8	10.0
1960 (April)[2]	57.3	80.4	50.0	86.2	95.3	89.0	30.5	35.7	32.6	44.8	39.1	41.6	10.3
1950 (April)	55.1	81.6	51.7	81.9	93.3	88.2	41.4	29.9	31.1	42.9	33.3	28.8	7.8
1940 (April)	52.4	79.1	34.7	88.1	94.9	88.7	41.8	25.8	18.9	45.6	30.5	20.2	6.1
1930 (April)	53.2	82.1	40.1	88.8	95.8	91.0	54.0	23.6	22.8	41.8	24.6	18.0	7.3
1920 (Jan.)	54.3	84.6	51.5	89.9	95.6	90.7	55.6	22.7	28.4	37.5	21.7	16.5	7.3
1900 (June)	53.7	85.7	62.0	90.6	94.7	90.3	63.1	20.0	26.8	31.7	17.5	13.6	8.3
1890 (June)	52.2	84.3	50.0	90.9	96.0	92.0	68.3	18.2	24.5	30.2	15.1	12.1	7.6

Percent Distribution

Decennial census:

Year													
1970 (April)	100.0	62.8	4.4	7.6	26.9	21.2	2.5	37.2	3.2	5.7	14.2	12.7	1.4
1960 (April)[2]	100.0	67.9	3.8	6.6	31.5	22.8	3.2	32.1	2.5	3.6	13.6	11.2	1.3
1950 (April)	100.0	72.2	3.7	7.7	34.4	22.4	4.0	27.8	2.2	4.3	12.9	7.5	.9
1940 (April)	100.0	75.4	4.8	9.4	35.3	22.4	3.5	24.6	2.6	5.1	11.5	4.8	.5
1930 (April)	100.0	78.1	5.9	10.0	36.9	21.5	3.8	21.9	3.4	4.9	9.3	3.9	.5
1920 (Jan.)	100.0	79.6	7.3	10.1	38.1	20.6	3.4	20.4	4.1	4.4	8.2	3.3	.4
1900 (June)	100.0	81.9	10.3	11.9	38.2	17.9	3.6	18.1	4.5	4.3	6.5	2.4	.5
1890 (June)	100.0	83.0	9.1	13.0	39.0	18.0	3.9	17.0	4.5	4.3	5.6	2.2	.4

SOURCE: Condensed from *Historical Statistics of the United States*, Volume 1, pp. 321–322.

[1]14 to 19 years for 1940 through 1946.

[2]First year for which figures include Alaska and Hawaii.

TABLE 2.4

United States Population, 1790–1910

CENSUS DATE	POPULATION	INCREASE OVER PRECEDING CENSUS	
		Number	Percent
1790	3,929,214	———	———
1800	5,308,483	1,379,269	35.1
1810	7,239,881	1,931,398	36.4
1820	9,638,453	2,398,572	33.1
1830	12,866,020	3,227,567	33.5
1840	17,069,453	4,203,433	32.7
1850	23,191,876	6,122,423	35.9
1860	31,443,321	8,251,445	35.6
1870	39,818,449[1]	8,375,128	26.6
1880	50,155,783	10,337,334	26.0
1890	62,947,714	12,791,931	25.5
1900	75,994,575	13,046,861	20.7
1910	91,972,266	15,977,691	21.0

SOURCE: U.S. Bureau of the Census, Statistical Abstract United States: 1965 (Washington, D.C.: U.S. Government Printing Office, 1965), p. 5. Adapted from Clough and Marburg (1968).

[1]Revised to include adjustments for undernumeration in Southern states; unrevised number is 38,558,371.

spired other hopeful authors to write in a similar vein. Concerned with the impending internal crisis, each of these romantic novels argued that man was not competitive and greedy but was essentially good, innately capable of living in peace with his fellow man. Environment had thwarted those noble impulses; different circumstances would nourish them. The key lay in abundance, for when man's material wants were filled, no reason for selfishness would remain. Modern technology provided the opportunity for man to create an ideal society, free of social conflict (Hays, 1957:51).

Far more prevalent than utopianism was the lingering doctrine of Calvinism. Persons who worshipped in the Calvinist tradition were presented with a serious theological and cosmological problem. If the ultimate aim of living was to be with God in heaven, and if God had already decided who would enter the kingdom of heaven and who would not, and if one could not earn one's way into heaven, then how was a person to know whether he or she was on God's "short list"? The answer to this ultimate question, evolved over the years, was this: God would provide a sign of grace to those who could count on an eternity in heaven; the sign would be good health, good fortune, and most importantly, the accumulation of material wealth.

Max Weber, in The *Protestant Ethic and the Spirit of Capitalism* (1958), has provided the classic analysis of the superb fit between the ideological foundations of Calvinism and other forms of Protestantism and the material and social structural needs of industrializing societies. As Hays has noted:

> Outspoken religious leaders of the day firmly argued that material success provided outward evidence of an inward moral and religious character. In fact, Russell Conwell (1843–1925) argued in his oft-repeated lecture, "Acres of Diamonds," that to make money honestly was both a Christian obligation and a form of preaching the gospel (Hays, 1957:23).

A sample from Conwell's famous presentation follows: "Money is power, . . . and for a man to say, 'I do not want money,' is to say, 'I do not wish to do any good to my fellowmen' " (quoted in Goldman, 1952: 70).

To the laws of God were added the laws of science. Herbert Spencer, an English economist–sociologist–popular lecturer, discovered in Charles Darwin's *Origin of Species* a model to explain and justify the hierarchy of social organization and a blueprint for societal progress. Eric F. Goldman describes the impact of Spencer's ideas as follows:

> Herbert Spencer had transformed Darwin's biological laws into social "laws" that made science say precisely what every conservative wanted said. Biological Darwinism asserted that all species of organic life had evolved and were evolving by a process of the survival of the fittest. According to Spencer's "Social Darwinism," society, too, was an organism that evolved by the survival of the fittest. Ex-

isting social institutions were therefore the "fittest" way of doing things, and businessmen who bested their competitors had thereby proved themselves "the fittest" to enjoy wealth and power. No wise man would try to interfere with this evolutionary process by social legislation. At best, the social legislation would not work as it was intended to work, and, in any event, it would have baleful results. Poverty and corruption were undoubted evils, Social Darwinism admitted, but they would be cured only by a centuries-long evolution resulting from the survival of the fittest. Meanwhile, as Henry George's friend had said, "nothing, nothing at all" could be done (Goldman, 1952:71).

The laws of biological science, discovered by Darwin and reinterpreted for higher-order beings by Spencer, added considerable weight to the theological justification for individual greed and unlimited, unabashed self-interest that was provided by Calvinism. As Goldman noted:

"The problem presented to systems of religion and schemes of government," ironmaster Abram Hewitt had pointed out, was to make men who were equal in liberty content with inequality in the distribution of property. Conservative Darwinism not only repeated the answer to the problem which conservatism had long been effectively using; its solution added all the authority of science. Conservative Darwinism created, as it were, a science of selfishness. Now John D. Rockefeller, with the same confidence that he had in his latest laboratory, could explain the Standard Oil trust to his Sunday-school class as "merely a survival of the fittest . . ." (Goldman, 1952:71).

Ideologically, Herbert Spencer's transmutation of Darwin's theory of biological evolution — Social Darwinism — provided a kind of scientific justification for the inherent right of the wealthy and powerful to hold their economic and social positions. In an age when science was beginning to be revered and when churches were losing membership, the Darwinian defense offered a more acceptable rationale for opposing social intervention in the structure of opportunities than did the theological defense of Calvinism. Yet, as Goldman

(1952) has pointed out, reliance on scientific theory to bolster a normative belief system also provided a powerful justification for reform efforts.

For the most part, reform theorists did not address the difficulties of extrapolating the processes of biological evolution to the development of social structures. Instead, they took adaptation to the environment as their theme, and pointed out that conservative thinkers had misconstrued Darwinian theory on the dimension of change. Darwin, said the reformers, did not posit a stable universe and made no suggestion that the current order of things was the ultimate in evolutionary development. A truly scientific position would recognize that change was ubiquitous, and that human beings, by reason of their higher intelligence and their will, had the power to intervene in environmental conditions and thus to change the configuration of social positions. The wealthy had no moral right to their financial holdings, and even if they might be somehow biologically superior to the poor, that situation was subject to change if the environment of the poor could be properly manipulated. In this way, reform thinkers attempted to undercut the scientific underpinnings of status-quo ideology and to claim for themselves a more rational and truly scientific foundation.

Theological and biological laws, perceived as timeless and universal, were cemented in a material sense by the laws of laissez-faire economics as interpreted by 19th-century intellectuals, religious leaders, and businessmen. In essense, these interpreters believed that the function of the "invisible hand" was to ensure that the overall well-being of a population was maximized by the consistent and aggressive pursuit of individual self interest. In other words, prevailing economic theory and belief suggested that the greedier one was, the better for society, and that social welfare would be maximized if everyone engaged in greedy, self-interested behavior.

It is no wonder that the Progressive Era was marked by an unprecedented concentration of wealth and power. Those who wished to be rich or were rich already could afford to be ruthless in seeking to further their interests. The laws of economics, biology, and theology combined to support such endeavors and to justify them in the eyes of most members of the society, from the poorest of wage-earners to the wealthiest industrialists.

SOCIAL ORGANIZATION

Competitive conditions during the Progressive Era are frequently described as fierce, but they cannot be truly characterized by such a blanket statement. Some industries — for example, food manufacturing and semidurable consumer goods — experienced dramatic growth in market possibilities, number of firms, and total output, and they were marked by intensive competition among firms. For other industries — primary metals, transportation, banking — the age of the "robber barons" (following the Civil War and preceeding the Progressive Era) had resulted in unprecedented consolidation of financial and industrial interests and in many cases a severe decline in free market competition.

The economic disparity between businesses enjoying empire-like status and businesses struggling for survival and growth was reflected in organizational developments. Industrialization and the competitive conditions surrounding it fostered collective economic enterprises of many kinds. Banding together in a common purpose was a potent way to amass social and economic resources, which could then be applied to the defeat of competitors and the boosting of group members' other interests. Significantly, it was during this time that businesses, collectivities, and other interest groups began to discover and to take serious advantage of the potential power of the federal government to shape competitive conditions and the allocation of resources.

Some collectivities sought to guarantee the continuation of concentrated economic power and to leave control in the hands of those who already held it. The "trusts" (money, beef, railroads, sugar) and some corporate mergers (e.g., Standard Oil) supported the status quo and made sure "their" Senators did the same, as did some business and trade organizations such as the National Civic Federation (an organization akin to today's Business Roundtable) (Weinstein, 1968). Other collective enterprises were founded to try to reallocate economic resources more favorably for "disadvantaged" groups — those who did not wield economic clout but wanted to do so. The Grange and the other agricultural cooperatives were intent on reducing the stranglehold of railroads and warehousers over the annual income of farmers (from whom they exacted heavy transportation and distribution fees). The National Association of Manufacturers, representing a host of small and medium-sized businesses, lobbied intensively in Washington to capture competitive advantage for themselves and to restrict public policies that heavily favored big businesses.

Farmers' organizations provide an example of economic coalitions that developed to secure competitive advantage for their members. In the 19th century farmers were particularly dependent upon short-term market conditions for their survival. Because of the influence of weather, pests, natural disaster, and similar factors on the size and quality of crops, farmers had relatively little control over the supply of foodstuffs. They had virtually no control over demand, and were highly dependent on prices. Following the Civil War, agricultural prices bottomed out, many farm mortgages were foreclosed, and

> . . . farmers became both discouraged and belligerent. In their predicament they joined in such action groups as the Grange, which had a membership of 1,500,000 in the Spring of 1874, and the National Farmers' Alliance, which had a membership of 100,000 in 1880 (Clough and Marburg, 1968:92).

The Grange and the other farmers' organizations quickly discovered that political action was the fastest route to economic stability. Encouraged by small successes, these groups gradually began to tackle larger, nationwide problems:

> Farmer groups attacked high railway rates, discriminatory rates, and poor service. They complained that the Burlington charged nearly four times as much in 1877 for hauling freight west of the Missouri as for hauling it east; that James J. Hill would not ship grain from elevators of less than a thirty-thousand-bushel capacity; that some roads charged twice as much as others for the same service, and that cattle cars were left long hours on sidetracks where there was no water or feed. These complaints finally got results, as for example, in the establishment of rate regulation (adopted by Minnesota in 1871), in establishing the constitutionality of such regulation (*Munn v. Illinois*), and in getting the Interstate Commerce Commission created in 1887 to deal with interstate commerce (Clough & Marburg, 1968: 92–93).

It must be noted, however, that it is not at all clear that the farmers achieved their aims in the establishment of the Interstate Commerce

Commission. Subsequent research has shown that the ICC served mainly to stabilize competitive conditions for rail transportation companies (see Mitnick, 1980).

Commodity collectives, agricultural cooperatives, and other networks and coalitions of agricultural, commercial, financial, and manufacturing organizations became more and more common during the era, as individuals discovered that they could better achieve their objectives by acting in concert on certain issues.

Labor unions certainly developed on the same principle of collective action for common benefit. Growth in union membership is shown in Table 2.5. It is readily apparent that union membership did not begin to approach its potential, yet the actions and objectives of labor unions had a dramatic impact on labor market conditions and public consciousness. The depression of 1873–1879 marked the first of a long series of bitter and violent strikes, culminating in the first nationwide strike, in the summer of 1877. Eric F. Goldman describes the sequence of events as follows:

> Trouble started when the principal railroads, refusing to decrease high dividends on watered stocks, decreed a ten percent cut in wages. First on the Baltimore & Ohio lines in West Virginia, then north and west all the way to Canada and California, the workers hit back. Their violent strikes provoked the use of troops by business-minded governments, and the use of troops provoked more violence.
>
> The turbulence reached a climax in Pittsburgh. Twenty-five people were killed and many more wounded when soldiers came into collision with a mob of strikers and strike sympathizers. Disorder ricocheted across the city. Barrels of liquor were tapped and drunk on the spot; stores were broken into for food, clothing, and furniture; long lines of freight cars were looted and set on fire. The incendiarism spread until the four-story Union Depot, two thousand cars, the railroad machine shops, a grain elevator, and two roundhouses with 125 locomotives had been destroyed. Two days later the city awoke to its hangover of ashes and caskets. Railroad executives and storekeepers wrathfully estimated their losses at five to ten millions; railroad workers sullenly went back to work with the wage cut intact. The nation, uneasy and irritated, wondered what America was coming to (Goldman, 1952: 26).

TABLE 2.5

Labor Union Membership, by Affiliation, 1897 to 1915

| YEAR | TOTAL UNION MEMBERSHIP (1,000) | | AMERICAN FEDERATION OF LABOR | | | INDEPENDENT OR UNAFFILIATED UNIONS, TOTAL MEMBERSHIP (1,000) |
| | | | Number of Affiliated Unions, | Total Membership (1,000) | | |
	BLS	Wolman	BLS	BLS	Wolman	Wolman
1915	2,560	2,583	110	1,946	1,968	614
1914	2,647	2,687	110	2,021	2,061	626
1913	2,661	2,716	111	1,996	2,051	665
1912	2,405	2,452	112	1,770	1,818	635
1911	2,318	2,343	115	1,762	1,787	556
1910	2,116	2,140	120	1,562	1,587	554
1909	1,965	2,006	119	1,483	1,524	482
1908	2,092	2,131	116	1,587	1,625	505
1907	2,077	2,080	117	1,539	1,542	538
1906	1,892	1,907	119	1,454	1,469	438
1905	1,918	2,022	118	1,494	1,598	424
1904	2,067	2,073	120	1,676	1,682	391
1903	1,824	1,914	113	1,466	1,556	358
1902	1,335	1,376	97	1,024	1,065	311
1901	1,058	1,125	87	788	854	270
1900	791	868	82	548	625	243
1899	550	611	73	349	410	201
1898	467	501	67	278	312	189
1897	440	447	58	265	272	175

SOURCE: *Historical Statistics of the United States,* Volume 1, Series D-940-945, p. 177.

In the 1890s union activity began to diverge from its initial coalition with the Populist movement. Under the leadership of Samuel Gompers, the American Federation of Labor emerged as the preeminent labor organization devoted exclusively to the welfare of employees. The older Knights of Labor, comprised of a strange mixture of workers, retail commercial people, and farmers, began to give way, and its Populist foundation garnered little comfort from the new union militancy:

> Samuel Gompers, master architect of the federation, was determined to keep the AFL tightly reined to the purpose of larger wages, better working conditions, and shorter hours for industrial labor. At times Populism seemed to offer so much to labor that Gompers wavered, but he was soon back to his original position. Complete cooperation between the unions and the Populist Party, Gomers wrote, was "unnatural." The Populist Party consisted mainly of "employing farmers," whose "purposes, methods, and interests" diverged from those of the "employed farmers of the country districts or the mechanics and laborers of the industrial centers" (Goldman, 1952:46).

With the creation of the United States Steel Corporation, the world's first billion-dollar trust, in 1901, many people in America became concerned that the concentration of power in the hands of giant corporations (and in the future, giant trade unions) would lead inevitably to a socialistic government. Goldman illustrates the commonly expressed concern:

> "It was bad enough to have million-dollar trusts run by a few men," the Chicago Evening Post expressed the widespread feeling, "but what is going to happen to the farmer, the worker, and the small businessman when we have billion-dollar combines maneuvered by a handful of men who have never been in a plant and who think of a factory as just another chip in a gigantic financial poker game?" (Goldman, 1952:57).

The excesses of industrial development seemed to have no redress other than state ownership of industry or the equally abominable federal control of industrial practices. What was to become of the free market?

We shall hold for the moment any argument that the free market had been long dead by the time the Progressive Era began. For now, it may suffice to note Hays' argument:

> despite . . . differences in the pace of organization, industrialists, shippers, farm-commodity organizations and labor unions developed in common a firm commitment to the existing economic order. Whereas in previous years many had expressed dissatisfaction with the "system" and had voiced the conviction that it could be cast aside, the new economic organizations accepted the implications of industrialism and concentrated on working out their destiny within it. Their very success in coping with day-to-day problems through collective action cemented their attachment to the new industrial society (Hays, 1957:69–70).

This contention is easily understood if one recalls that the predominant ideological structure insisted upon the moral and material superiority of self-interested action. Collectives such as trusts, unions, cooperatives, and others could easily be seen as being merely more powerful vehicles for achieving personal self interest.

Many businesses were getting bigger, not only because of normal growth, but because of the relatively new phenomenon of corporate mergers and acquisitions. Ralph L. Nelson, in his study of the three important merger movements in U.S. mining and manufacturing industries, maintains that the first such movement, peaking in 1890–1902,

> . . . was the most important of the major merger waves. It transformed many industries, formerly characterized by many small and medium-sized firms, into those in which one or a few very large enterprises occupied a leading position. It laid the foundation for the industrial structure that has characterized most of American industry in the twentieth century (Nelson, 1959:5).

Samuel P. Hays cautions against the inclination to explain major merger activity by the technological demands of mass production:

> It should not be thought that the vision of more efficient production stimulated the merger movement. To be sure, elements such as more efficient marketing were involved; but far more important was the desire of entrepreneurs to escape the rigors of competition, to form market power to intervene in impersonal economic conditions before which, as individuals, they had formerly stood helpless. Moreover, these efforts succeeded (Hays, 1957:52).

This theme of attempts "to escape the rigors of competition" is an important one for our purposes, and we shall return to it later.

Publicly held corporations, though growing in popularity because of their tax advantages and their ability to serve as a vehicle for accumulating capital, were not nearly as common as they are today. Many corporations were privately held, and few other businesses were incorporated. Of the stock corporations, Clough and Marburg observe:

> Gradually the stock company assumed a large role in the business community, and elaborate machinery was erected to manage investments in them. The New York Stock Exchange, which was founded in 1792 as a voluntary association of members to trade in Federal, state, county, and municipal bonds, became the most important of the many marts established in every major city to trade in stocks; and through these exchanges, brokerage concerns, investment houses, and investment divisions of banks and life insurance companies formed channels that led from those with savings throughout the nation to the industrial corporations. So effective was this machinery that by 1879, the number of stocks listed on the New York Stock Exchange numbered 174, and the volume of transactions in stocks attained $72,700,000. In 1886 there was a day when the volume topped one million shares. In 1905, when the railroad-building era was nearing its close, there were 374 stocks listed and the volume of sales was $260,500,000 (Clough & Marburg, 1968:185).

Hays notes that many corporations experienced substantial growth toward the end of the 19th century. One reason for this phenomenon was the Panic of 1893, when the stock market crashed, commercial and industrial credit was severely restricted, and many businesses went bankrupt and were forced to close. Hays reports that other circumstances of this period also favored corporate growth:

> Mass markets and mass production had ushered in an era of intense competition. But competition, constantly tending to push production beyond the capacity of markets, gave rise to uneasiness in the minds of businessmen; by driving prices downward it threatened both immediate profits and long-range industrial stability. Entrepreneurs looked for methods of manipulating market forces to con-

trol competition. They experimented with a variety of techniques before discovering the most effective one.

In the 1870s the pool, a gentlemen's agreement unenforceable at law, was widely used to establish minimum prices, to control production, and to divide markets. Such agreements, however, placed a severe strain upon the integrity of gentlemen; many succumbed to the temptation to cut their own prices (Hays, 1957:49).

Price-fixing and other restraint-of-trade practices were perhaps among the milder corporate behaviors that had begun to cause alarm among some sectors of society. Concurrent with industrial development, and probably because of it, social movements and social action organizations of many sorts emerged and contributed their philosophies, political demands, and normative prescriptions to American consciousness. Patriotic and hereditary organizations; women's groups such as the General Federation of Women's Clubs; social justice groups attempting to secure protection for children, immigrants, the mentally deficient, the insane, prisoners, and women; the Socialist Party; the Women's Christian Temperance Union; and many other groups used action and rhetoric to reassert the integrity and worth of individuals and their communities.

In summary, the turbulence of the times and the highly visible contrast between the upper class's conspicuous consumption and the inability of the lower classes to gain even a toehold promoted the development of organizational forms seeking to reduce the alienation of individuals in cities and factories and to better the conditions of their material lives (Veblen, 1953). Sociologically, the era epitomized the dichotomy between "community" (intimate, tradition-bound, local, satisfying) and "society" (impersonal, uncertain, cosmopolitan, alienating) that constituted a resonant theme in classical sociological theory (Toennies, 1940; Durkheim, 1947). For many, the central problem of the era could be defined as one of trust. In traditional societies, such as agrarian America, the rules for behavior were known by all, as were the sanctions for improper behavior. Smaller, simpler, closer-to-home mechanisms for economic production and distribution, furthermore, meant that persons could more readily identify the sources of many of their market-related troubles and effect remedies. Responsibility for the quality of goods and services could be located in individuals, with names known to all community members. This mode of social organization, despite faults and limitations, at least provided for the quality of the items they sold or bartered to others.

Industrial, urban society, on the other hand, not only discouraged this sort of personal responsibility but largely made it impossible. When goods were produced in factories and shipped to distant markets, when families no longer grew and stored their own food, when clothing was purchased in retail stores or through mail-order catalogs and not made by the user, how could consumers maintain any direct control over the quality, quantity, or price of goods and services? The law of supply and demand might provide an overarching rationale for consumer power in the marketplace, but clearly it provided no relief to individual consumers who found less and less basis for trusting the unknown persons and machines who made and sold the goods they could no longer provide for themselves.

For businesses, the central organizational problem concerned continuing or altering the resource allocation status quo. Some organizational forms developed to guarantee concentrated power and wealth, and others developed to allow aspirants to power a chance to gain competitive advantage. For "the people," reform and social action organizations, as well as other voluntary groups, seemed to be focused more on the problem of locating the individual in a new social order. Across the board, organizations began to discover the possibility of wielding political power by speaking and acting collectively.

A LIMITED ROLE FOR GOVERNMENT

Despite fears that industrialization would lead naturally and rapidly toward national socialism, the belief that the federal government should have a limited role in economic affairs was still widespread. As Table 2.6 shows, the growth of government during the Progressive Era is accounted for largely by the growth of the Postal Service, as more and more small communities had their own post offices established, and as cities began to require more postal employees to accommodate their burgeoning populations.

What may seem strange to modern readers is that the role of

government during this time was not limited to protecting "the public interest" as we might define it today, in terms of the voiceless consumer or the helpless worker. It was limited instead to acts that would help those whose primary function was the generation of wealth.

The functions of Progressive Era government, on both federal and state levels, are described as follows:

> In these decades of industrial growth, politics and government were called upon to be the instruments of material progress. No doctrinaire view prevailed as to the proper role of government in economic life. There was only the pragmatic assumption that the business of America was to create wealth and that government at all levels should contribute to this task. At times some leaders and groups pretended to believe in laissez faire, but they did not hesitate to take advantage of government if useful to their own particular method of creating wealth. The American economy involved a mixture of public and private stimulants, federal, state, and local assistance for capital, technical advice, generous tax concessions, and the use of legal power to lessen the rigors of competition. Such aid, often given in the absence of private resources, frequently ceased as private initiative supplied the deficiency, but the creators of wealth demanded that government stand prepared to assist when needed (Hays, 1957:17–18).

Recent research on the independent regulatory commissions, the origins and administration of antitrust legislation, and the relationship between the passage of a law and its regulatory implementation have contributed to a "revisionist" school of American history that substantiates the view that government's role until recent decades has been to protect businesses and not "the people" (see Mitnick, 1980). The Progressive Era, however, hosted a number of significant reform movements that made themselves felt in Congress and elsewhere in the government. Many of these reform movements were humanitarian in outlook; many constituted revolts against the excesses and evils of industrialism. These movements (to protect child and women workers, to prohibit the sale of alcoholic beverages, to reduce the power of the trusts, to eliminate corruption in government, to aid the poor and homeless, and to accomplish many other

TABLE 2.6

Paid Civilian Employment in the Federal Government, 1816–1915

	EMPLOYEES			COMPETITIVE CIVIL SERVICE EMPLOYEES (CLASSIFIED)	EXECUTIVE BRANCH				LEGISLATIVE BRANCH	JUDICIAL BRANCH[3]
YEAR	Total[1]	Washington, D.C.	All Other Areas		Total	Defense[2]	Post Office	Other		
1915	395,429	41,281	354,148	292,291	387,294	58,286	212,012	116,996	5,975	2,160
1914	401,887	40,016	361,871	292,460	393,555	57,989	212,973	122,593	6,132	2,200
1913	396,494	38,975	257,519	282,597	388,217	55,476	213,103	119,638	6,037	2,240
1912	400,150	38,555	361,595	217,392	391,918	60,015	214,770	117,133	5,942	2,290
1911	395,905	39,782	356,123	227,657	387,673	60,283	211,546	115,844	5,902	2,330
1910	388,708	38,911	349,797	222,278	380,428	58,320	209,005	113,103	5,910	2,370
1909	372,379	35,936	336,443	234,940	364,078	54,425	205,360	104,293	5,891	2,410
1908	356,754	34,647	322,107	206,637	348,479	50,665	199,904	97,910	5,825	2,450
1907				194,323						
1906				184,178						
1905				171,807						
1904				154,093						
1903				135,453						
1902				107,990						
1901	239,476	28,044	211,432	106,205	231,056	44,524	136,192	50,340	5,690	2,730
1900				94,893						
1899				93,144						
1898				89,306						
1897				85,886						
1896				87,044						

Year										
1895				54,222						2,731
1894				45,821						
1893				43,915						
1892				37,523						
1891	157,442	20,834	136,608	33,873	150,844	20,561	95,449	34,834	3,867	
1890				30,626						
1889				29,650						
1888				22,577						
1887[4]				19,345						
1886[5]				17,273						
1885[6]				15,590						
1884[7]				13,780						
1881	100,020	13,124	86,896		94,679	16,297	56,421	21,961	2,579	2,762
1871	51,020	6,222	44,798		50,155	1,183	36,696	12,276	618	247
1861	36,672	2,199	34,473		36,106	946	30,269	4,891	393	173
1851	26,274	1,533	24,741		25,713	403	21,391	3,919	384	177
1841	18,038	1,014	17,024		17,550	598	14,290	2,662	332	156
1831	11,491	666	10,825		11,067	377	8,764	1,926	289	135
1821	6,914	603	6,311		6,526	161	4,766	1,599	252	136
1816	4,837	535	4,302		4,479	190	3,341	938	243	115

SOURCE: *Historical Statistics of the United States*, Volume 2, Series Y-308-317, pp. 1102–1103.

[1] Excludes employees of the Central Intelligence Agency and the National Security Agency.

[2] War and Navy Departments; beginning 1881, includes mechanics and other workmen at army arsenals and navy yards.

[3] Estimated for 1908–15.

[4] Jan. 16, 1886–June 30, 1887.

[5] Jan. 16, 1885–Jan. 15, 1886.

[6] Jan. 16, 1884–Jan. 15, 1885.

[7] July 16, 1883–Jan. 15, 1884.

"social" goals) gained a great deal of attention nationwide and were successful in accomplishing some reforms. Business leaders at the same time were learning to be constantly alert to public pressures on government.

Hays reports:

> To avoid the antibusiness sentiment that might lead to detrimental legislation, business also became increasingly sensitive to public opinion. When laws to regulate business first appeared, industrial leaders, for example, William H. Vanderbilt of the New York Central Railroad, had assumed a "public be damned" attitude, blurting out that the public had no legitimate interest in what seemed to them essentially private affairs. Once convinced, however, that the threat of regulatory legislation was serious, business became more concerned with practical techniques to prevent such adverse results. Industrial leaders became more cautious in expressing their attitudes toward the public; they now argued that the public did have a legitimate interest in the conduct of private business, though they circumscribed the area of such interest as closely as they deemed politically practical. To prevent regulatory laws, they participated more actively in politics as candidates for office, as party officials, and in providing party financial support. Forced to accept regulatory commissions, they sought to influence them in their own interest, accepting such bodies as buffers between business and the public. A commission was worth the sacrifice if it would allay antibusiness feeling and if it could be rendered harmless by a judicious choice of personnel (Hays 1957:53).

It is during this era that substantial evidence for Murray Edelman's (1964; 1971) thesis concerning the political uses of symbols can easily be found. Reformers required action; the government responded to demands; the offenders, who were most likely to be coalitions of business leaders and government officials, learned quickly that a statutory law served as a powerful symbol to individuals who felt threatened with powerlessness in the face of increasing industrialization and concentration of wealth. Meanwhile, the law's implementation could be invisible to the public and could have nothing to do with the overt and formally expressed intent of the law. In short, business leaders learned that political efficacy often demanded discretion.

THE MUCKRAKERS AND PURE FOOD

The press, particularly the journalists who wrote for popular magazines, played an important role in bringing to public consciousness
the injustices and tragedies wrought by industrialization and the
social changes that accompanied it. Mowry and Grenier (1964) identify 1902–1912 as the "era of the muckrakers," coinciding with the
period in which Theodore Roosevelt and the Progressive Republi-
cans held national political power. They describe the function of the
"muckrakers":

> Like journalism, progressivism relied upon the moral and ethical
> efficacy of democracy to correct social evils once they were exposed.
> In most social upheavals, a vanguard usually brings old institutions
> into disrepute, paving the way for new ones. The muckrakers
> played this role. . . . They led the nation in the systematic uncov-
> ering of the strands of a giant web of control, linking politics, edu-
> cation, the press, religion, health, and high finance. . . . Trained in
> the Christian ethic and devoted to the people's right to know, the
> muckrakers revealed the corruption of public men and corporations
> in the name of morality, a heightened public awareness, and the
> common good (Mowry and Grenier, 1964:10).

A great deal of muckraking literature detailed the corruption and
inequities inherent in the practices of big business. Trusts and monopolies were special objects of public wrath, however much they
might be rationally justified in terms of economies of scale. Oddly,
however, the muckrakers who uncovered frauds and adulterations in
the food and drug industries recognized free market competition —
the relative absence of trusts and monopolies — as the prime stimulus
to such practices. If an intensely competitive industry produced immoralities of one sort, and monopolistic enterprise produced other
kinds of immoralities, perhaps the federal government was duty-
bound to intervene in the marketplace to protect the voiceless and to
ensure that the free market could operate without excesses.

Ida Tarbell's classic *History of Standard Oil* was published in
1904. In 1905, an investigation of the New York insurance and gas
industries, led by Charles Evans Hughes (a politician, not a journalist), uncovered appalling corporate practices, "among them bribes,

payoffs, and large campaign contributions" (Gould, 1978:59). David
Graham Phillips, a popular novelist, detailed corruption in Washing-
ton in his series, "The Treason of the Senate," published serially in
Cosmopolitan magazine between March and November, 1906, and
Upton Sinclair's infamous novel, *The Jungle*, also appeared in 1906.

If corporate financial chicanery was seen as appalling, what could
be said of Sinclair's book? The novel described the wretched existence of an immigrant family who labored in the meatpacking plants
of Chicago. Sinclair intended his book to be a powerful plea for socialist revolution; as he himself remarked, the book "aimed for the
hearts of the American people and hit them instead in their stomachs." The following passage provides a sample of the language that
horrified the American nation and its President:

> There was never the least attention paid to what was cut up for
> sausage; there would come all the way back from Europe old sau-
> sages that had been rejected, and that was mouldy and white — it
> would be doused with borax and glycerine, and dumped into the
> hoppers, and made over again for home consumption. There would
> be meat that had tumbled out on the floor, in the dirt and sawdust,
> where the workers had tramped and spit uncounted billions of [tu-
> berculosis] germs. There would be meat stored in great piles in
> rooms; and the water from leaky roofs would drip over it, and thou-
> sands of rats would race about on it. It was too dark in these storages
> places to see well, but a man could run his hand over these piles of
> meat and sweep off handfuls of the dried dung of rats. These rats
> were nuisances, and the packers would put poisoned bread out for
> them; they would die, and then rats, bread, and meat would go into
> the hoppers together. (Sinclair, 1906:135).

President Roosevelt appointed an investigatory commission to
verify Sinclair's tale of filth and fraud in the making of processed
meats (only a few pages of the book relate practices such as the use
of tubercular animals, offal, and putrid carcasses to make "canned
hams," and the story of the laborer who slipped and fell to a lower
level of the plant and was thereafter shipped out to an unsuspecting
public bearing the label "Durham's Pure Leaf Lard"). The commission indeed reported to the President that Sinclair's story was essentially accurate; the Meat Inspection Act of 1906 was promptly enacted
by Congress.

Popular commentary on adulterated and misbranded foods was carried on more by state agricultural and food inspection officials, chemists, members of Congress, and representatives of various groups such as the General Federation of Women's Clubs than by "muckrakers" per se. On the subject of patent medicines there were two series of popular magazine articles decrying the immorality of patent-medicine vendors — one by Samuel Hopkins Adams in *Collier's Weekly*, the other by Edward Bok and Mark Sullivan in *The Ladies Home Journal*. These series seem to have been quite influential in spurring the passage of the 1906 Pure Food Act and in ensuring that the act contained provisions to regulate the content and labeling of medicines.

CONCLUSION

The economic, organizational, and ideological themes of the Progressive Era — e.g., the structural changes brought by industrialization and an increasingly urban population, the theological and scientific justifications for laissez-faire capitalism, the growth of collective action organizations — constitute some of the major themes of the pure food controversy as well, as the next chapters suggest. In brief, the arguments from consumer "representatives" and businesses supporting a federal pure food law were these.

Consumer advocates of pure food legislation used to good advantage a number of strong arguments for a federal law. Most appealing was their citation of the constitutional duty of Congress to "promote the general welfare," by which they called for safeguarding the public from the harm wrought by unscrupulous business principles, and by which they justified demands for accurate food and drug labels. Consumers with sufficient labeling information were in a position to make the informed market choices that were necessary to prevent misallocations of economic resources.

On the other hand, business advocates of federal pure food legislation gave little more than an obligatory nod to free market justifications. Their arguments were much more clearly directed toward reducing competition than to securing it. In particular, the fact that federal legislation would give some businesses a distinct competitive advantage over others became an essential bargaining point, clothed in expressions of concern for the public welfare.

The federal government, viewed by almost all interested groups as a tool of self interest (and in some cases, a powerful weapon in the competitive armamentarium), seemed itself to have no clearly articulated notion of which "public interest," if any, it was to serve. Thus, as we shall see, the government's seeming ambivalence about its own role in regulating private enterprise allowed many public interests to be served at the same time, though perhaps none of them as completely or as satisfactorily as the interested groups might wish.

three

Poisons and Fraud: Consumer Interests in Pure Food and Drugs

TODAY MOST AMERICANS WOULD ACKNOWLEDGE THE EXISTENCE of something called a "consumer movement," even though they might have a difficult time if they were asked to identify the persons, groups, and actions associated with that movement. At the turn of the century there was no distinct consumer movement that was recognizable as either an entity or a concept. Consumers were not considered to be a class of people different from other classes; the consumer classes included *all* people who engaged directly or indirectly in the economic function of consumption. Many of these same people, of course, were producers as well.

The absence of a consumer movement — a recognizable group of people or coalition of groups, mobilized to act, with a resource base and a set of objectives — did not mean that no one spoke for consumers or that possible inequities or difficulties in the consumer's role went unnoticed. In the case of food and drugs, consumer problems were considered by many to be acute. "The consumer's position" was represented by numerous spokespeople in the various levels of government, in Congress and the press, in club meetings and lecture halls, and in trade and professional journals and pamphlets. Indeed, the consumer position on pure food and drugs was so well represented that it is practically the only set of interests connected with the Pure Food Act that has survived in our cultural memory.

What distinguishes the earlier articulations of consumer concerns about food and drug adulterations from similar but more recent concerns is the lack of clear separation of interests between "consumers" and "business" at the turn of the century, which is the subject of this study. Many of those who spoke of the need for consumer protection spoke also of the need for the federal government to protect honest, reputable manufacturers and tradespeople from unfair competition on the part of adulterators and misbranders.

In the interests of clarity, however, a separation of interests has been imposed in this book; the interests of consumers and businesses were not identical, however compatible they might have been. Chapters 4 and 5 present evidence on business interests in a pure food and drug law, and this chapter examines the central issues of food and drug adulteration that were of concern to consumers and their spokespeople.

Table 3.1 provides some evidence on the growth in popularity of the pure food and drug issue, in the number of magazine and journal articles published on the subject in each year from 1890 to 1909. (It should be noted that the table includes only periodicals; most of the press coverage of food and drug issues occurred in local newspapers.) The table shows a very mild interest in food and drug adulterations during the period 1890–1897, with press exposure increasing during the Spanish–American War (1898) and in the following two years, when Congress held a set of widely publicized hearings on adulteration. After 1901 the number of articles on the subject continued to increase dramatically as more and more interest groups became involved in the issue. Interestingly enough, interest did not abate much after the Pure Food Act was passed in 1906; the number of articles on pure food and drugs continued to show relative stability in numbers from year to year.

The issues arousing (or perhaps reflecting) this storm of media attention can be condensed into three sets. First, there was considerable alarm in some circles about the extent of poisonous and dele-

TABLE 3.1

Articles on Food and Adulteration Listed in Reader's Guide to Periodical Literature, *1890–1909*

Year	FOOD — GENERAL		FOOD — ADULTERATIONS, LEGISLATION		TOTAL	
	Number of Articles	% of Column Total	Number of Articles	% of Column Total	Number of Articles	% of Column Total
1890	5	2.8%	4	2.9%	9	2.9
91	2	1.1	0	—	2	.6
92	2	1.1	0	—	2	.6
93	1	.6	0	—	1	.3
94	1	.6	3	2.2	4	1.3
1895	2	1.1	0	—	2	.6
96	2	1.1	0	—	2	.6
97	0	—	0	—	0	—
98	2	1.1	3	2.2	5	1.6
99	7	4.0	3	2.2	10	3.2
1900	18	10.2	15	11.0	33	10.5
01	7	4.0	3	2.2	10	3.2
02	13	7.3	1	.7	14	4.5
03	11	6.2	9	6.6	20	6.4
04	16	9.0	10	7.4	26	8.3
1905	16	9.0	14	10.3	30	9.6
06	25	14.1	32	23.5	57	18.2
07	18	10.2	14	10.3	32	10.2
08	11	6.2	9	6.6	20	6.4
1909	18	10.2	16	11.8	34	10.9
	N = 177		N = 136		N = 313	

terious adulterations being foisted upon unsuspecting consumers. Second, some of the more cool-headed consumer "advocates" were concerned about economic adulteration or outright fraud — the substitution of worthless or lower-valued products for items of greater value. Finally, consumers and their advocates suggested that, under the rules of the free market, they had a right and a duty to *know* what they were purchasing and consuming; that is, they felt that they had a right to products that were accurately labeled and that provided them with sufficient information to make informed market choices.

The second major consumer issue was not so emotionally engaging as the first, but may have been more effective in securing broad-based support for a federal pure food law. Economic adulteration or commercial fraud did not directly endanger life and limb (except in the sense that inadequate nutrition contributed to ill health), but it did cheat the consumer of receiving full expected value for money expended. If consumers were not getting what they paid for, then a classic misallocation of resources was in place. Several consequences of this misallocation were described. For individuals, fraud resulted in a roundabout loss of income; that is, the expected and actual purchasing power of a dollar were not identical. The expected value of a dollar might be expressed in terms of the nutritive value of food, the status value of imported products, or the therapeutic value of drugs; the actual value received fell considerably short. Judeo–Christian morality was brought to bear on this aspect of commercial fraud: "Thou shalt not steal," businesses were told.

For the economy, fraudulent practices resulted in lessened ability to compete for manufacturers of honest products, which created inefficiencies or "warps" in what should be a laissez-faire market promoting the public welfare. Fraud also subjected certain classes of individuals to more widespread economic effects. For the working class, it was crucial that adequate nutrition be received from food purchased. If fraudulent substitutions lowered the nutritive value of food and thus adversely affected the health and vigor of working people, industry could certainly expect lower productivity from its employees.

The issues of poisonous adulteration and commercial fraud were embedded in a third issue: the consumer's right to know exactly what he or she was purchasing. Demands for accurate labeling of food and medicinal products were both a critique and a vindication of a free market economy. The critique concerned the decrement of knowledge about products available to the consumer. For example, when pickles were canned in a factory and not in one's own kitchen, one had no way of knowing what ingredients were used or whether proper canning processes were employed, and one had no particular reason to trust that faraway pickle packer. In effect, the people's diet was in the hands of strangers, and there was no guarantee — indeed, no incentive — that manufacturers would provide adequate and accurate labeling information to their customers. On the other hand, this small adjustment in marketplace activities — a uniform requirement for accurate labeling — would not mean government control of the economy. Accurate labels would allow consumers ready access to the information needed to make informed market choices, and thus would actually bolster the efficacy of free competition among producers. These consumer issues are discussed in greater depth in the sections that follow.

POISONOUS AND DELETERIOUS ADULTERATION

In 1883, Dr. Harvey Washington Wiley was appointed Chief of the Bureau of Chemistry at the U.S. Department of Agriculture. Educated in chemistry and medicine at Hanover College, Indiana Medical College, and Harvard University, Wiley is often credited with being the "father" of the Pure Food Act. Mark Sullivan (1946:519), a journalist involved in the pure food controversy and a contemporary of Wiley's, called him "a very mountain among men, a lion among fighters." Indeed, by all accounts, Wiley's influence on the passage of the Pure Food Act was critical. He was not, however, primarily a "crusader" or a "consumer advocate." He was for most of his adult life an official dedicated to public service, science, and the American nation, including its industries and its economic strength.

By Wiley's own account (1930:177) his first ten years in federal office were devoted to "extensive and exhaustive investigation of adulterations and misbranding of foods" and to "the development of the beet-sugar industry." Wiley was angered and upset by America's dependence on foreign sugar supplies. It was insufferable that the richest nation on earth should be subject to the whims of foreign markets in the supply of one of its most desired goods. With considerable financial backing from the USDA, Wiley conducted a series of laboratory, field, and manufacturing experiments, first with sorghum, then with beets, to establish the agricultural, processing, and packing techniques that would provide a reliable and profitable domestic source of sugar for the nation.

Wiley was convinced quite early that a federal law prohibiting the adulteration and misbranding of foods and drugs would benefit not only consumers, but domestic industries as well. During the course of the struggle, however, Wiley's interests in pure food came to be clearly associated with the consumer's position, and he was among the most vocal antagonists of the businesses and industries that opposed federal pure-food legislation.

Wiley's initial investigations of food adulteration involved taking samples of various foodstuffs and subjecting them to chemical analysis to determine the presence and the proportions of various ingredients in them. The results of these analyses were published in ten parts of the Bureau of Chemistry's Bulletin 13, "Foods and Food Adulterants." The first four parts appeared in 1887. By 1893, four more parts of the Bulletin were published. Together these first eight parts described the results of chemical analyses of controlled samples of various foodstuffs and beverages, including dairy products; spices; alcoholic beverages; lard; baking powders; sugar, syrups, honey, and candies; tea, coffee, and cocoa; and canned vegetables. (Part 9, dealing with cereals and cereal products, appeared in 1898, and Part 10, "Preserved Meats," was published in 1902.)

These studies found considerable adulteration in many of the products that were examined. Commercial adulteration (or fraudulent substitution, to which we turn in a subsequent section of this chapter) constituted the bulk of findings, but poisonous and deleterious adulterants were present in sufficient quantities to justify to Wiley a continued investment in research, as well as some judicious lobbying for a federal law to control the use of noxious substances in food and drink.

The popular press — the newspapers, circulars, magazines, and journals of the day — paid little heed to the official reports of the Department of Agriculture. The ten parts of Bulletin 13 were highly technical and not easily digested; they could not readily be turned into interesting news copy. These studies, however, provided a solid foundation of documentary evidence that became valuable later to those who wished to prove that food adulterations were common practice among manufacturers and retailers.

In addition, Wiley's early technical work significantly influenced the actions taken by a new scientific organization (of which he was a founder and an active participant) — the Association of Official Agricultural Chemists. AOAC members, who were employed by state and local health departments, food and dairy inspection agencies, and related governmental units, did not suffer from the journalist's distaste for the technical; they knew how to read and interpret Bulletin 13, and they knew how explosive its content could be. At the AOAC annual meeting in 1895, Henry A. Huston's presidential address included a call for a greater focus on the human diet, particularly with respect to "the growing use of preservatives." At the same time a food legislation committee of the AOAC was appointed, and two years later Harvey Wiley became chairman of the food standards committee. By 1897, and thereafter, the AOAC was an active organizational lobbyist for a general pure food law (Anderson, 1958:122–123).

The Spanish–American War of 1898 brought the first (and it seems only) public food scandal. The press reported that tons of rotten meat had been shipped to American troops in Puerto Rico and Cuba, its odor masked under visible layers of boracic acid.* The War Department, seeking to avert a massive and potentially distracting public outcry, requested that Harvey Wiley's team of USDA researchers investigate the allegations.

Wiley was personally and vehemently opposed to the use of boracic acid (commonly called borax) as a preservative. He was, however, apparently loathe to contaminate his interpretation of scientific evidence with his personal opinions, and he reported forthrightly that his investigation for the War Department revealed little use of preservatives in Army meats. In fact, Wiley reported that he found "no samples in poor condition and no trace of any preservatives except a very small amount of saltpeter in corned and luncheon beef." Not disputing reports of putrid meats and resulting illness among soldiers, Wiley suggested that the problem lay in the improper saving of opened cans of food in a tropical climate, and in nutritional imbalance in the overall diet of soldiers (Anderson, 1958:128).

Factual or not, the wartime meat scandal did have public policy repercussions. Mason (1900:67) noted that "the army-beef imbroglio" had led to the passage of several state pure food laws. More importantly for the domestic meatpacking industry, Germany in 1900 banned the importation of American meat products (*Nation*, Dec. 5, 1904:472), and Congress began to exhibit a renewed interest in the issue of pure food.

In 1899 the Senate Committee on Manufactures appointed a

---

*The (then) current term for boric acid.

United States Pure Food Investigating Committee and instructed the members to hold hearings and provide evidence on the question of food and drug adulterations. Lengthy hearings were held during 1899 and 1900 in Chicago, Washington, and New York, producing a wealth of testimony and statistical evidence on the nature and extent of adulteration. Harvey Wiley served as an expert witness, along with other members of the AOAC, and also assisted the Senators in questioning others who testified at the hearings. The press began to pay attention.

The lead article in *Science* for June 9, 1899, reported on the committee's first activity, a two-week-long hearing held in Chicago. Fraudulent adulteration occupied most of the report, but some attention was paid to poisonous adulterants as well:

> Professor A.S. Mitchell, Chief Chemist of the State Board of Health and Pure Food and Dairy Commissioner of Wisconsin. . . . described particularly the antiseptics and preservatives which were on the market under various tradenames, such as "freezem" and "freezine," and so forth. "Freezem" was shown to be a dilute solution of formaldehyde, while "freezine" was composed chiefly of sodium sulphite. The question of the use of preservatives was discussed by the experts before the Committee, and the universal opinion was expressed that they were all unwholesome ("Senatorial investigation of food adulteration," 1899:794).

The Nation (May 25, 1899) also commented on the Chicago hearings, entitling its editorial "The Poison in Our Food" and linking the Chicago findings with those from state-directed pure food investigations in Pennsylvania and Connecticut. *The Nation* hypothesized that toxic food additives and preservatives were especially harmful to invalids and others in poor health, and the editor seemed to believe that poor health was a chronic condition for Americans:

> To perfectly robust individuals these chemicals may be comparatively harmless, but Americans are a nation of dyspeptics, and salicylic acid, the favorite preservative used here, has been pronounced by the Paris Academy of Medicine especially injurious to dyspeptics. Their life is made wretched by the systematic food poisoning for the profit of dishonest dealers; salts of zinc or copper in a dish of canned peas, for example . . . may result in a sleepless night,

colic, headache, loss of a day's work, and general misery; and this may go on indefinitely, rendering life a burden, without any suspicion in the victim of the real cause (*Nation*, May 25, 1899:391).

State investigations were also yielding evidence on the extent of adulterated foods. The Boards of Health of Massachusetts, Nebraska, and Kentucky were among those in the forefront of the efforts to secure convincing proof of the extent and harmfulness of adulterations. Federal and state hearings and the activities of state and local agencies produced a mass of evidence and prompted journalists to report cheerfully that as much as 15 or 20 percent of America's food supply was adulterated.

In March 1900 the *Journal of the American Medical Association* reported some findings of the Massachusetts State Board of Health's investigation of frequently adulterated foods. The Board found that "the use of antiseptics in milk is decidedly on the increase, weak solutions of formaldehyde being apparently the favorite." The editor asserted that the concentration of formaldehyde in milk, "while perhaps not actively toxic, is *decidedly open to the suspicion of being unwholesome*" (emphasis added). The Journal's conclusion was that if Massachusetts, one of the few states to actively enforce a pure food law, experienced widespread adulterations, then "a worse condition of affairs" could be expected to exist in most other states (*JAMA*, March 3, 1900:564–565).

The statistical reports and the testimony generated by agencies and hearings, respectively, were far from conclusive, as the *JAMA* editor's cautious phrase, "decidedly open to suspicion," illustrates. Scientifically grounded criticisms focused on two crucial points. First, if the samples analyzed by state and federal agents were seized for suspicion of contamination, then the results did not truly reflect adulteration in the total food supply and any extrapolation made from those results, particularly the 15 to 20 percent figure, was grossly overstated. In methodological terms, a biased sample selection procedure makes it impossible to generalize findings accurately to the population. The second and perhaps more central criticism was this: Even if valid and reliable evidence of the extent of adulteration could be secured, no one had yet provided convincing evidence that preservatives, coloring agents, and the like were truly harmful to humans (*Independent*, May 16, 1901; Jan. 5, 1905). Should anyone be concerned about the health effects of adulteration, or was the whole issue, quite literally, a tempest in a teapot?

Harvey Wiley recognized this flaw in the pure food argument better than anyone and, fortunately for the law's advocates, he was in a position to do something about it. Beginning in 1902 and continuing for five years, Wiley tested the health effects of common food additives on his infamous "Poison Squad," authorized by a special act of Congress. Characteristically, his plan for establishing the harmfulness of preservatives, coloring and flavoring agents, and other artificial additives combined impeccable science with a flair for the dramatic. The Poison Squad consisted of a dozen young, healthy male volunteers from the Bureau of Chemistry who agreed to obey strictly Wiley's dietary prescriptions for a year and to have all their excreta, so far as was humanly possible, collected and analyzed. In his autobiography, Wiley (1930:216) describes the intent of the experiments:

> I wanted young, robust fellows, with maximum resistance to deleterious effects of adulterated foods. If they should show signs of injury after they were fed such substances for a period of time, the deduction would naturally follow that children and older persons, more susceptible than they, would be greater sufferers from similar causes.

Over an initial ten-day period a "normal ration" of food and drink was established for each subject, one that would "keep their bodies in a state of equilibrium," that is, at a constant weight. Wiley continues:

> We began the experiments by adding to that normal ration one of the common food preservatives of that day — borax. To six of the squad we gave this compound in the form of boracic acid, and to the other six borate of soda. Since we had eliminated all other variables in the diet we could measure quite distinctly the effect of this adulterant on metabolism. When the digestion of any of the squad showed signs of being impaired we released that member and gave him a "holiday" of several days, so that he could rest up and get ready for the next test.

The results of the Poison Squad experiments were published in seven parts, beginning in 1904, in Bulletin 84 of the Bureau of Chemistry. Each part described the health effects of one of the following food additives: "Boric acid and borax, salicylic acid and salicylates, sulphurous acid and sulphites, benzoic acid and benzoates, formaldehyde, sulphate of copper, and saltpeter" (Wiley, 1930:220).*

If Bulletin 13 had been ignored by the press, Bulletin 84 was an immediate sensation. The *Washington Post* published a series of reports by George Rothwell Brown, describing in ever more outrageous terms the conditions under which Wiley's young men nourished themselves (Anderson, 1958:151). Songs and poems were penned, cartoons were drawn, endless jokes were made, and even Wiley himself, although he treated his experiments with deadly and dispassionate earnest, could not resist taking a humorous approach to his work from time to time. Wiley, who could write a decent line of verse, keynoted a banquet, shortly after beginning the Poison Squad experiments, by poetically inviting the guests to enjoy their "chemical feast," and then naming all the adulterants that might be found in the dishes before them. Oscar Anderson (1958:151) gives us the following excerpt from Wiley's letters to friends who had jokingly volunteered for "Poison Squad" duty:

> You will begin with a diet of borax garnished with salicylic acid — with a dish of alum on the side. You will then have a course in chromatics — beginning with the beautiful yellow of oleomargarine and including the appropriate green of the French canned peas. Rochelle salts, bicarbonate of soda, acid phosphate, and basic alumina phosphate will be found delightful entrees. Please report for duty about September 10th. Blanks for wills and coroners' certificates must be furnished by the guests.

How could people make informed judgments about their diets, their health, and the value of the products they purchased if they did

---

*Many of these chemicals tested so long ago by Harvey Wiley, along with other common "adulterants" of the Progressive Era such as saccharin, coal-tar dyes, and chicory, have been subject to continuing controversy. Sulfites, for example, used by restaurants to retard spoilage and browning of lettuce and other foods, have recently been linked to allergic reactions ranging from coughing and shortness of breath to abdominal pain, shock, and loss of consciousness. A report in Better Homes and Gardens notes, "The Food and Drug Administration (FDA) currently is studying the issue of sulfite sensitivity to see if health warnings should be included on products containing sulfites" ("Salad bar hazard," 1985:74).

not know what they were consuming? How could honest businesspeople avoid the pressure to conform to commonplace adulteration?
To drive home his point that "the ethics of pure food" was and should
be the major rallying point for the supporters of regulatory legislation, Wiley emphasized the potential for hidden dangers in favorite
foods, as in the poem below, delivered to the second meeting of the
National Pure Food and Drug Congress in 1899 (reprinted in Anderson, 1958:126–127).

> We sit at a table delightfully spread,
> And teeming with good things to eat,
> And daintily finger the cream-tinted bread,
> Just needing to make it complete
> A film of the butter so yellow and sweet,
> Well suited to make every minute
> A dream of delight. And yet while we eat
> We cannot help asking "What's in it?"
> Oh, maybe this bread contains alum and chalk,
> Or sawdust chopped up very fine,
> Or gypsum in powder about which they talk,
> Terra Alba just out of the mine.
> And our faith in the butter is apt to be weak,
> For we haven't a good place to pin it.
> Annato's so yellow and beef fat so sleek,
> Oh, I wish I could know what is in it?
> The pepper perhaps contains cocoanut shells,
> And the mustard is cottonseed meal;
> The coffee, in sooth, of baked chicory smells,
> And the terrapin tastes like roast veal.
> The wine which you drink never heard of a grape,
> But of tannin and coal tar is made;
> And you could not be certain, except for their shape,
> That the eggs by a chicken were laid.
> And the salad which bears such an innocent look
> And whispers of fields that are green,
> Is covered with germs, each armed with a hook,
> To grapple with liver and spleen.
> No matter how tired and hungry and dry,
> The banquet how fine; don't begin it

Till you think of the past and the future and sigh,
"Oh, I wonder, I wonder, what's in it."

Wiley's experiments earned for him the sometimes affectionate, sometimes derisive nickname of "Old Borax." The *New York Sun* called him "chief janitor and policeman of the people's insides," (Sullivan, 1946:520), reflecting the distaste that some opponents of a federal pure food law felt at what seemed to them to be sumptuary legislation. *The Nation* (Dec. 15, 1904:472), offering a less sensational view of the Poison Squad findings, briefly described the results presented in Part 1 of Bulletin 84 (boric acid and borax), and advocated Congressional passage of a general pure food law. The editors reminded their readers of the borax scandal of the Spanish–American War and the consequent German ban on importing American meat. They asserted that scientific evidence of the deleterious effects of borax, provided by Wiley's experiments, vindicated the German ban and made obvious the need for federal legislation to protect the public welfare, in terms of both physical and economic health.

Even the most rigorous science is always subject to methodological criticism. Shortly after *The Nation* described the first of the Poison Squad experiments, another scientist, H.H. Langdon (1905:9), wrote to object to the magazine's support of Wiley's findings. Langdon's attack on Wiley's methodology focused chiefly on its generalizability, and he offered as evidence of Wiley's empirical shortcomings his observation (one must note, without any support whatsoever) that the British ate lots of borax and were nevertheless very healthy!

Those who used borax as a preservative also attempted to make scientific attacks on the Poison Squad findings, producing their own expert witnesses at Congressional hearings to provide contradictory evidence or to cast doubt on the validity of Wiley's findings. Wiley was always given the opportunity to respond to such attacks, and he did so with such devastating logic and showmanship that his own views usually prevailed. Although he was an able defender of the experimental methods of science, Wiley was no stranger to the politics of public debate and the effect of a well-timed denouncement. Demolishing his attackers first on scientific grounds, Wiley would then point out that their testimony had been paid for by the companies using the questionable preservatives. The press responded euphorically to this unassailable finger-pointing.

All the hilarity, exaggeration, and sensationalism served a purpose: The press and thus the public focused their attention more than ever before on the issue of pure foods and beverages; when solid evidence of harm was needed to sway some fence-sitters in Congress, Wiley was able to provide it.

The Poison Squad experiments were among the more spectacular demonstrations of the toxicity of food preservatives and other additives, but they were by no means the only evidence available to advocates of federal pure food legislation. The Saint Louis Exposition of 1904 was the scene of yet another convincing demonstration of the harmfulness of food additives. A pure-food booth, organized primarily by members of the Association of State Food and Dairy Departments, was established adjacent to the exhibits of preserved-food manufacturers. Many of the products exhibited by companies were found also in the pure-food booth, with placards attached showing the names of the deleterious and adulterating substances contained in them. What made the crowds pause in horrible fascination, however, was the table on which garishly colored pieces of silk and wool were arranged, having been dyed with the colorings extracted from a number of popular canned and preserved foods. Silk and wool were animal tissues, as were human stomachs and intestines; what dyed the one would surely dye the other as well, and who knew what disastrous health effects all that artificial coloring might have on a person? Mark Sullivan (1946:524–525) explains why this exhibit was so effective in arousing public attention:

> As it happened, many Americans had an exceptional familiarity with the tints of the viscera, and a concern about them not shared by the non-medical laity of other nations, for the reason that some 15 or 20 years before there had been introduced into many of the public schools a new branch of learning, physiology. The science was imparted through vividly illustrated text-books and colored charts, of which the purpose was not merely to teach hygiene in the broadest sense, but particularly to inculcate the desirability of total abstinence from alcoholic liquors. . . . Many of the pictures in the physiology text-books were in pairs, in the "before and after" manner. The "before" pictures showed the normal coloration of the mechanism for metabolism. The "after-taking" pictures showed the coloration of the same organs and tissues as they would be when transformed by the consumption of specified quantities of alcoholic

> liquor. Since the impression meant to be made by the "after-taking" pictures was designed to be one of restraint, it followed that the colors in which the "after-taking" results were pictured had such a vividness and variegation as would have been, but for this detail of American education, unfamiliar to all except those who chanced to have made . . . unusual adventures into the farther reaches of the spectroscope.

> The result of familiarity with the tinting of the viscera thus brought about, and the concern about it that had been implanted, was that many Americans felt an acute disquiet about any departure from the conventional in the coloring of the internal organs. In short, the average American examined the display in the aisles of the St. Louis Exposition with intentness and minuteness, and passed on with a readiness to listen favorably to any agitator who thought Congress ought to do something about the use of artificial coloring in food.

Statistical evidence of widespread adulterations, experimental data on the harmfulness of food additives, and the curious mixture of science and morals represented by the St. Louis exhibit created powerful support for a federal law to control harmful additives in foods and beverages. Wiley had intended his Poison Squad experiments to include adulterated medications, but these tests did not take place. The evidence on drug alterations, to which we now turn, was much less scientific and even more emotionally charged than that concerning adulterated food.

THERAPEUTIC POISONS: ADULTERATED DRUGS

Medicines occupied a special place in concerns about deleterious adulteration. American medical practice at the turn of the century was not so heavily drug based as it is now, and control over the distribution of medicines was exercised through normative rather than legalistic channels. A number of reputable pharmaceutical companies had already established themselves as suppliers of "ethical" preparations — what we now call prescription drugs. The term "ethical drug" derived from a cooperative understanding between drug companies and physicians. Since many drugs were beneficial when used under a physician's direction, but were potentially dangerous in the hands of the medically uninformed, such drugs should not be advertised directly to the public. Ethics dictated that drug companies should inform physicians of the properties of these medicines, and physicians then should determine for whom and under what conditions they should be used.

Although many of today's reputable pharmaceutical manufacturers existed at the turn of the century, they did not control the market for medicines. With 2,276 manufacturers of medicinal products listed in the U.S. Census of Manufacturers of 1900, it is obvious that the large pharmaceutical houses did not yet exercise the considerable market power that they later claimed. Mail-order medicines, over-the-counter products, the special mixtures of local druggists, and the mysterious bottles of the snake-oil vendors were quite popular with consumers. Most of these remedies were classified as "patent medicines" (more accurately named proprietary medicines, for they were legally protected by trademarks and secret formulas, not by patents), and these were the focus of public attention and criticism.

Common knowledge has it that the press first sounded the alarm on patent medicines, and indeed, journalists were important in spreading the issue nationwide. The medical community, however, had decried for decades what Edward Bok, publisher of *The Ladies' Home Journal*, called America's "accursed passion for self-doctoring" (April, 1905). Bok linked the therapeutic problem of self-medication with the resultant problem of unwitting alcohol and narcotic addiction.

The *Journal of the American Medical Association* and *American Medicine*, in 1900 and 1901, respectively, began new campaigns to educate physicians to the evils of so-called patent medicines. Proprietary remedies were denounced on several scientific and ethical grounds. Their secret formulas opposed the needs of medical science by fostering lack of uniformity, inadequate therapeutic information, and fraudulent promotion. Their use by laypeople circumvented the physicians' role in health care. Physicians' testimonials — an especially touchy problem — violated the medical code of ethics. Finally, the active ingredients of proprietary remedies were often highly addictive and dangerous drugs — alcohol, morphine, cocaine, opium. This latter complaint eventually led to Women's Christian Temperance Union opposition to patent medicines, when it was demonstrated that women who bitterly opposed the use of alcohol in any form were consuming quantities of it in their daily tonics.

In February 1900 the *Journal of the American Medical Association (JAMA)* printed as its lead article an address on medical ethics by Dr. Samuel C. Busey, President of the Medical Association of Washington, D.C. In the name of science, morality, and good medicine, Dr. Busey reminded his colleagues that it was unethical according to the code of their profession for them to patent, dispense, or attest to the effectiveness of proprietary remedies — "secret medicines." Alluding to the harm wrought by false science, Dr. Busey wrote:

> Proprietary pharmacy is the most pretentious of the artful devices of empiricism. The daily mails bring to every physician the advertising bulletins of proprietary pharmacists, filled with certificates of physicians, setting forth the wonderful virtue of some special compound, mixture, tablet, or pill, each of which is extolled as a panacea for diseases having no etiologic or pathological relation to each other, and the credulous practitioner goes forth on his daily rounds enthused with the single idea that he has at last discovered a remedy with which he can drug, dose, or feed every patient, and, when the day's work has been finished, congratulates himself with the accomplishment of the highest aims of a beneficient science (Busey, 1900:259).

These were strong words indeed to members of a profession that had already claimed for itself the prerogatives of "special" or "secret" medical knowledge, including the assumption that patients were to trust their physicians implicitly. In Dr. Busey's initial address and throughout a series of articles in *JAMA*, the evils of malicious deception and wrongdoing on the part of greedy medicine vendors were painted as hardly greater than the evils of self-deception and ignorance on the part of physicians who unwittingly aided the deceivers and violated the public trust.

Two months after Busey's address appeared, *JAMA* published the first article of an eight-part series titled "Relations of Pharmacy to the Medical Profession." This series examined a number of drug-related concerns, but its most acrimonious analysis, and indeed the bulk of its content, was reserved for the evils of "proprietary pharmaceuticals."

Part 1 of the "Relations" series set the stage for physician rejection of secret remedies by discussing the need for national pharmacopeias. "The secrecy and lack of uniformity in medicines" during the Middle Ages was said to have led to the development of dispensatories — compendia of drug formulas produced by "various medical authorities." When these proliferated and lost their value as uniform reference works, city governments began to issue local pharmacopeias, which were superceded in the 19th century by national collections of formulas. These attempts to standardize medicinal preparations acknowledged physicians' need for drugs of known, consistent therapeutic value (*JAMA*, April 21, 1900:987). The onslaught of proprietary medicines in the later 19th century threatened the scientific, ethical, and social structural positions of physicians by promoting self-dosing and by circumventing the accumulation of empirical knowledge about medicinal effects. These concerns are illustrated in the following passage:

> . . . their identity, strength and purity can rarely be determined by chemical or physical tests, and . . . their therapeutic value must consequently be estimated through their therapeutic or physiologic effects, which must necessarily, from such complicated mixtures, be largely empirical. When to this is added the ever-present danger of altering . . . the preparation by the manufacturer, through the best of motives, which may, however, unfavorably affect its therapeutic use or value, the status of these preparations becomes exceedingly questionable. . . . (*JAMA*, "Relations," April 21, 1900:988).

In the absence of a national information exchange on the positive and negative consequences of drug use, the physician's reliance on raw empiricism — that is, case-by-case determination of a drug's value — was potentially quite damaging to the medical profession's healing function and was certainly unsatisfactory from a scientific perspective.

Part 2 of *JAMA*'s series defined eleven classes of pharmaceutical products that would be considered in the remainder of the series, and then provided some evidence on the types of patent medicine frauds that currently existed. The author noted that "patent medicines" were not in fact patented, because the manufacturer would have to disclose the formula in order to obtain a patent. "Secrecy," the author continued, "is the vis medicatrix of all 'patent medicines,' since this admits of the most mendacious misrepresentation to bolster up their alleged virtues and puff them to a credulous public" (*JAMA*, "Relations," April 28, 1900:1049).

Part 3 examined the uses and misuses of drug trademarks. In some cases a trademark specified a guaranteed degree of purity, strength, and quality, but for most drugs, trademarks merely engendered confusion. *JAMA* recommended that "trade-names should be supplanted as early as possible by pharmaceutic ones . . ." (*JAMA*, "Relations," May 5, 1900:1116). Part 4 (May 12, 1900) expressed concern about the lack of standardization in the training of pharmacists, and then hammered once again at secret medicines. Several examples offered in this article sounded the theme that was later to be trumpeted in the popular press: that many secret remedies were "furnishing plenty of work for the undertakers":

> "Essence of Oats," some ten years ago, vaunted as a most wonderful restorative, was found to be a preparation of morphine. More recently a preparation made from a plant . . . growing in the everglades in Florida and only collected at the risk of sacrificing human life, was recommended in a New York medical journal as a cure for the opium and morphine habit, but was found on analysis, to be a preparation of opium (p. 1179).

Part 5 (May 26, 1900) concerned more subtle frauds: drugs with published formulas that were either misleading or could not be duplicated by independent pharmacists. If anything, these frauds were even more reprehensible than cases in which the formulas were kept secret. Such drug promotions seemed on the surface to comply with the requirements of medical ethics, but for their mendacious "forthrightness" they were to be doubly damned. Part 6 (June 2, 1900) dealt with elixirs and other mixtures with accurately provided formulas and known therapeutic values. No objection to prescribing these trademarked medicines by physicians was offered.

Part 7 (July 7, 1900) reopened the question of trademarks, printing a letter from a pharmacist–manufacturer, R.W. Gardner, who objected to the journal's position on trademarked medicines. The writer maintained that trademarks were an essential protection of the man-ufacturer's investment in his products, and that physicians would be less easily duped by fraudulent advertising if they received better pharmacological training in medical school. *JAMA* agreed only in part; if manufacturers would provide full information and "pharma-ceutically descriptive titles" for their preparations, then both business and medicine would be joined by ethical means to a common end:

> . . . the manufacturer who adopts the above two propositions and carries them out honestly and honorably will add prestige to his products, dignity and reputation to his name, which, on the label of a bottle, would be worth more than any copyrighted proprietary title (p. 29).

Part 8 of the series (July 14, 1900) lamented the "decadence of elixirs," the disrepute into which palatable medicinal compounds had fallen as a result of secrecy, lack of standardization, and simple fraud. If proper scientific controls and ample information were instituted, elixirs — sweet-tasting and easy for patients to accept — might regain favor with the medical community.

Concurrent with the publication of Part 6 on June 2, 1900, *JAMA* issued a position statement on the use of secret remedies. Acknowl-edging its own responsibility to serve as a clearinghouse of sorts for drug information, it promised to "make haste slowly," to protect all interests involved, including those of honorable drug manufacturers. Three recommendations were expressed in no uncertain terms:

1. Medical preparations, the composition of which is kept secret, should not have medical patronage.
2. Those which are directly advertised to the laity as remedies, or cure-alls for disease, should not have medical patronage.
3. Manufacturers of preparations designed for external use need not necessarily be required to furnish the exact proportions of the ingredients except in cases in which some of these are active or toxic agents (*JAMA*, "Secret Nostrums," June 2, 1900:1420).

JAMA also promised to stop accepting advertisements for proprietary remedies "on expiration of existing contracts." Although this policy had already resulted in the loss of $8,000 in annual revenue, *JAMA*

declared that financial considerations would not stand in the way of
its moral duty to the medical profession.

Throughout 1900 and 1901, numerous other articles appeared in
JAMA denouncing the prescribing and certification of "secret nostrums." Physicians who provided testimonials to the efficacy of secret
remedies, whether they did so because they were gullible or because
they were mercenary, were held not less responsible than the manufacturers for these unacceptable practices. Like Esau trading his
birthright for a mess of potage, physicians who were swayed by small
gifts, money, or the gratification of having their names in print nationwide were guilty of being the "willing tools" of nostrum peddlers
and of sacrificing the integrity and scientific beneficence of their
profession (*JAMA*, "Endorsed by physicians," Feb. 3, 1900; see also
Witherspoon, 1900; *JAMA*, "Dangers," July 21, 1900; *JAMA*, "Testimonials," July 13, 1901).

Ethical and scientific norms were inseparable in the epistemological foundation of medical practice. As healers, physicians were
committed to the highly moral enterprise of saving lives and alleviat-
ing suffering. As scientists they were committed to activities that
would enhance their healing abilities through the accumulation of scientific knowledge. Secret medicinal formulas thwarted both aims,
and in addition introduced the confounding elements of commercial
marketing, dedicated neither to healing nor to science. The physician
stood as intermediary between the suffering individual and the industrial and commercial pharmaceutical interests. This role required
the physician to assess the validity of manufacturers' claims and to
determine which medication would provide the highest therapeutic
value for individual patients, but physicians found themselves unable
to distinguish true scientific advances in pharmacology from harmful
and "purely commercial" frauds. Thus, to the extent that they relied
on drugs for healing, physicians could not be assured of engaging in
moral and efficacious behavior or of acting on the basis of scientific
fact.

JAMA argued strongly for procedures whereby the industrialization and commercialization of medicinal preparations could be ra-
tionalized to permit a stronger moral and scientific foundation for the
individual practice of medicine. Drug standardization, the elimina-
tion of secret formulas, and the use of chemically descriptive names
(today's generic names) were all practices that would augment

collective knowledge of healing techniques. They would permit physicians to fulfill more adequately their intermediary roles, and such changes could eliminate many of the evils of industrialization of pharmaceutical manufacturing while taking advantage of its enormous benefits.

The importance of accumulated capital in permitting large-scale research and development in pharmacology was not lost on the leaders of the American Medical Association. Indeed, they believed strongly that reputable drug manufacturers contributed a great deal to the advancement of science and medical practice, and that those manufacturers should be rewarded amply for their contributions. The competitive conditions of industrial capitalism were seen as generating too much fraud, too little valid information, and a dangerous situation for physicians and their patients. That poisons could heal had been known for millenia; the physician who unwittingly prescribed poison in too large a dose or in inappropriate circumstances, however, no matter how gullible, was still a murderer.

In 1901 the journal *American Medicine* picked up the themes of food and drug adulteration and patent medicine frauds. Forsaking *JAMA*'s analytical and exhortative style, *American Medicine* favored short, pithy news briefs and comments that made a single point. On July 6 the editors expressed their disgust with the inclination of "some physicians" to place the blame for drug frauds exclusively on manufacturers and then to generalize the evil to *all* manufacturers. "We should sweep and clean our own house," the editors wrote. Some manufacturers were undoubtedly unethical; many were not, but the same could be said for physicians as well ("Lay manufacturers and physicians" 1901: 2). Thereafter, *American Medicine*'s stories distinguished between reputable makers of foods and drugs and those whose greed drove them to commercial excesses.

Subsequent articles proposed various remedies for curing patent-medicine and food-adulteration evils. Pharmacists were encouraged to label secret medicines with a disclaimer of personal responsibility for their effects ("The sale of 'patent' medicines," August 3, 1901). Various schemes involving fraudulent advertising, purchase of testimonials, and financial wheeling and dealing were exposed ("A medicine selling scheme," August 10, 1901; "Success in advertising quackery," Nov. 23, 1901; "The market price," May 31, 1902). A tax on roadside nostrum advertisements was promoted as a way of compensating for the damage done by them although it is difficult to tell if the editors were objecting to the billboards themselves or the medicines they promoted ("The taxation of nostrum advertisements," Nov. 2, 1901). They further recommended that all canned foods be dated (July 12, 1902), that publication of instances of fraud be unceasing (Dec. 21, 1901), and that international standards for drug potency be established (Nov. 8, 1902). They were quick to recognize the potential value of Harvey Wiley's "Poison Squad" experiments. Briefly describing the experimental design, the editors commented, "The question of the possible harmfulness of boric and of salicylic acids will, we hope, be decided by the proposed plan" (A scientific test," Sept. 20, 1902).

An intriguing development emerged in *American Medicine* in 1902. Three years earlier, Professor Atwater of Wesleyan University in Connecticut had reported a series of experiments on the value of alcohol as human food. The Women's Christian Temperance Union, deeply committed to overcoming alcohol abuse and the consequent abuse of families by alcoholic husbands and fathers, was enraged at the very idea of associating what they considered to be a physically and socially destructive drug with food, a necessity of life.

JAMA had coolly dismissed both the outrage of the WCTU and the jubilance of antitemperance forces by asserting that the claim of alcohol to be a food depended entirely on one's definition of food. If food was anything oxidized and used by the human body, then alcohol certainly was one, along with many other toxic substances. But if foods were substances that were nutritious and beneficial to the body, then alcohol could not qualify (*JAMA*, "Alcohol as a food," Feb. 3, 1900, and "Shall alcohol be recognized as a food?" March 31, 1900). *American Medicine* went further, ridiculing the WCTU's misinterpretations and intolerant tactics and urging the prohibitionists to link politically the issues of temperance and patent-medicine frauds.

Many proprietary remedies contained substantial portions of alcohol; many relied for their "curative" powers on the effects of morphine, opium, and cocaine. All four of these drugs, though therapeutic to some degree, were known to be highly addictive. *American Medicine* raised the issue of drug and alcohol addiction caused by the use of remedies containing them, and discerned an apparent blind spot in the WCTU's stance against consumption of alcohol. On November 8, 1902, the journal reported: "Last year a great temperance reformer's portrait and testimonials were blazoned in every yellow journal in the country, extolling the virtues of a nostrum largely made up of alcohol. . . . Think of a crusade against beer, which contains only from 2 percent to 5 percent alcohol, while allowing the free sale of 'bitters' containing ten times as much" ("Why do not the temperance people" 1902: 720).

Three weeks later the editor received an angry letter from the WCTU's "Superintendent of the Department of Anti-Narcotics for Philadelphia County," asserting "in words of lofty and abstract glorification of the WCTU" the organization's dedication to remaining "wide awake to this evil." In an editorial on November 29, *American Medicine* asked, "When, and where, and how have you attempted to limit patent medicine alcoholism . . . ? In all of your crusades do you even now show one sign of recognition of the wisdom of adding knowledge to your zeal?" ("The W.C.T.U. and real temperance" 1902: 840).

Two weeks after that, on December 13, *American Medicine* published a letter from Mrs. Martha M. Allen. Given charge of the WCTU's national Department of Nonalcoholic Medication in 1895, she began an information dissemination campaign "against the medical use of alcoholic drinks by physicians." This work led her to study "disguised alcohol in the form of proprietary medicines," and she subsequently published a booklet titled "The Danger and Harmfulness of Patent Medicines." Mrs. Allen acknowledged that the WCTU's troops were not exactly in step with the generals: "Not all members of the Woman's Christian Temperance Union are in sympathy with the opposition to patent medicines, but the leaders everywhere are, so the multitude will follow in time." The editor of *American Medicine*, having received a copy of Mrs. Allen's booklet along with her letter, applauded it, though regretting that the "multitude" had not yet followed: "When the W.C.T.U. as a body takes up such work as that and stops its foolish struggles for impossible reforms, then it will accomplish its aims" ("The W.C.T.U. and 'Patent Medicines,' " Dec. 13, 1902). Those "foolish struggles" included attempts to gain legal prohibition, the teaching of temperance along with physiology in the public schools, and the banning of Army canteens.

One other issue was presented in *American Medicine*, the editors being less reticent than *JAMA* about making overtly political statements. The need for federal legislation to control poisonous, addictive, and worthless medicines seemed clear: "What is more absurd than to create drunkards and morphinomanics by government protection and sanction, and then to build asylums and hospitals by the same government wherein to lodge and care for them?" ("Government encouragement," Nov. 8, 1902:719).

In the same issue the journal attacked the advertising practices of patent medicine makers ("Drug-habits") and expressed skepticism that local and state laws could control medicine-induced drug addiction ("The sale of poisons and narcotics"). It did indeed seem irrational that the government should protect worthless remedies via trademark law and the absence of regulatory controls, and then be obliged to shelter the victims in federally supported institutions.

The popular press was not far behind the medical journals. The *Ladies' Home Journal* raised the public alarm in 1903, lambasting the unethical abuse of confidence by mail-order "doctors" and the entrapment of unsuspecting persons into debilitating addictions. Samuel Hopkins Adams, writing for *Collier's* in 1905 and 1906, continued these attacks on the patent medicine industry, addressing problems such as false advertising, the narcotic and alcohol content of specific patent medicines, and testimonials by religious leaders, physicians, and prominent members of the temperance movement (see Anderson, 1958).

Citing many medical references, Maud Banfield (1903), "The Journal's Trained Nurse," urged her women readers to understand that the "calmatives" they gave their children and the nostrums they took themselves were not only harmful to their health, but were the first step on the road to a drunkard's life. Banfield also reported that life insurance companies were opposed to the use of patent medicines, presumably because they shortened the lives of users and thus constituted a health hazard to consumers (and a financial hazard to insurance companies).

Banfield's theme was reiterated with greater force in a series of articles by Edward Bok (publisher of the *Ladies' Home Journal*) and Mark Sullivan in *Ladies' Home Journal* during 1904 and 1905. Bok (1904a:18) pointed out in the first of this series that the use of nostrums containing alcohol, opium, or cocaine established life-long drug habits, and he exhorted mothers to be more careful of their children's health, hitting again and again on the moral issue of a mother's duty to safeguard her children in all possible ways.

In his second article, Bok (1904b:18) described the consequences of relying upon "mail-order doctors" instead of one's own physician for therapeutic diagnosis. Women responded by the thousands to widely circulated advertisements urging them to write "the Doctor," who would give their cases his personal attention. Bok asserted, based on an anonymous "insider" account, that the letters were read by "the Doctor's" employees, who marked each with a number, depending on the particular ailment mentioned. Each number corresponded to a form letter, which was "made to look like a genuine letter and sent out." The anonymous reporter continued:

> The house has some four or five different "medicines" — all containing practically the same ingredients, as I afterward found out from the "chemist" of the establishment, but under different names. One of these is recommended as "especially fitting your case." Each letter contains a strong recommendation to try "not many bottles," but "just one," so as to lead the unwary on. The "Doctor" knows mighty well that the alcohol in his preparation will so exhilarate the patient as to lead her to a second bottle if she tries the first (Bok, 1904b:18).

Bok was unrelenting in his attacks on those who would take advantage of women's credulity and vulnerability. To dangle the promise of a cure for one's ailments, and then to "hook" the unsuspecting consumer with an alcohol or narcotic addiction, was, in Bok's judgment, as unscrupulous a practice as had ever been generated by the Industrial Revolution. In the remainder of his series Bok hammered away at the theme of the "alcohol, cocaine, or morphine appetite" aroused by the use of patent medicines (Bok 1905:18) but laid the blame for the most part on the consumer herself: "There is no evil in America today so great as this accursed passion for self-doctoring. . . . And it is upon this evil that a certain portion of the "patent-medicine" industry thrives, with all its horrors of deception, fraud, and dangerous ingredients" (Bok, 1906:20).

Bok's final article was entitled "Pictures That Tell Their Own Stories" (1905c:15). One picture illustrated the results of an experiment designed to dramatize the alcohol content of three popular patent medicines. A tablespoonful of each nostrum was placed in a can, "connected by rubber tubes to a gas burner and mantel, heat was applied, and the vapor gave brilliant illumination as follows:"

Hostetter's Bitters burned for	4 minutes
Peruna burned for	2 minutes 40 seconds
Lydia Pinkham's Vegetable Compound burned for	2 minutes 35 seconds
Beer burned for	20 seconds

Another photograph portrayed the label of Mrs. Winslow's Soothing Syrup, a preparation sold to quiet the tears and fussiness of teething children. The British label displayed the following statement, required by the English Pharmacy Act: "This preparation, containing among other valuable ingredients a small amount of Morphine, is in accordance with the Pharmacy Act hereby labelled POISON" (Bok, 1905c:15).

In 1905, when a federal pure food law seemed no longer an impossible dream, Senator Porter J. McCumber of North Dakota, a strong supporter of Congressional food and drug legislation, published in *The Independent* an article called "The alarming adulteration of food and drugs." He cited the following, from "one of the New Orleans newspapers," as evidence of the hazards of proprietary remedies and the need to control them:

> "The surgeons of the New Orleans Eye, Ear, Nose and Throat Hospital have noted the great number of patients entering that institution from the country around New Orleans suffering from partial or total blindness. An investigation has disclosed the fact that a cheap antiseptic, containing a large amount of wood alcohol, has been used throughout Louisiana. The city chemists have found 30 per cent, at least, of methyl alcohol in one of these specimens, rendering them totally unfit for internal administration, as methyl alcohol when taken internally acts directly upon the optic nerve. The majority of persons affected will not fully recover their eyesight" (cited in McCumber, 1905:30–31).

Dr. Horatio C. Wood, Jr., writing in *Popular Science Monthly*, alleged that "soothing syrups" — morphine compounds used to quiet unruly children — had caused "numerous enough" infant deaths. Still, the real evil foisted upon the unsuspecting public, he asserted, was the ". . . hundreds of children condemned from the cradle to a life of invalidism, to which the grave is preferable" (Wood, 1906:535).

Alleged poisoning of children provides a powerful call to action. There is little doubt that "soothing syrups" and other nostrums containing alcohol and narcotics were widely used. Given the state of medical record-keeping at the time, however, it is impossible to determine, with a few anecdotal exceptions, the extent of damage actually done by patent medicine consumption.

The case against poisonous food additives and preservatives was better documented, but not by much. For the most part, the proof of hazard resided in the experimental findings of Dr. Wiley, statistical reports of food sample analyses, and the logical deductions of chemists and physicians. The etiology of disease and death was certainly less well developed than it is at the present, so that actual accounts of death and illness resulting from toxic food additives were little more than oft-repeated and unsubstantiated anecdotes.

The Independent, which published Senator McCumber's blistering attack on adulterated foods and drugs in 1905, in the same issue offered an editorial word of caution. Citing the problems of defining adulteration and establishing appropriate standards, and noting that most official studies of adulterated foods and drugs were looking for adulteration and therefore did not properly control sample selection, the editor remarked: "Such an article as that we print on another page is, however truthful, liable to give a wrong impression to the casual reader" (*The Independent*, Jan. 5, 1905:50). Then, one of the first to do so, the editor clearly separated two consumer issues that before had been entwined in most of the literature:

> The substitution or misbranding of medicine is a dangerous practice. The misbranding and adulteration of foods is in most cases more of the nature of commercial fraud. . . . Adulterated food *harms* the consumer only when it contains ingredients more unwholesome than the ordinary; it *cheats* the customer only when it is sold at as high a price as the pure article. Positively harmful adulterants are now, thanks to the diligence of our chemists, quite rare. . . . The truth is bad enough without making it any worse by exaggeration or misconceptions (p. 51, emphasis added).

Thus the editor of *The Independent* clarified the issues from the consumer's perspective. The highly emotional issue of poisonous adulterants was, in the editor's opinion, blown out of proportion to the truth; further, the damage done was undocumented, except in a few cases. The less emotional (but perhaps ultimately more powerful) issue, which enjoyed abundant and authoritative documentation, was that of commercial fraud.*

COMMERCIAL FRAUD

Hinich and Staelin (1980:8–9) describe three types of food and drug adulterations that have been of concern to the federal government:

1. *"Potentially harmful" adulteration* includes the use of poisonous or deleterious additives, as well as contamination from manufacturing, processing, packaging, or storage procedures.
2. *Aesthetic adulteration* is defined as "food that contains substances that are nonhazardous but considered 'filthy' . . . for example, nondiseased fly specks or dirt in the foods."
3. *Economic adulteration* is "nonhazardous adulteration that degrades the general quality of a food as perceived by consumers."

The third type of adulteration occupied a great deal of attention during the controversy over the 1906 Pure Food Act. Many concerns were expressed about partial or total substitution of fillers or cheaper materials for the "real" article and about misbranding of imitations as genuine products. During this time economic adulteration was often referred to more simply as "commercial fraud."

Although concerns about hazardous adulteration and commercial fraud were often uttered in the same breath, it is important that they be recognized as separate and distinct issues. Hazardous adulteration was a public health concern. The evidence and examples used to illustrate this problem had to do with the harmful effects, to the human body, of various additives, preservatives, colorings, flavorings, and

---

The Independent began publication in New York City in 1848 as a religious weekly circular associated with Henry Ward Beecher's Congregationalist Church. During the antebellum period and the Civil War, emancipation was a constant theme, and Harriet Beecher Stowe became a leading contributor after the publication of *Uncle Tom's Cabin.* By the 1890s *The Independent* had converted to a secular magazine concerned with current issues. It ceased publishing in 1928 (Mott, 1938:377–379).

other substances not present in the "natural" commodities. Pure food advocates sought, for the most part, to ban the use of such additives altogether. Since physicians, chemists, pharmacologists, and other experts often disagreed over the absolute and relative toxicity of numerous food and drug additives, the very modern issues of the weight and authority to be given to scientific evidence and expert testimony occupied a fairly prominent position in this portion of the debate.

Fraudulent substitution, in whole or in part, of a cheaper product for a more expensive, higher-quality one did not directly affect public health, but it did affect the ability of consumers to know exactly what they were purchasing and to get the full value they expected from dollars spent on foods and medicines. Thus substitution distorted the proper allocation of economic resources. A moral disdain of thievery was substantially bolstered by this laissez-faire economic argument for regulation.

WHAT DO WE GET FOR OUR MONEY?

The difference between value expected and value received comprised the bulk of evidence offered on food adulterations in the hearings of the U.S. Pure-Food Investigating Committee and in the reports of state agencies and the Bureau of Chemistry.

Senator W. W. Mason of Illinois, a member of the Congressional fact-finding committee and a strong early advocate of federal pure food legislation, offered one of the early popular accounts of the Pure Food Investigating Committee's Chicago hearings. He began his article by stating that "The United States of America, the greatest food-producing country in the world, is suffering from the adulteration of food products. . . . There is hardly an article of food that has not been at some time more or less adulterated; flour, butter, cheese, tea and coffee, syrups, spices of all kinds, extracts, baking powders . . . " (Mason, W.E., 1900:548).

Many specific cases of partial or total substitution of cheaper goods for more expensive ones, and of failure to accurately label substitutions and imitations, were offered to the committee. For example, "More Vermont maple sugar is made every year in Davenport, Iowa, from cheap yellow sugar flavored with vegetable extracts than can be produced from all the maple trees in the whole state of

Vermont!" (Mason, H.B., 1900:67). According to witnesses, much of what passed for the genuine article was neither maple sugar nor from Vermont, and yet these spurious goods commanded premium prices. Testimony was also offered on the selling of oleomargarine colored to resemble butter; jellies and jams made from peels, cores, and glucose; artificial "whiskies" manufactured from water, artificial flavorings, and grain alcohol; "pepper," "cinnamon," and other spices that were largely or wholly ground nutshells; and coffee containing high portions of chicory, grain, or both* (U.S. Senate Doc. 141, "Adulteration of food products," 1900; *Science*, June, 1899).

Over the next few years, many other reports were made on the nature and extent of fraudulent foods and drugs. The Bureau of Chemistry generated some of these reports, but more of them originated within state departments of agriculture and public health. Senator McCumber, for example, cited a 1904 paper by Professor Ladd, Food Commissioner of North Dakota, indicating that fraudulent practices in food and drug manufacturing were widespread. Some of the examples Commissioner Ladd included were the substitution of glucose for maple syrup; substitution of lard for butterfat in candies, condensed milk, and ice cream; and adulteration of phenacetin** with a much cheaper chemical (McCumber, 1905). The following example is typical of the portions of Commissioner Ladd's paper that were quoted by Senator McCumber:

> Many of the catsups offered for sale in the State [North Dakota] were made from the waste products from canners — pulp, skins, ripe tomatoes, green tomatoes, starch paste in considerable quantity, coal tar colors, chemical preservatives, . . . the whole highly spiced and not always free from saccharin. In other instances the basis for the catsup was largely pumpkin (McCumber, 1905:29).

As a final example of the types of commercial fraud described by witnesses before the Senate Committee, House Report No. 1426

---

*The reader will observe that many of these "adulterated" goods (with the possible exception of spices that are really nutshells) are legitimately sold in today's market, properly labeled.

**Phenacetin was an aniline derivative commonly used to reduce fever and relieve pain. Acetanilid, a less desirable substitute for phenacetin, became popular in the 1880s "mainly because of its cheapness" (R. Adams, 1931:137).

(May 10, 1900:8) contains the following excerpt from a farmer's bulletin providing instructions for the proper use of Gilt-Edge Butter Compound:

> Take a pint of fresh unskimmed milk and as much of the compound as you can heap on a silver ten cent piece and thoroughly mix the compound and the milk together in the churn with as much salt as is necessary to salt one pound of butter. Add to this one pound of soft butter and churn until the mass has come to butter, then you will have two pounds of butter and no milk.

THE ECONOMIC EFFECTS OF ADULTERATION AND MISBRANDING

Estimates of the extent of food adulteration varied widely, as did calculations of the economic costs of adulterated food purchases. R.O. Brooks, formerly New Jersey State Chemist and also Food-Inspection Expert for the Pennsylvania Dairy and Food Commission, estimated that total economic loss from foods was one billion dollars annually from all sources, including "adulteration, factory and domestic waste, inappropriate nutrition, etc." (Brooks, 1906:457). He then estimated that Americans spent about six billion dollars on foods and beverages annually, of which roughly 15 percent were adulterated, resulting in an economic loss of $900 million, or 90 percent of the total estimated loss. Brooks cited other figures as well, including an estimated $150 million loss annually calculated by Dr. McNeal, Ohio's dairy and food commissioner, and Dr. Abbott's calculation of an annual loss of $300 million (Dr. Abbott being, for 20 years, chief food inspector for the State of Massachusetts).

Senator McCumber (1905:29) borrowed his estimates of economic loss from adulterations from the Secretary of Agriculture's calculations, based on "reports from the food commissioners of the several states and from such other sources as he could command." On balance, the Secretary had found, by aggregating these various reports, that about 15 percent of all food and beverage purchases were adulterated, resulting in an annual economic loss of $1.175 billion.

To be conservative, in his official reports the Secretary cut this figure in half. Senator McCumber, concerned about adulterated products that were consumed but never subjected to government investigation, insisted that the figure should be doubled, not halved.

Obviously, whatever the actual figures might have been, "economic loss" in these discussions did not refer to the equivalent of lost gross national product, for the spurious goods were being sold. The term referred instead to the value lost to consumers when they unwittingly paid premium prices for inferior goods. Occasionally the issue of lost nutritional value was raised, for example when "cream cheese" that contained no cream was purchased. For the most part, however, the issue concerned consumers' right to purchase that which they thought they were purchasing, and the demand was not for a ban on substitutions and imitations, but for accurate labeling. If labels accurately described the goods being purchased, then the force of consumer choice in a free market would be protected.

PROTECTING THE POOR AND IGNORANT

Most of the popular literature on commercial fraud expressed the general theme of the consumer's right to know the content of purchased products. Some authors, however, explicitly raised a different (though related) theme — that of the need to protect the poor and the ignorant from the deceitful practices of dishonest manufacturers.

Irritating enough to the middle class, the effects of fraud on the poor were damnable. A number of writers expressed alarm at the apparent inclination of Congress to favor "special interest" legislation concerning adulterated or misbranded imported foods, for example, and their lack of interest in guaranteeing honest, inexpensive foods for those who could least afford to be cheated and most often were.

Harry B. Mason, writing for *The American Monthly Review of Reviews* (January 1900), admitted that "so far as public health is concerned the great majority of adulteration is not harmful. But where it is not harmful to the consumer's health it is to his pocket-book." Continuing, Mason struck the theme of protecting the poor from their own ignorance:

> Currant jelly made from apple cores and olive oil made from cotton seed are perhaps no more productive of systemic disturbance than the articles for which they are dishonestly substituted, but they are

deleterious to the purse of the poor man who pays for and thinks he is getting the pure articles (Mason, 1900:69).

Dr. Charles A. Crampton, Chief Chemist of the Internal Revenue Office, also wrote forcefully on this subject:

> The keynote of modern propaganda in respect to methods of control of food adulteration may be given in three words — vis., *an honest label!* No one wishes to deprive the poor man of his right to use a cheap and wholesome substitute for a more expensive article of food; it would be an unwarranted interference with the rights of both producer and consumer to prohibit the sale of such an article. . . . But it should be sold under its true name and upon its own merits — not as or for the article of which it is an imitation or a substitute (Crampton, 1900:943).

W.J. Ghent, arguing from a socialist perspective on industrial production, which was quite popular at the time, provided the following analysis of "commodity graft" or commercial fraud:

> It is in the cheaper grades of goods that the commodity graft finds its working field. . . . The greater temptation would naturally lie in debasing the dearer commodities — if only such commodities could be sold. But those who buy the dearer commodities have obviously the means to make effective their demand for good qualities, and they will not take the poorer. . . . It is thus upon the working class that the burden of debased commodities mainly falls. The working class produces the standard commodities, but it cannot buy them back (Ghent, 1906:1190).

Ghent used the U.S. Bureau of Labor's breakdown of the average working-class family's food budget to illustrate the extent to which the working class was being defrauded in their food purchases. For example, milk, butter, and cheese, accounting for 16.12 percent of the average food budget, were said to be adulterated as follows: milk preserved with formaldehyde; the cream removed from "cream cheese" and "cheese made of lard, cottonseed oil, and metallic salts"; oleomargarine substituted for butter, "renovated butter" made from "unsalable butter in various degrees of putrefaction," and fake butter made by "the solidifying of skim milk" (Ghent, 1906:1191). Ghent continued this analysis through numerous categories of working-class food purchases, concluding that those who could least afford to be cheated were being cheated the most.

An editorial in *The Nation* (July 30, 1903:88) declared that "the consumer of impure food is cheated even when he is not poisoned." Briefly examining some of the "special interest" legislation that had been passed by Congress (including the tax placed on oleomargarine, accurate labeling provisions for some imported products, and a law preventing the misbranding of certain cheeses as to their alleged geographical origin), the editor continued by decrying the lack of Congressional protection for the poor:

> Congress . . . does not concern itself with the "pure maple sugar" which never saw a maple tree, the "comb honey" made of paraffin and the indispensable glucose, the lowgrade flour whitened with alum, the diluted acetic acid which passes as vinegar, the red wood and charred peanut shells in spice boxes, or the strawberry jam made of flavored and tinted glucose and gelatin mixed with timothy seed, all of which are domestic products. The workingman may be sure that his *petits pois* and cognac are all that could be desired, however much doubt there may be as to his bread and salt.

Surely, in a free market one should be able to purchase inexpensive and nutritious foods, even if they were not "the real thing." In the absence of general federal oversight, however, there was no guarantee against fraud. Special-interest legislation to guard the quality of imported foods and specialty items was seen by these writers as an insult to the poor, who had no such safeguards for the food they could not produce themselves.

DRUGS AND COMMERCIAL FRAUD

In the case of drugs, public expressions of concern over commercial fraud carried much less weight than did arguments about the deleterious ingredients found in patent medicines. Medicines were supposed to cure or relieve the symptoms of illness; the public bought them for this purpose and expected them to perform this function. If they did not perform as expected, it was not always immediately obvious to the consumer. Even today assessing the efficacy of drugs is a time-consuming and often uncertain process. In the late 1800s proof of efficacy was almost entirely a matter of "raw empiricism"; one tried a bottle or two and if one felt better, the product worked.

The larger concern over adulterated and misbranded drugs was closely tied to negative health effects. Even worthless but not inherently harmful patent medicines came under attack. In the first place, many patent medicines contained one or more of alcohol, opium, morphine, or cocaine — all addicting chemicals consumed by innocent victims. In the second place, consumers who relied on patent medicines to cure their real illnesses were not inclined then to seek the services of physicians; their health could easily suffer by their unwarranted trust in medicines possessing no curative or palliative powers. In the case of drugs, then, the issue of commercial fraud (e.g., why should one pay a dollar for a small bottle of water, alcohol, and coloring and flavoring agents?) was far overshadowed by the public health issue.

THE CONSUMER'S RIGHT TO AN ACCURATE LABEL

Deleterious adulteration and commercial fraud converged in the issue of accurate labeling — the consumer's right to know what he or she was purchasing. Even Harvey Wiley, the most devoted of pure-food advocates, did not wish to deny persons the right to consume poisonous or inferior goods if they chose to do so.

In the final hearings on the Hepburn Bill (S.88, which passed into law) Dr. Wiley told the Senate Committee on Manufactures, in response to a question about the prohibition of substances that harmed relatively few people, "I am not advocating the prohibition of the use of benzoic acid by anybody who wants to use it. I would be in favor of putting benzoic acid in a little salt-cellar . . . and letting the people use it if they want to" (Wiley, 1929:31).

Over and over, the theme of consumer protection through adequate labeling information was reiterated. Proponents of the new law argued that patent medicines should be labeled with a complete description of their contents, so that mothers would *know* they were dosing their babies with alcohol and morphine, and all users would know if they were being defrauded by worthless "medicines." Users of imitation or "rectified" whiskey should *know* that they were not purchasing genuine aged whiskey. No one complained that oleomargarine was unwholesome, only that when it masqueraded as butter, consumers were being cheated.

On the other hand, the use of toxic chemicals in foods and drugs seemed indeed to be a case in which the federal government's mandate to secure the general welfare outweighed the free-market dictates of unfettered consumer choice.

Peter Temin begins his recent book on U.S. drug regulation with the statement, "In pursuit of 'errorless ball,' government policy toward medicinal drugs has progressively removed control over drug choices further and further from the consumer" (Temin, 1980:1). The decline of consumer choice is, of course, a common theme in current literature on business–government relations, and it has a considerable factual basis. The call for greater consumer choice via fewer government controls can, however, represent a view as myopic as that which promotes the federal government as a panacea for all social problems. To perform its free market role appropriately, "consumer choice" must be geared to *current* environmental conditions, not to those of the past. If consumers no longer have access to full and accurate product information, it is no good pretending that they do.

This yearning for "the good old days" is quite a common phenomenon, and it is understandable, in a way, because "the good old days" represent our mythical representations of a simpler, better, less confusing time. Such yearnings are by no means confined to modern human beings. Dr. Wiley prefaced the account in his autobiography of the battle for pure food legislation by looking backward:

> In the good old days preceding and immediately following the War between the States, there was little need of protection of the people from impure, adulterated and misbranded foods and drugs. The great bulk of the people raised most of what they ate and depended upon the standard, simple and proved remedies to overcome most of the general ills that then afflicted and still afflict humanity (Wiley, 1929:199).

What happened to these "good old days?" In a word, industrialization. Wiley himself mentions the "increasingly centralized population" as a force driving the society's increased reliance on manufactured foodstuffs; as people moved away from farms, foods had to be "imported" into the cities and could not be consumed while they were absolutely fresh. Distribution and transportation networks, as Hays (1957) has noted, made possible the mass marketing techniques that allowed mass manufacturing to be profitable. Newspapers and magazines, enjoying wide circulation, provided an excellent medium for product advertising.

Technological innovations tumbled one after the other into the manufacturing arena, making possible more efficient production and distribution. At the same time, they also contributed to the consumer's lessening basis for trust in the word of manufacturers and distributors. For example, automated canning facilities, however much they may have reduced deaths and illnesses from improperly home-canned goods, also removed control over the product from the consumer and placed it in the hands of the manufacturer and his employees. When you pull fresh loaves of bread from your own oven, you know that the ingredients are flour, salt, water, yeast, and oil. When the bread is bought from a bakery, a measure of trust in the baker becomes necessary for the consumer to be satisfied with the product. Bread from a grocery store, mass-produced elsewhere and trucked in, cannot on the face of it be determined pure and wholesome by the purchaser.

Industrialization, then, generated not only a wealth of heretofore unseen products, many of which were beneficial and desirable, it also made it impossible for consumers to know precisely what they were purchasing.

The free market was not, after all, a foolproof mechanism for the efficient allocation of resources. The removal of food manufactures from home and community generated enormous potential for fraud and abuse; industrialization and cross-country distribution eliminated the foundation of trust and accountability between buyer and seller. If manufacturing and commercial interests could not be trusted to behave honestly, then consumers would have to transfer their trust to the government, which could assure them that the product information on which they depended was accurate.

Accurate labels would protect the rights of people to use margarine, glucose syrup, coffee mixed with chicory, or worthless tonics if they chose to do so. Labeling regulations would prevent manufacturers from misrepresenting cheap products as expensive ones. In short, accurate labels would ensure that consumers had the information needed to make informed market choices. Only the federal government could make such a guarantee effective across the nation.

The story usually ends here, but consumer interests were not the only issues at stake vis-a-vis pure foods and drugs in the Progressive Era. Businesses, too, had enormous vested interests in the passage of a federal law.

four

The Dimensions
of Competition

ALTHOUGH THE 1906 PURE FOOD ACT IS SEEN TODAY AS CON-
sumer protection legislation, the pure-food movement did not find its
only supportive voices among consumers and their unofficial representatives; the movement did not reflect the mythical battle between
"the people" and "the interests." It is true, of course, that there was
a great deal of business opposition to the idea of regulating interstate
commerce in foods, beverages, and drugs, but the controversy preceding the passage of the 1906 act was also marked by a number of
manufacturing and retail voices speaking favorably of such a law.

Just as there was no true "consumer movement" expressing "the
consumer position" on pure food and drugs, it was equally the case
that there was no "business position." Business leaders did not act in
unison, perceiving their interests to lie with all others like themselves; there was no clear dichotomy between "business" and "society." Instead, business leaders formed, abandoned, and reconstituted
coalitions that could be responsive to political conditions and that
could maximize the power of collective action to influence those conditions favorably.

Some business representatives, such as H.J. Heinz, offered their

108

unqualified support for a federal food and drug law. Others, such as the American Proprietary Association (representing "patent medicine" vendors), were unequivocally opposed to federal intervention in their markets. Most involved businesses expressed support for the *idea* of a federal law, but chose to argue for or against various particulars in the many bills that were presented to Congress. Support, opposition, and *ad hoc* arguments alike arose from businesspeople's perceptions of how the law would affect their own operations.

These perceptions reflected common interests among business communities only in the most abstract sense: All were dedicated to the goals of survival, growth, and profits. The political positions of businesses on the pure food law were only occasionally articulated in terms of free enterprise ideology and support for overall economic development; free-market justifications received little more than an obligatory nod from the business community. The arguments pro and con were based much more on each business's or industry's or industry segment's desire to maintain or strengthen its own competitive position in the marketplace; they were much more clearly directed toward reducing competition than to securing it.

George Stigler's (1971) "economic" theory of regulatory origin suggests that businesses seek to use the coercive power of government to serve their competitive interests. He identifies four "policies" that can be promulgated by the government to assist businesses: "direct subsidy, control over entry, powers affecting substitutes and complements, and price-fixing" (Mitnick, 1980:113). Richard A. Posner extends Stigler's analysis by maintaining that "regulation can protect industries by bringing about shared rules for behavior — rules which ensure higher than competitive rates, protection from potential competitors, and so on" (Mitnick, 1980:117).

In the pure food and drug debate, three of these five outcomes were sought directly by businesses (control over entry, powers affecting substitutes and complements, and shared rules); a fourth — price-fixing — was indirectly involved in the attempts of some businesses to have federal or state taxes imposed on the products of their principal competitors, under the guise of concerns about adulteration and mislabeling. These competitive interests were bolstered by moral arguments, made by business representatives, concerning honesty and integrity in business dealings, and by appeals to Congress and to uninvolved segments of industry to protect industrial productivity by ensuring that workers were adequately nourished (and not cheated of nourishment through commercial fraud). Indeed, the moral and economic justifications for passage of a food and drug law were well mixed; business interests in economic health and productivity had not yet become ideologically distinct from "public" interests in safe, healthful, accurately labeled products (see Vogel, 1981).

The right of businesses to defend their own interests by entering and attempting to influence public policy debates was not seriously questioned, despite some concerns about the enormous economic and political power of the "Trusts." David Graham Phillips' popular book, *The Treason of the Senate* (1906; reissued 1964), was one expression of these concerns that money and clout translated into ineffective government. In Congress and elsewhere, however, there was little argument. Many journalists, scientists, public officials, and members of Congress made public declarations of business's right to self-defense — not in the shrill tones that have characterized recent such declarations, but in the matter-of-fact tones of entitlement. This feeling of entitlement seems almost to have disappeared in the intervening decades. Recall, for example, the words of Irving Shapiro (of DuPont and the Business Roundtable) when the Consumer Protection Act was finally killed in 1978 after aggressive lobbying and "grassroots" organizing on the part of businesses: "There are some dangers in all this. One is that the public will perceive that businessmen are running around Washington acting like elected officials, trying to take over the running of the country. If business steps over that line, it will be in worse trouble than it has ever known before" ("Going Public," May 30, 1978:22).

No such caveats and hesitancies were felt to be necessary to justify the participation of business leaders in Progressive Era political affairs. To most of those who thought and wrote about the pure food issue it seemed beyond the scope of consideration that businesses should be denied the right to participate in political decisions that would affect them, or that their right to a voice should be abridged. After all, since competition was the keystone of the economy and the theoretical guarantee of its efficiency, businesses should be free to compete in the political as well as the purely commercial arena.

Four rationales for passing federal food and drug legislation were offered by and on behalf of businesses. First, the possibility that workers were cheated of proper nutrition or became ill from poisonous adulterants and "patent medicines" posed a problem in the efficient use of human resources (a moral and economic argument). Second, the growth of interstate commerce meant that a uniform federal law would be more rational and cost-effective than complying with a multitude of state laws, and that reputable manufacturers needed protection against adulterators and misbranders located in other states (arguments for shared rules to promote honesty and integrity). Third, the need to increase exports, to absorb increased production, was hampered by the tarnished reputation of U.S. processed foods overseas (general economic interest arguments). Finally, as discussed in Chapter 5, the interests of businesses in securing protection from their domestic competitors were expressed in legislative components of numerous trade wars among food and drug companies. Firms and industries whose market position was threatened by newer, cheaper products entered the legislative domain to seek protection against their competitors via federal laws (arguments for control over entry, control over substitutes and complements, and price-fixing through "punitive" taxation).

To establish a context for subsequent analysis of these issues, the next section examines the economic status and competitive conditions of the most important industries involved in the manufacture of foods and drugs during the Progressive Era.

COMPETITIVENESS IN THE FOOD INDUSTRY

Summary data from the Census of Manufactures are presented in Appendix A for every industry involved in the manufacture of food, beverages, and drugs for the period 1870–1909. The fact that *thirty* separate industries are so identified is a clue to the importance of these activities to the economy, as well as to the conditions of competition facing businesses so engaged. Table 4.1 presents summary data for all food, beverage, and drug industries combined, which can be compared with the data in Table 4.2, for all U.S. industries covered by the Census of Manufactures. Table 4.3 shows, for each category of data, the percentage of all U.S. industries represented by the food, drug, and beverage industries.

The statistics for the number of establishments partially reflect the conditions of U.S. industry overall and food and drug businesses

TABLE 4.1

Census Data on Combined Food, Drug, and Beverage Industries, 1870–1909

		NUMBER OF EMPLOYEES		
YEAR	NUMBER OF ESTABLISHMENTS	Adult Males	Adult Females	Children
1870	35,711	142,235	13,673	6,119
1880	43,629	166,264	24,982	11,309
1890	49,917	253,266	52,939	10,213
1900	74,759	320,117	65,876	12,907
1904	55,785			
1909	67,233			

	NUMBER OF EMPLOYEES			
	Proprietors	Salaried Employees	Wage Earners	TOTAL EMPLOYEES
1870				161,997
1880			224,356	224,356
1890		61,367	319,742	381,109
1900		66,909	400,357	467,266
1904	57,637	78,948	457,103	593,688
1909	71,035	125,787	513,940	710,762

	CAPITAL (thousand $)	SALARIES (thousand $)	WAGES (thousand $)	COST OF MATERIALS (thousand $)	VALUE OF PRODUCTS (thousand $)
1870	335,816		45,463	660,762	845,359
1880	491,374		75,090	1,123,862	1,370,859
1890	904,594	50,217	128,285	1,645,955	2,052,615
1900	1,687,148	68,515	181,115	2,336,232	2,864,543
1904	1,979,983	86,578	225,202	2,543,173	3,543,792
1909	2,808,427	141,383	277,030	3,526,647	4,893,424

SOURCE: Calculated from the U.S. *Census of Manufactures,* years noted.

Note: The total number of employees by age and sex categories and by type (proprietors, etc.) do not correspond because of inconsistencies in the available census data. Figures were not consistently available for all food, drug, and beverage industries by each type of breakdown.

TABLE 4.2

Census Data on All U.S. Manufacturing Industries, 1870–1909

		NUMBER OF EMPLOYEES		
YEAR	NUMBER OF ESTABLISHMENTS	Adult Males	Adult Females	Children
1870	252,148	1,615,598	323,770	114,628
1880	253,852	2,019,035	531,639	181,921
1890	355,415	3,327,042	803,686	120,885
1900	512,254	4,110,527	1,029,296	168,583
1904	216,180			
1909	268,491			

		NUMBER OF EMPLOYEES		
	Proprietors	Salaried Employees	Wage Earners	TOTAL EMPLOYEES
1870				2,053,996
1880				2,732,595
1890		461,009	4,251,613	4,712,622
1900		396,759	5,308,406	5,705,165
1904	225,673	519,556	5,468,383	6,213,612
1909	273,265	790,267	6,615,046	7,678,578

	CAPITAL (thousand $)	SALARIES (thousand $)	WAGES (thousand $)	COST OF MATERIALS (thousand $)	VALUE OF PRODUCTS (thousand $)
1870	2,118,209		775,584	2,488,427	4,232,325
1880	2,790,273		947,954	3,396,824	5,369,579
1890	6,525,156	391,988	1,891,228	5,793,269	9,372,437
1900	9,817,435	403,711	2,322,334	8,373,170	13,004,400
1904	12,675,581	574,439	2,610,445	8,500,208	14,793,903
1909	18,428,270	938,575	3,427,038	12,142,791	20,672,052

SOURCE: Calculated from the U.S. *Census of Manufactures,* years noted.

TABLE 4.3

Census Data for Food, Drug, and Beverage Industries as a Percent of All U.S. Industries, 1870–1909

		EMPLOYEES		
YEAR	NUMBER OF ESTABLISHMENTS	Adult Males	Adult Females	Children
1870	14.2	8.8	4.2	5.3
1880	17.2	8.2	4.7	6.2
1890	14.0	7.6	6.6	8.4
1900	14.6	7.8	6.4	7.7
1904	25.8			
1909	25.0			

	EMPLOYEES			
	Proprietors	Salaried Employees	Wage Earners	TOTAL EMPLOYEES
1870				7.9
1880				8.2
1890		13.3	7.5	8.1
1900		16.9	7.5	8.2
1904	25.5	15.2	8.4	9.6
1909	26.0	15.9	7.8	9.3

	CAPITAL	SALARIES	WAGES	COST OF MATERIALS	VALUE OF PRODUCTS
1870	15.9		5.9	26.6	20.0
1880	17.6		7.9	33.1	25.5
1890	13.9	12.8	6.8	28.4	21.9
1900	17.2	17.0	7.8	27.9	22.0
1904	15.6	15.1	8.6	29.9	24.0
1909	15.2	15.1	8.1	29.0	23.7

SOURCE: Calculated from the U.S. *Census of Manufactures,* years noted.

in particular. The Panic of 1873 likely accounts for the relatively small growth in the total number of businesses from 1870 to 1880 (Table 4.2), but it should be noted that the number of food businesses grew at a much higher rate for the same period (Table 4.1). Appendix A shows that this dramatic growth, despite generally unfavorable economic conditions, is attributable to growth in these specific industries: baking powder producers, bakeries, dairy establishments, canners and preservers, patent medicine manufacturers, and meat-packers (see Appendix A). Table 4.3 shows further that food and drug establishments accounted for 17.2 percent of all industry in 1880, up three percent from 1870.

Consistent growth patterns are documented in Tables 4.1 and 4.2 through 1900, but the lingering effects of the depression of the 1890s and the effects of the first of the great merger waves are seen, beginning in 1904. The overall number of U.S. manufacturing enterprises declined in 1904 to less than half the number existing in 1900; the decline in four years was 137 percent. In contrast, food and drug industries experienced a mere 34 percent decline in the number of enterprises from 1900 to 1904. As the tables in Appendix A show, many food and drug classifications continued to exhibit growth in the number of businesses and others experienced only minor decreases. Interestingly, among the four specific food industries registering sharp declines in the number of businesses, only cane sugar shows any sign of real contraction in terms of number of employees and capitalization, and even that industry shows consistent growth in the value of goods purchased. Table 4.4 provides the relevant data.

Continuous increases in number of employees, capitalization, and value of goods produced are apparent for cider and vinegar, confectionery, and flour and milling. This suggests that the very marginal producers closed their doors or were swallowed by other enterprises between 1900 and 1904, leaving larger, more heavily capitalized, more productive businesses in these industrial categories.

By 1909, most of the thirty food and drug industries were experiencing resurgence in number of establishments and the other statistics gathered in the *Census of Manufactures*. Indeed, Table 4.3 suggests that the industry concentration that began to flower in 1900–1904 may have received a setback over the next five years as many new businesses began again (as they had in the 1880s and the early

TABLE 4.4

Selected Summary Census Data for Cider, Confectionery, Flour, and Cane Sugar Industries, 1880–1909

INDUSTRY AND YEAR	NUMBER OF ESTABLISHMENTS	NUMBER OF EMPLOYEES	CAPITAL (thousand $)	PRODUCT VALUE (thousand $)
Cider and Vinegar				
1870	728	2,041	1,845	3,472
1880	306	1,257	2,152	3,418
1890	694	3,388	5,858	6,649
1900	1,152	2,257	6,188	6,455
1904	568	2,514	7,520	7,265
1909	963	3,073	10,879	8,448
Confectionery				
1870	949	5,825	4,995	15,923
1880	1,450	9,801	8,487	25,637
1890	2,921	27,211	23,327	55,997
1900	4,297	39,211	35,155	81,291
1904	1,348	42,729	43,125	87,087
1909	1,944	54,854	68,326	134,796

TABLE 4.4

Continued

INDUSTRY AND YEAR	NUMBER OF ESTABLISHMENTS	NUMBER OF EMPLOYEES	CAPITAL (thousand $)	PRODUCT VALUE (thousand $)
Flour and Milling				
1870	22,573	58,448	151,565	444,985
1880	24,338	58,407	177,362	505,186
1890	18,470	63,481	208,474	513,917
1900	25,258	42,863	218,714	560,719
1904	10,051	59,623	265,117	713,033
1909	11,691	66,054	349,152	883,584
Cane Sugar				
1870	772	25,896	30,793	119,325
1880	49	5,857	27,433	155,485
1890	393	7,529	24,013	123,118
1900	832	16,143	184,246	240,970
1904	344	15,799	165,468	277,285
1909	233	15,658	153,167	279,249

SOURCE: Calculated from the U.S. *Census of Manufactures*, years noted.

and late 1890s) to enter highly competitive markets for processed foods and drugs.

Clough and Marburg (1968:76) have described the conditions under which commercial agriculture and the downstream manufacturing it supported became both possible and profitable:

> The commercialization of agriculture, the growing of a limited number of crops for sale in an impersonal market rather than many crops to fill the needs of the immediate producer, was in evidence well before 1850, as in the case of cotton. But it was only after that date that transportation facilities, farm machinery, and a money economy were well enough developed to make the change dramatic. It was then that farmers gave up growing their own wheat and carrying it to the local grist mill to be ground into flour, preferring instead to buy their flour at the local store. They gave up raising sheep needed to produce wool for their own clothes and moved both spinning wheel and loom into the back attic, whence they were to be dug out years later by antique dealers and "summer folks." They stopped churning their own butter or making their own cheese. Even dairy farmers sometimes purchased oleomargarine. And in some cases they even gave up growing fruits and vegetables for themselves, claiming that it was cheaper to buy canned or frozen foods in the nearby shopping center.

Hampe and Wittenberg (1964:46) have called the period from 1850 to 1940 the "third revolution" in American agriculture, characterized by the movement of farming into the age of modern technology. According to these analysts, a number of trends and factors converged, particularly in the last half of the 19th century, and encouraged the industrialization of food production and distribution. These trends and factors included settlement of the West, farm mechanization, mass transportation, an increase in highly specialized farming and a drastic decline in self-sufficient farms, expansion into new markets (domestic and foreign), the growth of farmers' organizations such as the Grange, and the rise of educational opportunities providing modern technological and scientific information, incentives, and values to young future farmers.

With such favorable conditions, and with the explosion in agricultural technology (including breeding knowledge and planting and harvesting techniques as well as farm machinery), it is no wonder that food, the most basic of industries, continued throughout the period under consideration to constitute a large portion of all American industry. It is surprising, however, that statistics for the combined food and drug industries do not seem to show the effect of bankruptcies and mergers seen in the figures for aggregated U.S. industries. It is necessary to examine the evidence for specific industries to see that, despite the existence of complex and intense patterns of competition, concentration *was* beginning to develop in many food and drug industries during the Progressive Era. With economic concentration came more powerful political voices from the business sector to speak not for all businesses, but for their own.

In the following sections statistical and historical data are presented for several of the major food and drug industries. Makers of baking powders, butter and cheese, and oleomargarine are held for examination in Chapter 5. Table 4.5 presents some baseline data on growth rates for all food, drug, and beverage industries during the period 1870–1909. The figures show the percent increase (or decrease) from one reporting period to the next and for the entire forty years in the number of establishments, number of persons employed, capitalization, and dollar value of goods produced. Table 4.5 will serve as a basis for comparison with the specific industries discussed in subsequent sections.

Flour and Milling

Table 4.6 shows the relative importance of the flour and milling industry in terms of its percentages of the establishments, employees, capital, and product value of all U.S. food, drug, and beverage industries. Table 4.7 shows the patterns of growth and decline exhibited by this industry from 1870 to 1909.

Examining these two tables together, it is easy to see that this was an industry marked by early (and somewhat successful) attempts at concentration. In 1870, flour and grist mills accounted for almost two-thirds of all food establishments,* employed more than one-third of all food workers, produced more than half the total food product

---

*Unless otherwise noted, this term is used hereafter to include drug and beverage establishments as well.

TABLE 4.5

Selected Census Data on Combined Food, Drug, and Beverage
Industries: Percent Growth Between Reporting Periods, 1870–1909

YEAR	PERCENT GROWTH IN:			
	Number of Establishments	Total Employees	Capital	Value of Products
Baseline 1870	(35,711)	(161,997)	($335,816,000)	($845,359,000)
1880	22.2%	38.5%	46.3%	62.2%
1890	14.4	69.9	84.1	49.7
1900	49.8	22.6	86.5	39.6
1904	(−25.4)	27.1	17.4	23.7
1909	20.5	19.7	41.8	38.1
Total % growth, 1870–1909	88.3%	338.8%	736.3%	478.9%

SOURCE: Calculated from the U.S. *Census of Manufactures,*
years noted.

TABLE 4.6

Selected Census Data on the Flour and Milling Industry as a
Percentage of All U.S. Food and Drug Industries, 1870–1909

YEAR	NUMBER OF ESTABLISHMENTS	TOTAL EMPLOYEES	CAPITAL	VALUE OF PRODUCTS
1870	63.2%	36.1%	45.1%	52.6%
1880	55.8	26.0	36.1	36.9
1890	37.0	16.7	23.0	25.0
1900	33.8	9.2	13.0	19.6
1904	18.0	10.0	13.4	20.1
1909	17.4	9.3	12.4	18.1

SOURCE: Calculated from the U.S. *Census of Manufactures,*
years noted.

TABLE 4.7

Selected Census Data on the Flour and Milling Industry: Percent Growth Between Reporting Periods, 1870–1909

	PERCENT GROWTH IN:			
YEAR	Number of Establishments	Total Employees	Capital	Value of Products
Baseline 1870	(22,573)	(58,448)	($151,565,000)	($444,985,000)
1880	7.8%	(−0.1%)	17.0%	13.5%
1890	(−24.1)	8.7	17.5	1.7
1900	36.8	(−32.5)	4.9	9.1
1904	(−60.2)	39.1	21.2	27.2
1909	(16.3	10.8	31.7	23.9
Total % growth, 1870–1909	(−48.2%)	13.0%	130.4%	98.6%

SOURCE: Calculated from the U.S. *Census of Manufactures*, years noted.

value, and was supported by almost half the capital available to food industries. Virtually every community had at least one mill; milling then was close to being still a cottage industry. The roller process for milling, applied in the 1870s, began the trend toward obsolescence for the traditional stone grist mills and made possible the efficient mass production of flour and other milled grain products. Concentration and mass production, however, did not exclusively characterize this industry until much later in the 20th century.

Victor S. Clark (1929:267–268), in his volume *History of Manufactures in the United States*, reports on some of the collective pursuits of the milling industry during the Progressive Era:

> About the time the roller process was introduced in the United States, conflicting patents for flour-mill machinery burdened the industry with so much litigation that the lead producers formed a protective association to defend themselves against this flood of lawsuits. Eventually the original motive for the existence of this society, which was known as the Millers' National Association, lost its former

importance, and it assumed other functions, such as looking after railway charges and claims for its members, standardizing products, and maintaining prices. Local mill consolidations occurred at Minneapolis, which was the country's greatest flour-manufacturing center, and elsewhere, but never acquired national importance until 1899, when some twenty-four important mills, at points as far apart as New York City, Minneapolis, and Superior, were brought together in a single corporation. This combination, the United States Flour Milling Company, had an output of 40,000 or 50,000 barrels a day when its mills were running to capacity; but it did not exercise an appreciable control over prices. In general the big milling companies were the most extensively engaged in the export trade; while custom flour mills or gristmills, and the small local merchant millers, supplied a relatively larger share of the domestic consumption.

By 1909 the number of milling establishments was half what it had been in 1870, a reduction of 10,882 mills over 40 years. The number of persons employed in the industry increased only 13 percent (compared to a 339-percent increase for combined food industries). The value of goods produced, on the other hand, had almost doubled by 1909, and the industry's capital had increased by 130 percent. Although these gains are modest when compared to those of combined food industries (see Table 4.5), it is apparent that the average size, capitalization, and output of mills increased considerably over this period.

Breads, Crackers, and Bakery Goods

Tables 4.8 and 4.9 present summary data relevant to the bread, crackers, and bakery goods industry (hereafter called the baking industry). Concentration in this industry is masked in the aggregate statistics by the industry's substantial growth over the period. On all measures the baking industry grew much faster than did the combined food industries, and by 1909 it had assumed a reasonably prominent place among those industries.

After noting that manufacturers of breakfast cereals in the Central Western states (what we would now call North Central — "be-

TABLE 4.8

Selected Census Data on the Bread, Crackers, and Bakery Goods Industry as a Percentage of all U.S. Food and Drug Industries, 1870–1909

YEAR	NUMBER OF ESTABLISHMENTS	TOTAL EMPLOYEES	CAPITAL	VALUE OF PRODUCTS
1870	9.9%	8.7%	3.0%	4.4%
1880	14.7	10.0	3.9	4.8
1890	21.0	13.8	5.1	6.3
1900	20.0	14.9	4.8	6.1
1904	32.7	18.5	6.2	7.6
1909	35.6	20.3	7.6	8.1

SOURCE: Calculated from the U.S. *Census of Manufactures,* years noted. See Appendix A and Table 4.1.

TABLE 4.9

Selected Census Data on the Bread, Crackers, and Bakery Goods Industry: Percent Growth Between Reporting Periods, 1870–1909

| YEAR | PERCENT GROWTH IN: | | | |
	Number of Establishments	Total Employees	Capital	Value of Products
Baseline 1870	(3550)	(14,126)	($10,026,000)	($36,908,000)
1880	80.2%	59.2%	91.1%	78.3%
1890	63.9	134.6	138.9	95.1
1900	42.3	31.6	77.1	36.8
1904	22.2	57.9	51.0	53.5
1909	31.3	31.6	74.0	47.2
Total % growth, 1870–1909	574.0%	921.7%	2,023.6%	975.3%

SOURCE: Calculated from the U.S. *Census of Manufactures,* years noted.

tween Niagara Falls and Minneapolis") had combined to control the
market by the early 1900s, Clark (1929:268–269) reports on the birth
of Nabisco and the great firms of the baking industry:

> Consolidation was also the order of the day in the baking industries.
> By the middle nineties several large companies, representing for
> the most part combinations of plants associated by their location or
> by common sources of capital, occupied conspicuous positions in
> this business at New York City and at other important population
> centers. In 1898 the New York City Biscuit Company, The Ameri-
> can Biscuit and Manufacturing Company, the United States Baking
> Company, and the United States Biscuit Company consolidated as
> the National Biscuit Company with a total capital of $55,000,000.
> There had been severe competition in the industry for some time
> previously, and the combined companies from the first operated as
> one. The new corporation controlled the cracker and biscuit trade
> between the Atlantic Ocean and the Rocky Mountains, operating
> 139 plants, or about 90 percent of all the larger bakeries in the coun-
> try. It started out with a settled policy of reducing its percentage of
> profit but of simultaneously increasing its total profit by multiplying
> its sales. In spite of the large share of the commercial baking busi-
> ness, at least in certain lines, that the consolidation controlled, the
> first report of the President said: "We have no monopoly. . . . We
> always expect to have a great deal of competition. We propose to
> get the business and hold it by selling better goods, by furnishing
> them in a better condition to consumers and at lower prices . . .
> than our competitors are able to do." A very large increase in sales
> testified to the wisdom of this policy — so large, indeed, that it was
> at times impossible to fill the demand for goods. This was accounted
> for partly, however, by scientific advertising and the distribution of
> products in attractive sanitary packages. Within two years the com-
> bination's annual consumption of flour exceeded 2,000,000 barrels.
> At this time the National Biscuit Company was said to have a work-
> ing agreement with the Pacific Coast Biscuit Company, which was
> organized almost simultaneously and controlled the biscuit, cracker
> and cake trade of the three Coast states, not to operate west of the
> Rocky Mountains, while the Pacific Coast company shipped none of
> its products east of that boundary. Notwithstanding the existence of
> these large corporations, however, many small cracker-manufactur-
> ing companies were formed during the next few years, particularly
> in the South.

Hays (1957) analyzed the effects of the introduction of small packages — sealed and easily shipped — on the market for crackers. Prior to this innovation, crackers were shipped in bulk and sold from open barrels. New packaging forms made a considerable contribution to the formation and success of national baking companies.

Despite the emergence of giant corporate bakers like Nabisco and the Pacific Coast Biscuit Company, small bakers continued to proliferate, serving local markets for freshly baked and specialty items. These bakeries, of course, participated little if at all in interstate commerce, and although they were largely responsible for the rapid increase in the number of baking establishments, their relative contribution to the industry's capital and product value was less significant.

Canning and Preserving

Tables 4.10 and 4.11 present data on the phenomenal growth of the canning and preserving industry from 1870 to 1909. According to Clark (1929:270), the canning industry's growth was marked by several "outstanding developments," including

> . . . the establishment of pineapple canning in Hawaii; additions of the first importance, like condensed soups, to the older range of products; increased specialization of plants and processes; and the extension of scientific control to all stages of production, from the vegetable field and the orchard to the warehouse for finished goods.

One of the most important scientific advances for this industry occurred in 1874 — "the invention of the pressure kettle, or retort" (Hampe and Wittenberg, 1964:116). Industrial application of the pressure retort meant that canned foods could be sealed and stored under the most sanitary conditions, and that botulisms and other virulent organisms could be kept out of the finished products with a much greater degree of accuracy. By reducing the risk of food poisoning, canners could increase the levels of trust in their products. Tomatoes, fruits, vegetables, fish, and seafoods, canned and distributed nationwide, became an inexpensive and reliable source of food for many American families.

TABLE 4.10

Selected Census Data on the Canning and Preserving Industry as a Percentage of All U.S. Food and Drug Industries, 1870–1909

YEAR	NUMBER OF ESTABLISHMENTS	TOTAL EMPLOYEES	CAPITAL	VALUE OF PRODUCTS
1870	0.9%	5.9%	1.4%	1.4%
1880	1.2	14.8	1.9	1.5
1890	2.6	16.7	2.9	2.6
1900	3.8	11.7	4.1	4.2
1904	7.1	13.6	6.6	5.4
1909	7.4	13.1	6.6	5.8

SOURCE: Calculated from the U.S. *Census of Manufactures,* years noted.

TABLE 4.11

Selected Census Data on the Canning and Preserving Industry: Percent Growth Between Reporting Periods, 1870–1909

YEAR	PERCENT GROWTH IN:			
	Number of Establishments	Total Employees	Capital	Value of Products
Baseline 1870	(311)	(9,488)	($4,629,000)	($12,112,000)
1880	67.2%	250.3%	106.1%	65.9%
1890	152.7	91.8	175.9	169.8
1900	116.1	(−14.2)	164.0	123.3
1904	38.6	47.7	88.5	58.3
1909	26.6	15.1	40.3	47.4
Total % growth, 1870–1909	1,501.3%	879.5%	3,872.6%	2,231.8%

SOURCE: Calculated from the U.S. *Census of Manufactures,* years noted.

Concentration in the canning industry proceeded slowly, and was barely in evidence by 1909. As Clark (1929:270–271) reports:

> Unlike so many other food manufactures, canning did not fall into the hands of a few great corporations, although certain packing firms entered this field on a large scale; and in some localities, like Alaska, California and Hawaii, where the business was highly standardized and was centralized geographically, big company control was the rule. In addition to these large corporations, trade associations of canners were organized, which performed numerous services, such as standardizing prices, securing favorable freight rates, and conducting joint publicity campaigns for their members. In 1907 a National Canners' Association, embracing companies in all parts of the country, was formed, which in addition to the usual functions of such a body maintains a laboratory to study problems of practical interest to the industry. A similar association, also with a special research department, was organized by canners using glass containers.

As it turned out, the canners' trade associations were among the most active business voices in the pure food controversy.

Canners were bound in many instances to locations near the source of their foodstuffs. Massachusetts hosted codfish canneries; Maryland produced canned oysters; Maine was a leading producer of canned lobster and sardines. Hawaiian pineapple, California fruits and vegetables, Wisconsin peas, and Alaskan salmon were other items canned near their sources. Propitious conditions for marketable agricultural products such as these did encourage the development of large regional canners. According to Clark (1929:271),

> Among the largest corporations in the business were the Alaska Packing Company, whose chief product was canned salmon, and the California Fruit Canners' Association. The latter company was organized in 1899, with a capital of $3,500,000, to consolidate the principal plants in that state canning fruits and vegetables. When in full operation throughout the season its output was more than 50,000,000 cans annually, or three-fourths the total product of California, which was the leading state in this industry.

Canning, like farming, was a risky business, and not only for obvious reasons such as crop failure, insect damage, or the wrong type of weather. Stephen Potter (1959) tells the story of H.J. Heinz's brush with bankruptcy early in his career as a Pittsburgh canner. Heinz had scouted the surrounding farms for the cucumbers of highest quality for pickle-making and contracted with those farmers to purchase their entire cucumber output the following year. To Heinz's great dismay, that next year produced a bumper crop of cucumbers. Obligated to pay for all the wagonloads that seemed to roll without ceasing into Pittsburgh, it took Heinz a number of years to recover from the financial blow of an exceedingly good season of cucumbers.

Clark (1929:271) reminds us of some of the scientific and technological developments that helped to reduce the risk of operating a cannery:

> By the end of this period growers raised certain fruits and vegetables, like pineapples, peaches and tomatoes, of uniform size to fit standard containers. Plant selection had also enabled the grower to produce crops that ripened simultaneously, as in the case of peas, where it is important that all the pods on a vine should mature at the same time for easy harvesting. During the period we are discussing, machinery was invented to shell peas without taking the pods from the vine, to husk corn, to peel tomatoes, and to perform other preparatory cannery operations that had previously required manual labor. Notwithstanding these technical improvements, however, the greatest advances in this branch of food preparation were due to the chemist and the bacteriologist, whose labors insured a more wholesome and palatable product than before.

The great success of these developments can be seen in an industry growth rate that far exceeded that for the food industries combined. On the other hand, it is important to remember that many of these scientific and technological advances also produced the conditions that made possible a public controversy over food and drug adulterations and, eventually, a federal law.

Meatpacking

Table 4.12 presents data on growth rates in the meatpacking industry, 1870–1909. Data on meatpacking as a proportion of all food industries is not reported because the proportions are consistently quite small.

TABLE 4.12

Selected Census Data on the Meatpacking Industry: Percent Growth Between Reporting Periods, 1870–1909

YEAR	PERCENT CHANGE IN:			
	Number of Establishments	Total Employees	Capital	Value of Products
Baseline 1870	(259)	(6,485)	($22,125,000)	($62,140,000)
1880	236.7%	320.9%	123.4%	388.5%
1890	56.8	79.7	138.8	86.0
1900	(−17.0)	62.5	61.6	40.0
1904	7.7	11.4	26.1	16.7
1909	34.4	22.4	59.5	48.6
Total % growth, 1870–1909	533.6%	1,576.4%	1,633.0%	2,105.6%

SOURCE: Calculated from the U.S. *Census of Manufactures,* years noted.

(Interested readers may calculate this data from Table A.23 in Appendix A and Table 4.1.)

The number of packing establishments showed a fairly steady increase over the period, from 259 in 1870 to 1,641 in 1909. The industrialization of meatpacking is evident in the much greater increases in employment, capitalization, and value of products. Toward the end of this period about ten billion pounds of pork, beef, mutton, and veal were processed every year (Clark, 1929:264). The stockyards of Chicago were the scene of much of this activity. Far behind Chicago in productivity, but important secondary meatpacking centers nonetheless, were Kansas City, New York, Indianapolis, and Saint Louis, with St. Joseph, Missouri, and Fort Worth, Texas, increasing in importance by the turn of the century.

Some of the developments encouraging the rapid growth of the meatpacking industry are reported by Clark (1929:264):

> . . . the substitution of mechanical refrigeration for natural ice refrigeration, about 1890, enabled the packing house to dispense with

its enormous ice house in favor of a more compact and efficient power plant, and freed it from the climatic limitations that had previously prevented, in some cases, the choice of what would otherwise have been the most convenient and economical site for operation. . . . Simultaneously scientific research was called in to assist in the technical progress of the industry, and soon made itself an indispensable aid in discovering and preparing by-products, and in perfecting and controlling preserving processes. Division of labor and organization of operations in packing houses had already reached a degree of efficiency and economy not likely to be radically bettered.

The statistics presented in Table 4.12 and Appendix A do nothing more than hint at the degree of concentration that characterized this industry. Slaughterhouses and and meatpackers were quick to take advantage of all that modern production technology had to offer them; they were quick, also, to capitalize on the refrigerated rail car to develop nationwide markets for their products. The economies of scale in this industry were so great that concentration seemed almost inevitable. What is interesting, however, is the degree to which the meatpackers, or the Beef Trust as some called them, were able to gain control of substitutes, complements, and by-products as well. Clark (1929:265) reports:

Five great corporations acquired a controlling position in the packing industry. These firms worked in agreement so as to exclude effective competition either in purchasing live-stock or in selling products. A Government report published immediately after the World War states that Armour and Company, Swift and Company, Morris and Company, Wilson and Company, and the Cudahy Packing Company together with their subsidiary and affiliated organizations, not only exercised "a monopolistic control over the American meat industry," but that they had secured control, "similar in purpose if not yet in extent, over the principal substitutes for meat, such as eggs, cheese, and vegetable-oil products," and were rapidly extending their power "to cover fish and nearly every kind of foodstuff." Such a development was natural enough, because all these branches of food preservation and marketing were centered around the cold-storage warehouse and the refrigerator car; and in some cases the products mentioned were the logical backload for highly specialized transportation equipment that would otherwise have been partly idle and would have collected an unemployment dole from the consumer. But the public was peculiarly sensitive to attempts to monpolize the food trade, and farmers and graziers naturally resented being forced to sell to a solitary buyer. Moreover powerful industrial interests were aroused against some of the packers' operations. Independent cottonseed-oil men resented their entering this industry; tanners witnessed with a jealous eye their growing domination of the domestic rawhide and heavy leather market, and manufacturers of fertilizer viewed with disfavor their operations in this particular field. Some of the largest soap manufacturers in the country found their products imitated under new names by packers controlling direct supplies of raw materials. Altogether the array of forces hostile to the intrusion of packers into other lines of business was imposing but helpless. To be sure an attempt to form a great merger of the three leading companies, in 1902, was relinquished in face of a threatened Government suit and public opposition. But 17 years later these three firms, together with two associates which had grown in the meantime to something approaching equal stature, were reported to control the production and distribution of about three-fourths of the fresh meats entering into general trade in the United States, and in addition to possess "a very great competitive advantage in more than a hundred products and by-products — ranging in importance from hides and oleomargerine [sic] to sand paper and curled hair." They also controlled more than half of the export meat production of the Argentine, Brazil, and Uruguay, and were heavily interested in Australian packing enterprises. They were the largest distributors of butter, eggs, and canned goods in the country, and either individually or jointly were the country's largest rice merchants and extensive manufacturers of breakfast foods and staple groceries.

With the largest packers organized into a trust, competition in the meatpacking industry was limited to those small producers who served primarily local or specialty markets. By the early 1900s, it seems, there was virtually no competition in this industry.

Distilled and Malt Liquors

The rather erratic growth patterns in the distilled liquor and malt liquor industries are shown in Table 4.13. As state prohibition began

TABLE 4.13

Selected Census Data on the Distilled Liquors and Malt Liquors Industries: Percent Growth Between Reporting Periods, 1870–1909

	PERCENT CHANGE IN:			
YEAR	Number of Establishments	Total Employees	Capital	Value of Products
Distilled Liquors				
Baseline 1870	(719)	(5,131)	($15,545,000)	($36,191,000)
1880	17.4%	26.7%	56.0%	13.5%
1890	(−47.9)	(−17.8)	27.9	153.8
1900	119.8	(−18.0)	5.0	(−7.1)
1904	(−16.8)	64.9	53.9	35.6
1909	(−23.9)	15.2	44.6	55.9
Total % growth, 1870–1909	(−14.7%)	62.3%	366.1%	465.6%
Malt Liquors				
Baseline 1870	(1,972)	(12,443)	($48,779,000)	($55,707,000)
1880	11.1%	110.7%	87.0%	81.4%
1890	(−43.0)	32.7	154.9	80.8
1900	20.9	20.6	78.6	29.9
1904	1.4	38.4	24.2	25.7
1909	(−7.6)	14.9	30.2	25.6
Total % growth, 1870–1909	(−28.3)	436.3%	1,275.9%	572.7%

SOURCE: Calculated from the U.S. *Census of Manufactures,* years noted.

to spread and the country moved toward adoption of the 18th amendment to the Constitution, annual consumption of alcoholic beverages (including liquors, beer, and wine) increased, from under 15 gallons to more than 26 gallons per capita, between 1889 and 1914. California was far and away the leader in wine production, but wineries also made important contributions to the economies of several northeastern states. New York and Pennsylvania led in the production of beers and malt liquors, and distilled liquors were produced mainly in Illinois and Kentucky. Clark (1929:275) notes that the official figures for distilled liquors were almost certainly severely understated: "the number of illegal stills seized by Federal officers in 1898 was 2,391," he reports, "and ten were said to escape detection for every one captured by the authorities."

The growth patterns shown in Table 4.13 (based on data in Appendix A) are erratic only in part because of the stormy economic conditions of the era. Much of the seesaw of growth and decline in the distilled spirits industry is attributable to attempts to form trusts and consolidated companies, only some of which were successful. Clark (1929:276–277) recounts some of the details of these efforts to corner the market for distilled liquors:

> Of the three branches of the liquor manufacture, distilling was the most highly speculative and was more largely monopolized by great corporations. No historical continuity existed between the early whiskey pools of the seventies and eighties and later combinations in this business, but both were begotten by similar conditions and the precedents of the pools doubtless influenced the practices of the trusts. The Distilling and Cattle Feeding Company, which took over the business of the Distillers and Cattle Feeders Trust in 1890, like its predecessor fell into financial difficulties five years later and passed through a receivership and a stormy reorganization. Competition, the prejudice of customers against its alleged monopoly, and unsatisfactory distributing arrangements, interfered with its sales and profits. Moreover the Supreme Court of the State of Illinois handed down a decision declaring that the Company had exceeded its powers under its charter because it had purchased or leased distilleries, not to operate them, but to shut them down in order to eliminate competition.

> In 1896, soon after the Company was placed in the hands of receivers and this court decision was delivered against it, the American Spirits Manufacturing Company was organized under the laws of New York State, to take over the principal distilleries of the old company; but only 16 or 17 of the 84 establishments originally controlled by the former corporation were retained and the remainder were either sold or dismantled. Two years later, a second combination, The Standard Distilling and Distributing Company, was incorporated under the laws of New Jersey to unite the distilleries

outside of those controlled by the American Spirits Manufacturing Company. The establishments owned by each combination were widely distributed geographically and the two groups, operating under an amicable agreement, produced about the same quantity of corn spirits annually. In 1899 the Kentucky Distilleries and Warehouse Company was incorporated, also under the laws of New Jersey, to combine the Bourbon or Kentucky whiskey manufacturers of the United States, and the Standard Distilling and Distributing Company was represented on its directorate. This combination was said to embrace at the time of its organization 57 firms. The same year The American Spirits Manufacturing Company, The Kentucky Distilleries and Warehouse Company, The Spirits Distributing Company, The Standard Distilling and Distributing Company, and The Distilling Company of American formed a new consolidation, The Distilling Company of America, with an authorized capital stock of $125,000,000. Powerful as was this group, however, it at once encountered formidable opposition from the independent distillers of Kentucky, who were organized as an association and controlled half the Bourbon output. At no time, therefore, did the trust or group of trusts have a complete monopoly on the trade.

The malt liquor and beer industry was subject to fewer efforts to achieve concentration. Breweries continued throughout the period to serve primarily local markets. Despite a net loss of 558 breweries from 1870 to 1909, it is apparent that growth and modernization were occurring, for total employment, capital, and product value rose steadily. In 1870, average capitalization of breweries was $24,736, and they employed an average of six persons each. By 1909, the average brewery employed 47 people and enjoyed capitalization of $474,652.

As we shall see, the brewers had relatively little to say about the federal pure food law, as the controversy developed, although some companies supported the passage of such a law. Distillers, on the other hand, found their market position challenged by the "rectifiers" — manufacturers who could produce a reasonable imitation of eight-year-old Kentucky whiskey almost overnight. Both of these groups — distillers and rectifiers (both are included in statistics for the distilled liquors industry) — had a great deal to say about federal involvement in interstate commerce in beverages. Wineries, too, found themselves involved in the fight for accurate product labeling. (Statistics on vinous liquors are found in Table A.22 in the Appendix.)

Patent Medicines

The Progressive Era was the time for great expansion, rather than concentration, in the drug business. Table 4.14 shows the patterns of growth for the patent medicine industry, on each measure far exceeding the aggregate growth rates for all food, drug and beverage industries (see Table 4.5).

This phenomenal growth in the industry was not attended, on the whole, by comparable growth for individual establishments. The industry's growth resulted from the proliferation of small, independent businesses. In 1870 the average patent medicine enterprise had almost $21,000 in capital, employed seven or eight people, and produced about $51,000 in goods. After 40 years average capitalization had risen only to $27,441, eleven people were employed by the average enterprise, and the average value of output had *fallen* to about $39,000 per year.

James Harvey Young's fascinating volume, *The Toadstool Millionaires* (1961), provides a detailed and colorful history of the American patent medicine industry. "Most of the 'doctors,' " he reports, "died broke. Expensive habits, poor management, a run of bad luck, drained off the proceeds" (Young, 1961:195). The few who were successful in the industry depended on heavy advertising, the fateful winds of consumer preference, and sometimes the help of addictive ingredients (including opium and morphine). Hostetter's Bitters, Radam's Microbe Killer, and Fletcher's Castoria were among the most popular and profitable remedies; those that did not survive or enjoyed only brief success numbered in the tens of thousands.

When the patent medicine makers saw their collective commercial interests threatened by the prospect of federal legislation that would require accurate content labeling, they formed the Proprietary Association of America to defend their interests in Washington. Well funded and politically powerful, the PAA was one of the few business organizations that remained continuously and bitterly opposed to a

TABLE 4.14

*Selected Census Data on the Patent Medicine Industry; Percent
Growth Between Reporting Periods, 1870–1909*

YEAR	PERCENT GROWTH IN:			
	Number of Establishments	Total Employees	Capital	Value of Products
Baseline 1870	(319)	(2,436)	($6,668,000)	($16,258,000)
1880	76.5%	65.2%	59.3%	(−9.7%)
1890	100.2	133.3	75.1	122.2
1900	79.8	83.5	100.1	82.7
1904	37.1	87.2	103.2	97.0
1909	31.2	27.5	32.2	20.9
Total % growth, 1870–1909	1,041.7%	1,587.2%	1,398.8%	773.1%

SOURCE: Calculated from the U.S. *Census of Manufactures*,
years noted.

federal pure food law (Congressional Record, House, June 29,
1906:9655). We shall hear more from them in Chapter 5.

Summary

It is clear from this brief overview of some of the most important food,
drug, and beverage industries that no single characterization could
serve to describe all of them. As some of these industries enjoyed
dramatic growth, others contracted, others grew modestly, and still
others experienced erratic patterns of growth and decline. Some industries, such as meatpacking, were highly concentrated by 1900;
some were virtually atomistic, like patent medicines; and most were
in varying stages (and types) of concentration and collective action.
There were vast differences in the degree to which food industries served foreign, national, regional, or local markets, and
there was great variance in the degree to which the industries had avail-

able and had taken advantage of modern production and distribution technology.

With these competitive conditions facing them, it is no wonder that the food, drug, and beverage industries expressed many different positions on the issue of a federal pure food law. Their basic concerns, however, can be condensed into four categories — worker efficiency, export markets, interstate commerce, and trade wars, or competition between and within industry segments. The first three issues are discussed in the following sections, and the fourth issue is the subject of the next chapter.

FRAUD, NUTRITION, AND WORKER EFFICIENCY

If workers were being cheated of an adequately nutritious diet by adulterated foods, and if they were also subject to illnesses and addictions induced by poisonous food additives and proprietary remedies, then they could not be expected to provide a full day's labor for their daily wages. This was an inefficiency that could not be tolerated by businesses committed to increasing productivity.

In a brief summary of U.S. food-control legislation, R.O. Brooks (1906:453) asserted that health-related and ethical concerns over poisonous and deleterious adulterations were far less important than commercial concerns:

> From the first laws up to the present time, pure-food legislation has considered principally the economic and commercial aspect of the question. The earliest laws dealt with the adulteration of wines, beers, tea, and coffee, these being the most important commercially, and frequently also from a revenue standpoint. . . . The whole subject of food adulteration and its control is almost entirely an economic and commercial-ethical question, the hygienic aspect of it being relatively unimportant, although — unfortunately for the success of many a pure-food law — the most talked of.

Reiterating the definition of "food as the primary form of capital," Brooks suggested that the "economic and commercial-ethical question" of adulterated food had unintended consequences for all businesses, not just for those engaged in the manufacture and sale of foods and drugs. "One of the principal factors determining the industrial efficiency of the laborers of a nation," Brooks declared, "is found in the quality and quantity of the food consumed" (1906:453). Thus workers who purchased and consumed adulterated foodstuffs and medicines could not labor efficiently; if the adulterants were poisonous, workers became ill, and if they were merely fraudulent, workers were robbed of the nutrition necessary to sustain optimal output.

This theme had been sounded two years earlier, on December 15, 1904, by *The Nation*. In an editorial report on some early results of Dr. Wiley's Poison Squad experiments, *The Nation* noted that "daily doses of four or five grammes [of borax] usually bring about loss of appetite and decreased efficiency for work."

Two difficulties arise in attempting to interpret the strength and validity of this argument for federal pure food legislation. First, since industrial and epidemiological record-keeping at the turn of the century was primitive by current standards, there is no way to determine the truth of the argument. We do know that many industrial laborers were extremely poor, and we may deduce that many of them were malnourished as well. Neither the extent of malnutrition resulting from fraudulent adulteration or of food and drug-induced illnesses nor their effects on worker efficiency, however, can be ascertained. It is interesting that the appearance of this argument coincides roughly with the development of Frederick Taylor's scientific management theories and practices, and with the budding systems concept of the human body as a machine. Inputs to the machine (nutritious food, appropriate incentives) were linked directly to outputs (productivity, efficiency), especially for workers who were in effect extensions of the machines they operated.

The second difficulty is that business representatives themselves seem not to have voiced this concern, although clearly it would be in the best long-term interests of business to support any effort that promised to enhance the efficiency and productivity of workers. The argument sounds suspiciously like a rationale offered *to* business leaders to secure the kind of broad-based support for federal legislation that would outweigh the opposition of (or squabbling among) small, geographically dispersed but quite vocal food and drug manufacturers. This problem of unknown intent does not arise in the other business-related arguments for a federal pure food law, since there is

considerable evidence that businesspeople were quite involved in issues of foreign trade, interstate commerce, and trade wars.

FOREIGN COMMERCE

Several issues involving international trade were part of the public
debate over the pure food law. American farmers, manufacturers, and
distributors saw the potential for a profitable export trade and wished
to protect those possibilities. In the absence of a U.S. food law, this
was a difficult task; many European countries, protected by fairly rigorous pure food laws of their own and seeking as well to protect their
domestic producers from foreign competition, forbade the importing
of various U.S. food products. At the same time, many of the European goods imported into the U.S. enjoyed high demand, providing
American manufacturers with considerable competition.

Some businesses charged that the Europeans were "dumping"
— exporting goods of inferior quality that they were not allowed to
sell at home — and getting away with it because of the snobbery of
American consumers who wanted to see the word "imported" on
product labels. Retaliatory tariffs and import–export bans were also
part of the discussion, and sometimes were used in federal attempts
to assist U.S. food exporters.

Hampe and Wittenberg (1964:55) describe the condition of U.S.
agricultural exporting:

> The export trade in agricultural commodities expanded tremen-
> dously until the end of the nineteenth century. A major item in this
> trade was grain. . . . After the Civil War, the trend of grain exports
> continued upward until the turn of the century. Corn exports hit a
> peak in 1897, when 8.9 percent of the crop was exported. Wheat
> and flour exports reached their maximum in 1901, when 31.4 per-
> cent of that year's crop was exported. . . . Exports of meats and
> meat products, which had been relatively insignificant before the
> Civil War, soon came to rank third in importance. The packing in-
> dustries produced more than the home market could readily absorb,
> and export volume was important in taking up the slack, particularly
> in the case of pork products.

Clough and Marburg (1968:77) note that "between 9 and 14 percent of the value of all American farm products, exclusive of cotton, was exported" from the 1870s on. Exports of manufactured foods were not so considerable, yet they did represent profit to existing exporters and the promise of market expansion to many other producers.

To the federal government, exported agricultural and manufactured food products formed a critical portion of foreign policy and domestic growth:

> It was through foreign trade that the United States was able in its early days to get the manufactured goods it needed; it was through the anticipation of exports that it was able to borrow capital from abroad; and it was through foreign trade that it obtained whatever raw materials it lacked (Clough and Marburg, 1968:119).

Protective tarriffs had long served the interests of domestic manufacturers in Europe *and* the United States. Free trade, it seemed, was fine as an economic theory, but when it came to allowing one's native sons to lose the competitive battle in the international market, many nations — including the United States — understandably balked. Clough and Marburg (1968:119–120) describe some of the protective measures of the era:

> Although duties were lowered by European nations in the early 1860s, the trend of protective rates was upward after the economic depression of 1873. Most European states wanted to protect their traditional agricultural crops from overseas competition; and overseas lands, notably America, wanted to get the advantages of industrial production. It was clear that greater exchange value per unit of human input, or energy expended, could be obtained in industry than in agriculture (after 1873, prices for agricultural goods fell more rapidly than industrial goods and generally remained low in terms of man-hours of work), and success in modern warfare required the mass production of mechanized weapons. So generally recognized were these two facts that from 1876 to World War II world manufacturing increased much more rapidly than world trade. . . .
>
> The United States, along with many other industrially undeveloped nations, undertook the building of tariff walls to protect their manufacturers — a policy favored by the industrial North and opposed

by the agricultural South. Rates were pushed up to about 47 percent ad valorem during the Civil War (Act of 1864), reached 49.5 percent ad valorem with the McKinley Act of 1890, and after a slight reduction in the Wilson–Gorman Act of 1894, were increased still further by the Dingley Act of 1897. Then in the Payne–Aldrich Tariff Act of 1909, rates were adjusted on the basis of competing nations' costs of production and could be changed by the President in case of foreign discrimination against American goods.

The need for a federal pure food law became obvious to the U.S. exporters when they began to see a trend toward stabilization in the domestic market for agricultural products, in terms of sales volume and prices, and the consequent need to depend upon foreign commerce to absorb any increases in output. Just at the point where U.S. firms needed to rely on exporting to accommodate increased production, the borax scandal of the Spanish–American War was widely publicized at home and abroad. Subsequent media reports, particularly a number of exaggerated stories of the extent of U.S. food adulteration, based on testimony provided during Senate hearings, carried to Europe the news that American food products were poisonous and fraudulent.

Germany, France, and other nations banned or restricted the importation of many American processed foods (H.B. Mason, 1900; *Nation*, December 15, 1904; Brooks, 1906; Kolko, 1963:98–107; Clough and Marburg, 1968). These restrictions had little actual effect on the overall level of U.S. exports of manufactured foods (see Figure 4.1), but they were threatening to exporting manufacturers and those who sought to enter export markets to counter domestic price stabilization by expanding foreign trade.* In 1901 agricultural products, valued at $949 million, accounted for 65 percent of all U.S. exports. By 1905 agricultural products represented only 55 percent of exports, and their value had dropped to $825 million (*Historical Statistics*, Series K-251-255).

Food manufacturers engaged in foreign commerce argued that a federal pure food law would act as a badly needed sign of good faith

---

*See Hampe and Wittenberg (1964:55) for a general statement of domestic and foreign trade conditions. Overall food price stability is demonstrated by indices in Fabricant (1940). Annual figures (1899–1910) on production, exports, imports, and domestic consumption of manufactured foods appear in Shaw (1947:30, 273, 280, 290).

FIGURE 4.1

Manufactured Food Values 1869–1910

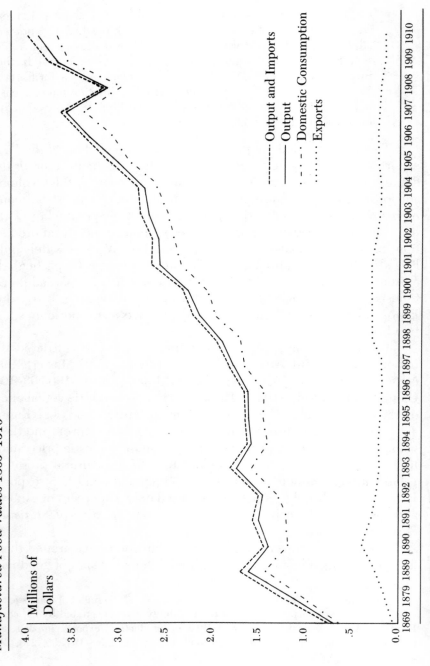

SOURCE: From data presented in Shaw (1947:30).

to European markets and governments. According to business leaders' testimony, the federal government could "do much toward preserving the reputation of American foods abroad . . ." (Senate Document 141, 1900:20). It seemed unthinkable that the United States, of all major nations, should be the only one without a uniform system of guaranteeing the quality of food products and the accuracy of their labels.

INTERSTATE COMMERCE

This issue, the final business issue to be examined in this chapter, was as explosive and almost as widely publicized as the consumer issue of poisonous adulteration. In an age that stressed personal morality as well as free competition, how was it possible for honest manufacturers and retailers to compete successfully against those who adulterated and defrauded?

In the closing days of Senate debate on S.88, which became the Pure Food Act of 1906, Senator Heyburn (chief shepherd of the bill in the Senate) read the following letter to his distinguished colleagues:

> As chairman of the pure-food committee of the National Retail Grocers' Association, I wish to inform you that your bill meets my hearty approval and endorsement. We have requested the retail distributors of food products throughout the United States to write their Representatives in Washington, urging them to support the passage of this measure. Our committee stands in readiness to go to Washington at any time, should our services be required.
> Yours, very truly,
> A.W. Farlinger
> Chairman Pure Food Committee
> National Retail Grocers' Association
> (*Congressional Record*, Senate. Feb. 20, 1906:2719)

More such letters were produced in support of the law's passage; they came from individual business owners and from large, powerful associations. Other Senators rose to provide similar evidence of their business constituents' support of federal regulation of the content and labeling of foods, drugs, and beverages. Why were they so concerned?

As mass marketing became both possible and profitable in the Progressive Era, more and more manufacturing firms sought to expand the boundaries of their markets beyond their home states. As the volume of interstate commerce increased, demands for a federal pure food law increased as well. State agricultural, health, and food-inspection officials desired the protection such a law would offer to their citizens who could not otherwise be guaranteed that foods and drugs obtained from other states would be unadulterated and properly labeled. Businesses also argued for a federal law, insisting that, although interstate commerce offered virtually unlimited possibilities for commercial growth, it raised unanticipated difficulties that could only be resolved at the federal level.

Many business representatives, testifying before Congressional committees and subcommittees, pointed out inconsistencies, in terms of both statutory requirements and enforcement practices, in state laws governing the purity and labeling of food and drugs. On July 30, 1903, *The Nation* reported Dr. Wiley's shocking testimony that "a food manufacturer requires the services of a lawyer to see that the laws of the different States are complied with merely in the matter of printing labels." The testimony of business leaders was summarized as follows in a Congressional document:

> The chief objection, especially from the standpoint of the manufacturer, to leaving the matter in the hands of state governments is the lack of uniformity in state laws, which makes necessary different kinds of labels according to the state to which the goods are to be shipped. It is also urged that the state laws are insufficient from the lack of appropriations necessary to enforce them, and through the lack of sufficient knowledge and efficiency on the part of the officials charged with their enforcement (Senate Document No. 141, 1900).

Packaging and content requirements also varied greatly among the states. Charles A. Crampton noted in 1900 (p. 943) that "a manufacturer whose goods are retailed extensively all over the Union must put them up in a dozen different ways to suit the laws of different States."

Meeting the various state requirements governing labeling,

packaging, and composition prevented manufacturers from taking full advantage of the economies of scale promised by mass production and marketing. Compliance with state laws was inefficient, costly, and a nuisance. Further, one could not predict when or how various state regulations might change; this fact introduced an unnecessary element of uncertainty into manufacturers' plans and projections. A federal pure food law, which would take precedence over (but would not supplant) state laws, would be a major step in overcoming these inefficiencies and uncertainties. In effect, such a law would provide a set of shared rules for food and drug industries, leaving them free to compete in national markets on the basis of price, quality, and regional product distinctions (and, not inconsequentially, reducing any advantage possessed by out-of-state or in-state manufacturers in the absence of federally imposed shared rules).

The second problem generated by the growth of interstate commerce was that reputable manufacturers in a state had no protection from the competition offered by adulterated or misbranded goods produced out of state. Most states had passed their own pure food laws by 1906, but as Brooks (1906:452) noted, "A State food-inspection department . . . cannot control or punish a manufacturer in another State where the laws are not enforced. Nor can a State regulate commerce in unbroken packages of foodstuffs between States. . . ." The interstate commerce clause of the U.S. Constitution provided the legal basis on which Congress could choose to regulate the manufacture and sale of foods and drugs. In the opinion of many business leaders, it was time for this clause to be invoked once again for their benefit.

Many business leaders argued for federal legislation on the grounds of their general inability to compete against dishonest, unscrupulous firms in other states. In the Senate's floor debate on S.88 (*Congressional Record*, February 19, 1906:2653) Senator Money of Mississippi reported a typical incident:

> I had a man, a grocer in a very small town in Mississippi, . . . who told me that he had received a circular from a concern . . . that proposed to sell him terra alba, or white earth, ground into an impalpable powder, not to be distinguished by appearance from flour, and notified him that he could get it at $6 a ton, for the purpose of adulterating flour, and saying that he could not afford to do without it, because all his competitors were using it.

Two days later, Senator McCumber of North Dakota read to his colleagues in the Senate a letter received from the President of the Western Canners Association:

> When the manufacturer of canned peas goes over into New York or even in his own State, he is met with a character of canned peas that looks exactly like his own in all respects, but he finds that where he has to pay $10,000, under the laws of the State of Wisconsin, for the sugar that is to go into the article he cans, his competitor pays only $750 for saccharine made from a coal-tar product. Of course he cannot compete in the market with that difference in the character of the goods used (*Congressional Record*, February 21, 1906:2764).

In further support of his bill the Senator noted that ". . . the fact that the brewers' associations are all in favor of this pure-food bill evidences the fact that they are satisfied that they manufacture a pure article . . ." (*Congressional Record*, Senate. February 21, 1906:2751).

A summary of testimony before Congressional committees in 1900 and 1901 concluded that "manufacturers would apparently be willing to label their goods properly if their competitors were required to do the same thing" (Senate Document No. 141, 1901:20). This theme was echoed in the pleas of Senator Porter J. McCumber in January, 1906:

> Every honest manufacturer in the United States is pleading for this bill, because he says that if he manufactures his goods in accordance with the pure-food laws of the several States or Territories, it is impossible for him to compete justly and fairly with the bogus articles that are put in competition with those manufactured by him (*Congressional Record*, Senate. January 18, 1906:1216).

Other members of the business community sought to protect the integrity of their local and regional specialties. There were many such specialties: Pennsylvania beer, New York cream cheese, Wisconsin cheddar, Kentucky bourbon and Tennessee sourmash, Michigan cherries, Maryland oysters, Washington salmon, Georgia peaches, and California olives were just a few. Clough and Marburg (1968:78) suggest that

By 1914 definite area specialization in agriculture had taken place. In this development the chief locational factors were the nature of the soil and climate, but in the same way as in industry, proximity to market, availability of labor, and adequate processing facilities also exerted an influence. Thus, cotton and citrus fruits could be produced only in the South, but around every large city there were to be found important truck farms, and within a radius of some 300 miles, one was able to find a "milk shed." The availability of cheap Mexican labor played a role in the location of fruit growing in California, and the presence of a large frozen-food plant in New Jersey explains why there is such extensive vegetable growing in its neighborhood.

The association of regional specialties with unique tastes and high quality, naturally, meant money in the bank to those producers of regional specialty items. But what was to prevent other entrepreneurs, perhaps even in faraway states, from seizing the names and regional identities of those specialty products and selling fraudulent items in their place? This was a twofold problem, representing immediate lost revenue to the authentic regional producers, as well as eventual loss of the good will of consumers who unknowingly purchased fraudulent, inferior products.

In 1902 Congress had passed a law requiring that foods be correctly labeled as to their place of production. This law provided some protection for famous regional products, but apparently it did not go far enough:

A man can pack cottonseed oil for interstate commerce and label it "olive oil," but if he is compelled to state that the "olive oil" is packed in Georgia or Alabama, the public becomes suspicious that it is getting cottonseed oil. A "New Orleans" molasses, packed in one of the glucose districts of Illinois, is open to the same suspicion. . . . Between products of the same class this 1902 law is effective, but between the imitation and the product imitated, it is of little avail, for raw materials can be shipped into a district famous for its cheese, jelly, syrup, wine or whiskey, and the label of the imitation then bears legally the name of that district which is in favor with consumers (Allen, 1906:55).

Arguing for passage of a new, stronger federal law to supplant the ineffectual 1902 act and to protect regional specialties, Allen continued (1906:55):

> . . . certain fruit, vegetable, dairy, and wine districts are known for the superiority of their products. The producers in these districts have the right to an honest market, while consumers should have the means to identify the foods from such districts should they so desire.

Similar arguments were heard for months on the floors of the House and Senate as the Pure Food Act neared passage in 1906. On January 18 Senator McCumber, speaking of the problems of regional specialty producers, criticized the practice of some domestic wineries of marking their bottles "imported." Senator Perkins of California responded indignantly:

> "The wine growers of California are in favor of this bill or any other pure-food measure that will give a market to our California wines and to our pure olive oil that is not adulterated with cotton-seed oil, and the jellies and jams and other products of our State. As my friend did not refer to California, I want him to understand that the wine makers and grape growers in California are in favor of this bill" (*Congressional Record*, Senate. January 18, 1906:1219).

Requiring that place of manufacture be shown on a product's label was an important clue to the product's integrity, but *content* labeling would be a much more effective deterrent to fraud.

Indeed, the California wineries, represented by the California Wine Growers' Association, were among those seeking such protection. The California growers were devoted advocates of state and federal pure food bills; their trade association, founded in 1862, seems to have been organized primarily to lobby the state legislature for protective laws and financial assistance for the industry (Carosso, 1951:29). The development of rail transportation had made it possible for California winemakers to send their products to the lucrative eastern markets as early as the 1860s. There, however, they encountered fierce competition from eastern producers, particularly those of New York and Ohio. Accusations of false labeling and unfair trade practices flew back and forth between the coasts as California struggled to secure a niche and a name for itself and the easterners fought to hold the markets they dominated. Vincent Carosso, historian of the California wine industry, writes (1951:34–35):

> As California became better known as a wine-producing area . . . and the demand for its wines grew, Eastern trades stopped calling California wine men counterfeiters. Instead, Eastern merchants in this period bottled anything that looked and smelled like wine under a California label, a practice that considerably damaged California's out-of-state trade as well as the general reputation of California wines. The many prizes, medals, and honorable citations California wine received at Eastern exhibits and fairs did not dispel the idea that the state produced mainly worthless imitations. The fight to gain a national pure-food law . . . indicates the length of the battle to prevent adulterations and to impress upon the Eastern market the real character of the California product.

CONCLUSION

In such a climate, doing business honestly and making and selling a quality product at a fair price was no guarantee of profit. Indeed, such practices could put firms at a comparative disadvantage in a market where regional or local specialties, product names, formulas, unique packaging, and advertising claims could be raided with impunity (see *Nation*, July 30, 1903; Brooks, 1906; Allen, 1906). Furthermore, in the absence of shared rules for the industry, the advantages a company could gain by implementing technological innovations might easily be offset by the disadvantages of increased costs or inability to meet the lower prices of adulterated or misbranded goods. This problem surfaced in the canning and brewing industries and may account for the strong support that a federal law gained from some of the leaders of those industries.

H.J. Heinz, perhaps the most dedicated food-industry advocate of pure food legislation, appointed a staff of three, including his son Howard, to assist the President and the Congress in any way to secure what Heinz felt to be a desperately needed food and drug law (Frasure, 1949; Potter, 1959). Robert C. Alberts (1973:171), one of H.J. Heinz's biographers, explains that Heinz

. . . knew that use of deleterious chemicals by unscrupulous food processors was hurting all other manufacturers in the industry by creating suspicion of the quality and purity of all products on the market. He felt his industry would not grow to major estate until it had earned public confidence. The way to earn that confidence was to work in partnership with a federal regulatory agency. Regulation would make the industry respectable and trusted — an achievement beyond any price. . . . He knew, moreover, that there was really no *need* for harmful chemicals — that good foods, properly processed, would keep without the addition of artificial preservatives. The speed of processing, the autoclaves, the whole state of the art, had advanced beyond such need. Processors either did not realize this, or they were unwilling to make the required capital investment in machinery, or they were preserving inferior materials by using chemicals.

Anne Lewis Pierce, a staff employee of the Bureau of Chemistry during the last few years of the pure food controversy, reported that

The Heinz Company took the lead in this reform, did pioneer work when government officials and legislators lagged. . . . The battle for pure food was won not so much by those who claimed that dirty, chemically preserved foods were unethical and unhealthful as by those who proved that they were unnecessary. And the House of Heinz was Dr. Wiley's first lieutenant in the charge over the top of this entrenched mistake (cited in Alberts, 1973:176).

Harvey Wiley himself acknowledged his and the nation's debt to H.J. Heinz, in a letter written to Howard Heinz in 1924 on the occasion of the company's dedication of the founder's statue: "I appreciate the loyalty with which your father and all of his staff stood by me in the darkest hours of my fight for pure food," wrote Dr. Wiley. "I feel that I should have lost the fight if I had not had that assistance" (Alberts, 1973:166; *A Golden Day,* 1929).

Frederick Pabst, founder of the Pabst Brewing Company in Milwaukee and known as "the Captain," was another industry leader who had overcome the need to use chemical preservatives or additives in his product and who lobbied for a federal pure food law to prevent others from using them. Technological developments, particularly direct-pressure carbonation, "made it unnecessary any longer to use artificial preservatives in Pabst bottled beer. This made the Captain anxious for a pure food law that would not only prohibit other brewers from adulterating their beer with sulphite of soda, but would also go a long way in convincing the public that beer was a pure and a safe beverage" (Cochran, 1948:204–205). Pabst was among the industry leaders who testified before the Congressional fact-finding subcommittee in 1899–1900, and he was instrumental in securing the support and lobbying efforts of the United States Brewers' Association (Cochran, 1948:206).

The need to rationalize the legal supports for manufacturing and interstate commerce seemed evident to many business leaders as they and their associates lobbied for Congressional action (see Senate Document 141, 1901; House Report 1426, 1900; Anderson, 1958; Kolko, 1963; Wiebe, 1962). Indeed, despite considerable evidence that many food and drug firms were *against* pure food legislation (a view supported almost entirely by Harvey Wiley), the authors of a major text on food industry management give full credit for the 1906 law's passage to the food industries and their trade associations (Hampe and Wittenberg, 1964). The business community's understanding of the strategic uses of regulation and public policy had begun to flower.

five

Trade Wars and Regulatory Policy

BY COMPARISON TO PROGRESSIVE ERA COMPETITIVE STRATEGIES, the modern corporate goal of "increasing market share" seems strangely gentle. In an ideological climate that encouraged the pursuit of self-interest as one's noble, God-fearing duty, there seemed to be little reason for business people to share the market with anyone else if it could possibly be avoided. Consequently, the more aggressive entrepreneurs of that time were frequently engaged in open campaigns to drive their competitors out of business. These campaigns were called, not inappropriately, the trade wars.

The trade wars of the Progressive Era (and of the Populist Era immediately preceding it) are a major reason for our belief that business competition then was hostile, cold, warlike, and implacably vicious. For those who served the god of laissez-faire capitalism, no tactic, no matter how underhanded, dishonest, or illegitimate, seemed too low if it promised to fulfill the higher purpose of generating wealth and, therefore, societal well-being. Highmindedness aside, the basic strategy of the trade wars was simple: Trick your opponents, unnerve them, get them to make mistakes, steal their clientele, and if all else failed, get the government to tax them out of business or have their products declared adulterated or fraudulent.

These battles within the food, drug, and beverage industries would not concern us here if it were not for the fact that many of the businesses involved were run by people shrewd enough to see the enormous advantages of using public policy to bolster private competitive strategy. It was not lost on Progressive Era business leaders that the coercive power of the federal government — with its powers to tax, spend, borrow, and regulate — was, if properly channeled, a much more efficient means of driving out the competition than was the collection of low-down tactics that must otherwise be used.

As we have seen, food, drug, and beverage businesses constituted at least 30 separate industries, not just two or three. The process of concentration within and across these industries had just begun, leaving much room for businesses to maneuver for position and to thwart the similar aims of their competitors. Intervening in public policy matters offered then, as it does now, a rich source of potential competitive advantage for businesses. The outcomes were uncertain, but the stakes were high, and judging by the vigorous efforts that were made to influence public policy, the economic benefits of successful legislative intervention were perceived to be great.

Some trade battles took place when traditional (or preexisting) industries were threatened by new industries competing for the same portion of the consumer market; that is, when products were threatened by substitutes. An example occurred when oleomargarine — a factory-produced, inexpensive substitute for butter — began to threaten the market domination of dairy farmers and creamery owners, who were for the most part undercapitalized and not mechanized, but who nonetheless held considerable political power, developed through decades of careful cultivation. This case is described more fully in the next section.

Other trade wars developed within industries, when manufacturers of "traditional," well-accepted products sought to continue to dominate a market threatened by newer and much cheaper product formulas. Bottled-in-bond whiskey distillers, perceiving an imminent erosion of their market, sought to destroy their competitors who produced "rectified whiskey" overnight and sold it at a much lower price. Many of the larger pharmaceutical houses were implacably opposed to any legislation that might possibly grant legitimacy to their itinerant competitors, the patent-medicine vendors. Yet another trade war, described fully in a later section, developed when traditional cream of tartar baking powder manufacturers sought to counter the threat posed by the newer, more effective, and much less expensive acid-based baking powders.

The trade wars had a substantial impact on the development of support for (and opposition to) a federal pure food law. They certainly provided a clear incentive for many businesses to become involved in the pure food battle in the first place; thus they contributed to the emergence of broad-based support for the law, as well as the development of powerful opposition. Because the food industries were "special interest groups," however, they also represented a hidden agenda of sorts — a complicating set of factors that perhaps slowed the progress of the pure food cause. Businesses not only went on record as "supporters" or "opponents" of pure food bills, they also spent considerable effort attempting to influence specific passages in the bills that were proposed and in promoting substitute bills, amendments, and rewordings that would offer them more advantages or would hurt their competitors.

WHAT'S BETTER THAN BUTTER?

Oleomargarine was first patented in France in 1869, first-prize winner in Emperor Louis Napoleon III's competition for butter substitutes. The first American patent was granted in 1873; the United States Dairy Company of New York began production about two years later. In 1881, 15 margarine manufacturing plants were operating in the U.S. Just five years later, that number had more than doubled, to 34. In 1884, however, New York became the first of several states to ban the sale of margarine. Congress passed the Margarine Act two years later, imposing a tax of two cents per pound on "imitation butter" and oleomargarine (Riepma, 1970).

Statistics on production and per capita consumption of margarine and butter provide scant evidence of serious threats to butter's market dominance before the 1940s. In 1886, when the Margarine Act was passed, six million pounds of margarine were produced, compared to 1,086 million pounds of butter; butter held 99.5 percent of the combined market. Through 1910, butter's market dominance never dropped below 92 percent (Riepma, 1970:148–149; *Historical*

Statistics, Series G-88-915), yet the threat of margarine was apparently felt quite strongly by the dairy industry. In state after state, and at the federal level as well, dairy lobbyists worked diligently and for the most part successfully to impose legal restrictions on the sale of their principal competitor.

Dairy interests were fortified by several important Supreme Court decisions. In 1894 the Court upheld the right of states to prohibit the sale of yellow margarine because of the possibility of its fraudulent substitution for butter, although in the same year the Court struck down state laws requiring margarine to be colored pink. New York's prohibition of the sale of margarine was also challenged, and the court ruled in 1888 that states did have the right to ban the sale of products deemed fraudulent or hazardous to the health of citizens. The constitutionality of the Margarine Act as a federal revenue measure was upheld by the court in 1897 (Riepma, 1970:113–116). The overall effect of these public policy decisions was to show the margarine manufacturers that their enemies were more powerful than they were. In a few short years the dairymen had succeeded in taxing margarine so that its price became unattractive, forbidding the use of coloring agents in it so that its appearance was equally unattractive (even though butter often contained yellow food coloring!), and defending the right of state governments to forbid its sale if they wished to do so. These were not insignificant accomplishments.

Congressional documents show quite clearly the dairy industry's strategy in seeking federal protection. In 1900 the House Committee on Agriculture recommended passage of the Grout Bill. The chief provisions of this bill were that "oleo margarine and other imitation dairy products [would be] subject to the laws of the state or territory into which they [were] transported" and that a ten-cent tax would be imposed on yellow margarine, making it a less acceptable substitute for butter (House Report No. 1854). In a report submitted with the bill the Committee defended these provisions on the grounds that yellow margarine provided unfair competition for real butter:

> . . . The counterfeit article . . . will no longer be accessible to hotel keepers, restaurant keepers, and boarding house proprietors at such prices as will be an inducement to deceive their guests, . . . and thus another class of consumers, who have been subject to imposition for more than 20 years, will be able to know whether they are

eating butter fat or hog fat when they spread their bread (House Report No. 1854:2).

A minority report was appended to the Committee on Agriculture's recommendation of the Grout Bill. After reviewing the testimony of distinguished scientists (including Harvey Wiley) on the wholesomeness of margarine, the authors maintained that the principal complaint with existing margarine laws was that dealers could easily substitute an unmarked wrapper for the existing package and thus fraudulently sell margarine as butter. The Grout Bill, they said, with its taxes and the priority given to state laws, would not prevent such fraud. They reminded Congress of certain testimony and evidence presented in committee hearings on the bill:

> Mr. Adams, Pure Food Commissioner of the State of Wisconsin, in his testimony before the Committee on March 7, 1900, said:
> "There is no use beating about the bush in this matter. We want to pass this law and drive the oleomargarine manufacturers out of the business."

> Charles Y. Knight, secretary of the National Dairy Union, in a letter to the Virginia dairymen, dated May 18, 1900, writes:
> "Now is the time for you to clip the fangs of the mighty octopus of the oleomargarine manufacturers who are ruining the dairy interest in this country . . ." (House Report No. 1854: 51).

Minority members expressed their dismay at the dairy lobby's attempts to gain what seemed to be unnecessary protection from competition via federal law:

> The Grout Bill would destroy the business of the legitimate oleomargarine manufacturers. In other words, Congress is being asked to ruin one industry to benefit another; and this, in the opinion of the minority, is a thing Congress ought not to do. The minority believe it to be class legislation of the most pronounced kind and would establish precedence which, if followed, would create monopolies, destroy competition, and militate against the public good (House Report No. 1854:51).

Minority views notwithstanding, the Grout Bill was passed in 1902. Yellow margarine was to be taxed at ten cents per pound; uncolored (white) margarine was subject to a nominal tax of one-fourth cent per pound. Dairy interests slackened their efforts to secure additional federal legislation and seem not to have been much involved in subsequent debates over the pure food law. One commentator wrote in 1906, "The butter people have secured all the special legislation they desire and of course take little interest in a general food law. In fact, a general food law may in the end restrict the use of artificial color in butter" (Allen, 1906:56). Margarine manufacturers, after an initial period of disarray, merely added a small packet of yellow food coloring to their packages of uncolored oleo, along with instructions to the consumer for blending the coloring into the margarine.

Available evidence makes it difficult to explain rationally the dairy industry's vigorous actions to restrain or prohibit the sale of margarine. Aggregate statistics indicate that margarine never accounted for more than eight percent of combined butter and margarine output during the period 1886–1910. There are some hints, however, of three factors that may have contributed to the bitter struggle.

First, regional (rather than national) competition may have provided the first spur to dairy's protection-seeking actions. In the 1870s, the first decade of margarine production, New York City was not only the site of the first manufacturer, but also bought one-fourth of total margarine output. One might assume that New York State and surrounding northeastern states accounted for a majority of margarine sales during this period. Could it have been the New York dairy interests who were first (and most) threatened by this new competition?

Second, the dairy and margarine industries were structured quite differently. Table 5.1 presents data from the Census of Manufactures for 1880 through 1909 and illustrates some of the differences. Margarine production was purely an industrial manufacturing operation. The factories were few, but more heavily capitalized, and they employed more workers and had much higher production values than the average butter producer. Butter, by contrast, was by and large a farm product, produced for personal consumption and local markets. Carroll D. Wright (1895:175), a Progressive Era Commissioner of Labor, reported that only 181 million pounds of butter were factory-made in 1890, compared to total butter production of 1,234 million pounds. Thus, 85 percent of butter produced that year came from farms and small local creameries.

Finally, the dairy industry argued that margarine production de-

TABLE 5.1

Industry Structures: Butter and Margarine, 1880–1909

	1880	1890	1900	1904	1909
Number of Establishments:					
Butter[a]	3,932	4,712	9,355	8,926	8,479
Margarine	15	12	24	14	12
Average Capital per Establishment (dollars):[b]					
Butter	7,371	11,679	9,523	5,294	8,407
Margarine	112,000	52,917	126,000	110,786	296,500
Total Employment:[c]					
Butter	9,724	16,952	21,177	19,064	23,487
Margarine	599	328	1,478	728	772
Employees per Establishment:[b,c]					
Butter	2	4	2	2	3
Margarine	40	27	62	52	64
Value of Output per Establishment (dollars):[b]					
Butter	6,547	13,303	14,024	18,842	32,381
Margarine	459,533	249,083	520,833	398,143	679,000

SOURCE: Department of Commerce, Bureau of the Census, *Census of Manufactures*, 1900 and 1910 (Washington, DC: U.S. Government Printing Office). (No data available on margarine production before 1880).

[a]All figures for butter manufacture are composites including cheese, butter, and condensed milk. Disaggregation is impossible from the census data provided.

[b]Means were calculated by dividing census categories (capital, employees, and value of output, respectively) by number of establishments.

[c]Includes salaried employees and wage workers, except for 1880, when no data were provided on number of salaried employees. Excludes owners and proprietors.

pressed the price of butter, forcing small butter producers out of business and cutting into the profits of remaining creameries. The minority report on the House Committee on Agriculture's recommendation of the Grout Bill (1900) attempted to rebut this argument:

> Two billion pounds of butter are produced in the United States annually, whereas only 83 million pounds of margarine were manufactured in the past year. . . . The argument that oleomargarine in any material sense controls the price of butter is not justified by the facts (House Report No. 1854:6).

Figure 5.1 illustrates the trends in margarine output, butter output, and butter's wholesale price per pound for the period 1886–1910. Although there seems to be wide variance between the two data sets (Riepma's 1970 history of the margarine industry and *Historical Statistics of the United States*) on tons of butter produced per year, a Pearson correlation coefficient of 0.898 between the two measures indicates that there is little statistically significant variance.

Figure 5.1 suggests that the wholesale price of butter and the amount of margarine produced followed a similar pattern of ups and downs over the years; the two measures are correlated, however, at only 0.20. Regression analysis showed no price effect when regressing annual margarine production on the wholesale price of butter, 1886–1910 (see Tables 5.2 and 5.3). In Table 5.3 neither the measures of butter production nor the measure for production of margarine explained a significant portion of the variance in butter prices; that is, there was no significant effect of margarine production on the price of butter (equations 1 and 2). It is interesting, however, that the other four equations do explain a significant amount of variance in their dependent variables. In particular, butter and margarine production seem to have been linked in a positive reciprocal relationship — the more of one, the more of the other.

Actually, growth in margarine production was wildly erratic, and the production figures seem to have been quite sensitive to changes in the legal environment (see Figure 5.2). Passage of the Federal Margarine Act in 1886, which imposed a two-cent-per-pound tax on oleo, seemed to have no inhibiting effect on margarine production; production for 1887 was 517 percent higher than for 1886. The 1888

FIGURE 5.1

Butter and Margarine Production and Wholesale Prices, 1886–1910

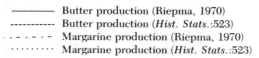

——————— Butter production (Riepma, 1970)
- - - - - - - - - - Butter production (*Hist. Stats.*:523)
· - · - · - · Margarine production (Riepma, 1970)
· · · · · · · · · Margarine production (*Hist. Stats.*:523)

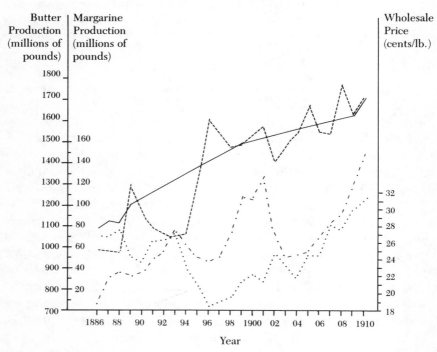

Supreme Court decision upholding the right of states to ban margarine sales was followed, however, by a 10.8 percent decline in margarine production in 1889. The 1894 Supreme Court decision allowing prohibition of yellow margarine had a much more drastic effect on production; tons of margarine produced declined by 46 percent over the period 1894–1896. The Grout Bill, passed in 1902, was followed by a 73.6 percent decline in margarine production for 1901–1903. From then on, however, margarine production rose fairly steadily from year to year.

TABLE 5.2

Correlation Matrix for Butter and Margarine Variables

	BUTTER PRODUCTION[a]	BUTTER PRICES[a]	BUTTER PRODUCTION[b]	MARGARINE PRODUCTION[b]
Butter production (tons per year)[a]	1.000	−0.161	0.898	0.622
Butter prices[a] (wholesale price per pound, at New York)		1.000	0.007	0.200
Butter production (tons per year)[b]			1.000	0.748
Margarine production[b]				1.000

SOURCE: [a]*Historical Statistics of the United States.* [b]S. F. Riepma, *The Story of Margarine,* 1970.

TABLE 5.3

Regression Results: Butter and Margarine

EQUATION	DEPENDENT VARIABLE[a]	INDEPENDENT VARIABLES	BETA	F	R^2	ANOVA F[b]
1	Butter price	Butter H	−0.465	3.522	0.026	2.294[ns]
		Margarine	0.489	3.902	0.173	
2	Butter price	Butter R	0.442	2.072	0.040	1.037[ns]
		Margarine	−0.323	1.109	0.086	
3	Butter H	Margarine	0.681	18.527	0.387	9.800[c]
		Butter price	−0.297	3.522	0.471	
4	Butter R	Butter price	−0.148	1.109	0.000	15.238[c]
		Margarine	0.778	30.473	0.581	
5	Margarine	Butter H	0.671	18.527	0.387	10.110[c]
		Butter price	0.308	3.902	0.479	
6	Margarine	Butter price	0.195	2.072	0.040	16.332[c]
		Butter R	0.747	30.473	0.598	

[a]Butter H = tons of butter produced annually (*Historical Statistics of the U.S.*); Butter R = tons of butter produced annually (Riepma, 1970); Butter price = wholesale price per pound of butter at New York (*Historical Statistics of the U.S.*); Margarine = tons of margarine produced annually (Riepma, 1970).
[b]Degrees of freedom for all equations = 2 and 22.
[c]Significant at the 0.001 level or beyond.

FIGURE 5.2

*Percent Change in Butter and Margarine Annual Production,
1886–1910*

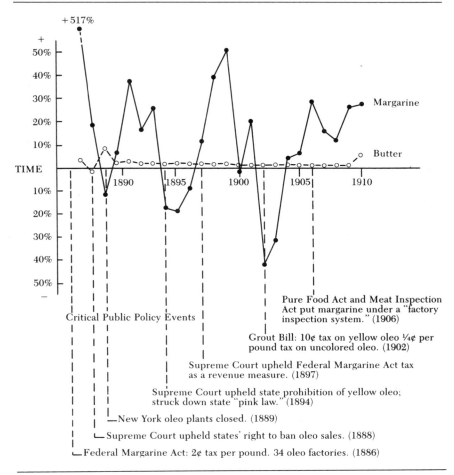

SOURCE: Calculated from Riepma (1970:148)

By contrast, increases in butter production remained essentially flat over the entire period of 1886–1910. The only year in which modestly high growth occurred was 1889 (with an 8.1 percent increase over 1888 production); for the remainder of the period, annual production growth ranged between less than one percent and 3.7 percent per year.

There is no evidence, in summary, that margarine production in any way depressed the price of butter or threatened its market domination. The evidence does, however, support the idea that the tendency of margarine production to grow very rapidly (in the absence of legal threats) was seen by the dairy industry as a serious challenge to its interests and particularly, one might suggest, to the interests of the larger manufacturers of dairy products. In the final floor debate in the Senate on the pure food bill (*Congressional Record,* Senate, February 21, 1906:2765), Senator Bailey argued staunchly against the bill on the grounds of its violation of states' rights and criticized Senator McCumber of North Dakota, one of the bill's chief supporters:

MR. BAILEY: Congress has taxed men out of the manufacturing business. I have no doubt that the Senator helped pass the oleomargarine law [the Grout Bill]. The very purpose of that law was to tax the manufacturers of oleomargarine out of business. It succeeded very largely —

MR. McCUMBER: True.

THE BAKING POWDER WAR

Around 1865, a new industry developed to produce and market cream of tartar baking powders. Cream of tartar was made from argols (wine lees), largely imported from France. As a yeast substitute it allowed the making of "quick" breads that did not have to rise before baking, and it soon became a mainstay for biscuits, pancakes, and the like. By 1875 several new forms of baking powder had been developed and placed on the market. Instead of using cream of tartar as the acid (to release gas when combined with soda and water to cause the bread to rise), these new powders used other acidic chemicals, especially tartaric acid, calcium acid phosphate, or aluminum phosphate; beginning in 1889 sodium aluminum sulphate (S.A.S.) was added to the list (Darrah, 1927).

The great baking powder war apparently erupted when the older cream of tartar powders began to lose market share to the effective and much less expensive powders that used other acids. Cream of tartar manufacturers responded with a vigorous campaign to have "alum" powders legally declared poisonous, or failing that to convince consumers that they were poisonous.

Alum was an astringent chemical sometimes used in pickling and with some medicinal applications as well. Alum was not tartaric acid, sodium aluminum phosphate, or any of the other substances used in baking powders to replace cream of tartar. Nonetheless, all baking powders not relying on cream of tartar as their active ingredient quickly came to be known as "alum baking powders," and the fight was on.

Table 5.4 shows several characteristics of the baking powder industry from 1870 to 1909. Although one can easily see the growth of the industry in terms of number of establishments, employees, and sales, these figures mask the internal dynamics of competition within the industry, particularly that between cream of tartar companies and others.

Senate Document 141 (February, 1901:4), the digest of testimony taken before the Senate Committee on Manufactures in 1899–1900 on the need for a federal pure food law, stated that "there is a decided preponderance of evidence to the effect that alum baking powder is positively harmful." A year earlier a document from the American Baking Powder Association (ABPA) had been introduced into Senate records, alleging that the wording of the pending pure food legislation was in part aimed directly at banning the sale of baking powders not based on cream of tartar and was an attempt by the Royal Baking Powder Company (and others) to seize a legal monopoly. ABPA complained that their representative had not been permitted to testify before the Senate Committee and that the written evidence they presented had been systematically ignored by pure food proponents in Congress (Senate Document No. 303, 1900:8–12, 39).

According to the ABPA report, of the 18 million pounds of cream of tartar baking powder produced annually, the Royal Baking Powder Company produced 90 percent, either directly or through controlling

TABLE 5.4

The Baking Powder Industry, 1870–1909

YEAR	NUMBER OF ESTABLISHMENTS	NUMBER OF EMPLOYEES	EMPLOYEES PER ESTABLISHMENT
1870	30	235	7.8
1880	110	1042	9.5
1890	150	1867	12.5
1900	191	2687	14.1
1904	164	3355	20.5
1909	144	3531	24.5

YEAR	VALUE OF PRODUCTS (thousands)	VALUE PER ESTABLISHMENT	AVERAGE CAPITALIZATION
1870	$ 895	$ 29,833	$ 8,300
1880	4,761	43,282	12,282
1890	7,407	49,380	23,920
1900	14,568	76,272	43,654
1904	19,043	116,116	80,689
1909	20,775	144,271	233,660

SOURCE: Calculated from the U.S. *Census of Manufactures,*
years noted.

Note: Beginning with the 1880 Census, the relevant line item is titled
"Baking and Yeast Powders." It is not clear whether the change (from "Baking
Powders") is merely a more accurate label or a composite of two industries.

interest in other companies. This was compared with 100.5 million
pounds per year of alum, alum phosphate, and phosphate powders
produced by 525 companies (note the unexplained discrepancy here
with the Census of Manufactures data in Table 5.4; no information
was provided on market shares or dominance among the 525 companies). The report's clear implication was that Royal did not suffer
gladly the competition from its smaller, less powerful, but thriving
industrial cousins.

Allegations of misconduct on the part of Royal exist elsewhere in

historical documents. Royal's game plan (as best it can be pieced together) could serve as an object lesson in aggressive strategic planning and environmental management. Their strategy seemed to have
three major thrusts: (1) consumer advertising and point-of-use intervention; (2) legislative efforts at both state and federal levels; and
(3) horizontal integration to cover bets on consumer preference
trends for the future.

On the company's advertising, a private lawsuit in 1888 between
two officers of Royal, William Ziegler and Joseph C. Hoagland, elic-
ited the following testimony before the Supreme Court of the State
of New York:

> (Mr. Ziegler) I have heard the testimony about what is called the
> "Alum War." I instituted it upon the part of the company. I em-
> ployed Dr. Mott [who testified on the health hazards of alum] per-
> sonally; it is possible that Mr. Hoagland may have made the money
> arrangement with him. . . . I got some [chemists] myself to give
> testimonials; I went over and saw Prof. Morton who had given an
> adverse opinion to get him to give a favorable opinion; I got him to
> change his mind . . . (quoted in Darrah, 1927:27–29).

Hoagland testified that, faced with declining profits in 1876, Royal
increased its advertising budget from $17,647 in 1877 to $296,084 in
1887. The theme of the advertising campaign was the unwholesomeness of alum baking powder:

> . . . We got the opinions of the Boards of Health and scientific men
> as to the question of whether alum was wholesome or not. Having
> obtained that evidence we published the names of all the alum bak-
> ing powders on the market. . . . During this time we began to ad-
> vertise with the newspapers more extensively than we had before
> making these investigations. . . . We engaged with the newspapers
> direct so as to get a reading notice [a disguised advertisement] un-
> der the regular heading of the papers; I would write these reading
> notices and they were put in the papers as reading notices, that was
> one method; there were others. . . . We employed all sorts of meth-
> ods in . . . showing this alum up as a deleterious substance . . .
> (quoted in Darrah, 1927:26–27).

The company's profits, according to Mr. Hoagland, increased from
$17,647 in 1877 to $296,084 in 1887. This growth was directly attributed to the success of the advertising campaign against alum
powders.

The American Baking Powder Association document presented
to the Senate in 1900 alleged that Royal's advertising contracts with
newspapers required that the papers *not* print any information contradictory to that contained in the Royal ads. A similar pressure tactic
— the "red clause" — was employed by patent medicine makers during the same period; one such clause read, "It is mutually agreed that
this Contract is void, if any law is enacted by your state restricting or
prohibiting the manufacture or sale of proprietary medicines" (Young,
1961:211). Such clauses provided a powerful financial incentive to
newspapers to work toward the best interests of their advertising
clients.

Evidence appended to the ABPA report showed "news items" on
cases of alum poisoning, including one case in which an entire family
was said to have died from eating baked goods made with alum baking
powder. Declaring that these "news items" had been fabricated and
paid for by Royal, ABPA then produced testimony from the Thomas
family of Somerset County, Pennsylvania — all alive and healthy —
who said that they had indeed been poisoned (though not fatally) by
accidentally ingesting some fragments of arsenical paint. In Sherman,
Texas, the report continued, Royal had sent "lady assistants" door to
door to "inspect the baking powders being used by women in the
community." Representing themselves as officials of various Pure
Food Commissions, they expressed horror and dismay if alum baking
powder was found on the shelf, and urged mothers to better protect
the lives of their children by switching to "pure cream of tartar" powder (Senate Document No. 303, 1900:14–15, 20).

Legislative efforts focused on both state and federal levels.
Cream of tartar companies produced a multitude of expert witnesses,
testimonials, and scientific reports at numerous hearings and official
proceedings to demonstrate that alum was a powerful drug and had
no business in the bread eaten by Americans. Harvey Wiley's agreement with this position strengthened their case considerably. Missouri passed a law in 1899 prohibiting the sale of alum powders. A
May 21, 1903 editorial in *The Independent* lamented this use of "pure
food laws for private purposes" in Missouri and other states:

Doubtless many of the members of these Legislatures were sincere in the belief that they were fighting a dangerous drug; but Circuit Attorney Folk, who has made so strong a fight against corruption in St. Louis, has shown that $1,000 bills were among the powerful arguments used. The effect of the law was to drive out the cheaper baking powders from the market and to give a monopoly of the business to the four firms manufacturing tartrate baking powders, which are combined in a trust of some form, and control all the cream of tartar sold in the United States.

The American Baking Powder Association's document presented in the Senate objected to the wording of S. 3618, the pure food bill before Congress in 1900. Section 5, Paragraph 1 of the bill defined adulterants as including "articles which enter into the composition of food." Section 6, Paragraph 6 stated, "It is adulteration of food if food contains any ingredient which may render such article injurious to the health of the person consuming it. . . ." The ABPA complained that "this section is directly aimed at so-called alum baking powders" (Senate Document No. 303, 1900: 1). "The ultimate aim" of the Royal Baking Powder Company, declared the ABPA report, was,

> . . . by the aid of national legislation prohibiting the manufacture and sale of alum baking powder, to accomplish in a wholesale way what it finds impossible to accomplish in detail by the passage of prohibitory legislation in the various States. . . . This is an unscrupulous endeavor to exterminate by strangulation a competition which it cannot meet, either in quality or price (pp. 10–11).

The third portion of Royal's competitive strategy seems to have been the acquisition of companies manufacturing sodium aluminum sulphate or phosphate baking powders. Federal Trade Commission proceedings show that such acquisitions were made secretly, and that Royal continued its advertising attacks on alum baking powders at the same time it was marketing such powders under names other that its own (Darrah, 1927:29–32; Federal Trade Commission, Docket No. 539).

A publication of the Calumet Baking Powder Company (Darrah, 1927) reports:

In 1901 William Ziegler, who controlled the Royal Company,

purchased through agents control of the Southern Manufacturing
Company (Richmond, Virginia), manufacturing S.A.S. baking powder. . . . While thus secretly owning the Southern Company, large
dividends were received from the sale of S.A.S. baking powder, but
nevertheless, Royal continued to publish its propaganda against
"alum" baking powder, claiming it was poisonous. It condemned
"alum" baking powder *with one side of the mouth* to fatten its profits
at the expense of the public and its competitors, *and with the other
side of its mouth* sucked in profits from the secret sale of the powder
it denounced as poisonous! (pp. 29–31; emphasis in original.)

Phosphate powders also seem to have been involved in this
acquisition-and-attack strategy. Royal's antiphosphate ads described

. . . phosphate as being made from old bones treated with oil of
vitriol. It pictured pans of old bones in its advertising to prejudice
the public against phosphate. While it was thus condemning phosphate it owned 49 percent of the capital stock of the Provident
Chemical Company of St. Louis, which manufactured and sold
phosphate to the very competitors Royal was attacking. . . . It also
secretly owned stock in a company which manufactured phosphate
baking powder (Darrah, 1927:32).

The response by manufacturers of alum baking powders (used
here, as it was used during the era, as a generic term to connote all
makers of non-tartaric powders) focused on issues of price, quality,
patriotism, and chemistry. The ABPA document of 1900 compared
the relative value of alum and cream of tartar powders. Two teaspoons
of cream of tartar were required to achieve the leavening power of
one teaspoon of alum powder. Since cream of tartar was five times
more expensive than alum powder (50 cents per pound versus 10
cents per pound), the actual price differential between the two products was 1,000 percent (Senate Document No. 303, 1900:4). On this
point the cream of tartar manufacturers could not argue.

On quality, "pure cream of tartar" seems to have relied on its
name to promote an image of high quality in the minds of consumers.
The Calumet rebuttal (Darrah, 1927) however, warns that

. . . in considering the unwholesomeness of cream of tartar we must
not be misled by the name. It is not a cream in any sense of the

word. It is not cream-like in its consistency. It does not rise to the top in the manufacture of wine, but is deposited at the sides of the cask and with the dregs at the bottom. It is not the most wholesome part of the grape but the least wholesome. It is not a food. It gives no heat or nutriment to the body when eaten, but passes through the system unchanged *like benzoic acid* (p. 95; emphasis added).

Benzoic acid, of course, was the preservative widely used in canned foods and abhorred by Dr. Harvey Wiley.

The patriotic element of the battle was a minor but nonetheless interesting interjection of deeply held cultural values into a commercial debate. The American Baking Powder Association made the point that cream of tartar was an imported product, negatively affecting the balance of trade. Thus the ABPA called on Congress to support the "great American industry" of bauxite (or cryolite) mining by *not* passing legislation that would require baking powders to be made of imported substances (Senate Document No. 303, 1900:4).

Knowledge generated by modern chemistry provided the heavy artillery for both sides of the argument. Cream of tartar manufacturers focused on the properties of alum, a powerful astringent drug listed in the U.S. Pharmacopaeia. Various chemical tests showed alum to be harmful to human health when ingested in large quantities; it was this evidence that found its way into the record of hearings of the Senate Committee on Manufactures. ABPA members had a two-pronged retort to this allegation. First, they declared, "alum" — the drug — was not a component of any manufactured baking powder. Alternatives to cream of tartar included a number of acidic or acid-like chemicals, but alum was not among them. The Calumet report (Darrah, 1927) claims:

> Laws were passed in two states and rulings made in a few others to this effect: "That every can of baking powder contains the following ingredients and none other . . ."; that the common names for the ingredients should be used, *but that any aluminum compound* used in baking powder should be designated by the use of the name "alum" (Darrah, 1927:35).

Why should the law demand that a thing be called something it was not? "This was very plainly an attempt to make the manufacturer of this type of powder call something 'alum' which was not alum" (Darrah, 1927:36). Alum, the drug, was not something a mother would knowingly feed her children in their daily bread.

The second chemistry-based argument focused on the residues left when bread was baked. Cream of tartar was a harmless substance, while alum was a potent drug. The ABPA responded that moisturizing, mixing, and baking transformed *all* baking powders into quite different chemical compounds. The ABPA document noted that cream of tartar is transformed by baking into Rochelle salts, "an irritant drug with purgative qualities." Alum powders, on the other hand, turned into hydrate of alumina ("a neutral substance with no harmful physiological effects") and sodium sulphate (Senate Document No. 303, 1900:4). When later evidence showed that the residue of alum powders also had purgative and diuretic qualities, the argument shifted to the *amount* of residue left in bread by the respective baking powders. S.A.S. powder, the Calumet company later declared, left a great deal less purgative residue in the bread than did cream of tartar powder, and this difference was increased dramatically when one considered that twice as much cream of tartar must be used to achieve the same leavening power as a measure of S.A.S. powder (Darrah, 1927:94).

The 1906 Pure Food Act contains, among others, the following definition of food adulteration: "any added poisonous or other added deleterious ingredient which may render such article injurious to health," with the proviso that externally applied preservatives were permissible if they could be removed by the user and instructions for removal were included with the product (Public Law No. 384, 1906). The proviso was included at the insistence of Senator Henry Cabot Lodge of Massachusetts, who supported a pure food law as long as it did not threaten to disrupt the codfish industry of his constituents. This definition left open the question of whether or not alum baking powder constituted a health hazard.

Thus, the formal definition of adulteration that was so offensive to the alum baking powder manufacturers remained in the law, but its operational definition was left to the judgment of the Secretary of Agriculture and the Chief of the Bureau of Chemistry. Although this concentration of power in the hands of two officials was objectionable to the ABPA, the passage of the law allowed them to shift battlegrounds and to take advantage of opportunities to present their case to the regulatory agency.

TRADE WARS AND PUBLIC POLICY

Intensive trade wars taking place within and between other food and drug industries also affected the debate over federal pure food legislation. Indeed, the trade wars seem to have been so broad-based and important that it is often difficult to determine from historical records whether the arguments for a food law presented in Chapter 4 could stand alone, or whether they represented merely another set of business tactics for competitive gain.

The battle between "ethical" drug makers (whose medicines were advertised only to physicians) and proprietary remedy manufacturers (the itinerant "medicine men" whose cures for baldness, catarrh, and "ladies' ailments" promised booming future revenues) provides yet another example of a trade war with important consequences for pure food and medicines.

Manufacturers of ethical drugs, represented by the American Pharmaceutical Association, lined up against the makers of proprietary remedies, who spoke through the Proprietary Association of America. The former favored a law that would drive the patent medicine interests out of business; the latter, obviously, felt that such attacks were unjustifiable attempts to prevent them from meeting apparent consumer demands.

The two series of articles, in *Collier's* (S.H. Adams, 1905a, 1905b, 1905c, 1905d, 1906a, 1906b, 1906c) and *Ladies' Home Journal*, (Banfield, 1903; Bok, 1904a, 1904b, 1905, 1906; Sullivan, 1906a, 1906b, 1906c) discussed in Chapter 3 appear to have been important in arousing public support for better controls on patent medicines, as were the efforts of the American Medical Association to convince the Women's Christian Temperance Union that alcohol in "spring tonics" and other remedies was as potent and dangerous as alcohol served in a tavern. Harvey Wiley, on the other hand, attributed much of the delay in passing the pure food law to the activities of patent medicine peddlers and their organizations, including the powerful Proprietary Association of America (Wiley, 1929; 1930).

Among the drug industry leaders who fought for laws to prevent further encroachment of patent medicines into therapeutic markets were the founders of Squibb, Inc., Abbott Laboratories, and Lederle Laboratories. Dr. Edward Robinson Squibb, according to a biographer, engaged in "a lifelong fight for pure drugs" via quality standards and legislation and was a sponsor of the first federal pure food bill, introduced into Congress in 1879. Squibb's death in 1900, however, prevented him from being a significant force toward the end of the pure food controversy (Mahoney, 1959:43–61; see also Beal, 1931). Dr. Wallace Calvin Abbott, founder of Abbott Laboratories, was an early partner in the American Medical Association's attack on patent medicines and continued his support for legislative action through his voluminous private and company publications. Dr. Abbott found himself engaged in an unfortunate battle with the AMA, however, over the capital-generating company bonds he advertised and sold to physicians; his lobbying partnership with the AMA was short-lived, but Abbott's commitment to pure drugs was not (Kogan, 1963:27–69; Mahoney, 1959:133–135). Dr. Ernst Joseph Lederle, founder of Lederle Laboratories in 1904, was a former Health Commissioner of New York City who had been active in tracing, identifying, and seizing contaminated milk and other adulterated food and drug products. To the pure food battle he contributed not only expert testimony in favor of a federal law, but also a great deal of evidence on the nature and extent of food and drug adulterations, amassed during his years of public service (Mahoney, 1959:158–163).

Whiskey makers engaged in another trade war that affected the pure food controversy. Distillers of bottled-in-bond liquors favored a pure food law that would declare competing products, especially "rectified" whiskies, to be adulterated. Rectified whiskies were solutions of grain alcohol, water, sugar, flavoring, and coloring. They were not aged and were easily and cheaply manufactured. Bonded distillers apparently saw little hope of having the rectified products banned outright, but they saw considerable advantage to themselves in having such goods labeled "artificial whiskey." Gerald Carson reports (1963:167–168):

> The bourbon distillers strongly supported the pure food bill. They had no objections to the proposed labeling feature which provided that compounded alcoholic beverages should be required to place

the words "imitation whiskey" on their packages while the aged product was entitled to use without qualification the term "whiskey." If this proposal became law it would put the blenders under a serious disadvantage.

Distillers actively entered the fray in the winter of 1904. The pure food bills before Congress at that time were the subject of hearings by the House Committee on Interstate and Foreign Commerce. Harvey Wiley, fearing that the rectifiers would succeed in having whiskey exempted from the bill altogether, "arranged to have spokesmen of the straight-whiskey interests of Kentucky present to argue their side of the question. This was not difficult to accomplish, for the Kentucky distillers, hard pressed by competition from the rectifiers, had come to see that the pure food law might be used to their competitive advantage" (Anderson, 1958:162).

Many of the Kentucky, Ohio, and Tennessee distillers of aged whiskey testified on behalf of a pure food bill before Congressional committees and sought to gain official sanction of their production methods. In fact, in the definition of adulteration cited earlier in this chapter, the specification of "added" poisonous or deleterious ingredients was a conciliatory gesture to the bottled-in-bond producers, who found it difficult to argue against allegations that their products soaked up "natural" toxins from the charred oak barrels in which they were aged.

Rectifiers, their supporters in Congress, and the National Wholesale Liquor Dealers Association argued vigorously that the bottled-in-bond distinction was purely a tax matter, that it was unfair to imply that a tax stamp on bottled-in-bond products was an assurance of high quality, and that it was nonsensical for the Congress to declare manufactured whiskies more deleterious than whiskies aged in oaken barrels (since it was true that the charring of the oak produced certain toxic chemicals that entered the whiskey solution). Claiming that their products were as wholesome as aged, bottled-in-bond liquors, and that their lower prices met a real consumer need, the rectifiers argued that to label their products "artificial whiskey" would be suicide in the marketplace. According to Anderson (1958:168), "it is possible that the pure-food bill would have become law in 1905 had it not been for the feud between the bottled-in-bond men and the rectifiers."

Potable substances were included under the definition of "food" in the 1906 Pure Food Act, but liquors were not singled out for special attention and, as in other cases, standards and regulations concerning adulteration and misbranding were left in the hands of the Secretary of Agriculture and the Chief of the Bureau of Chemistry (see Senate Document 141, 1901:11–14; *Congressional Record,* House, June 23, 1906: 9062–9066; Allen, 1906:56, 60–62; Anderson, 1958:157–182).

Canners who had developed the technology for producing canned goods without preservatives, such as H. J. Heinz, favored the law and actively supported its passage, even though it was never clear until the law finally did pass that preservatives would not be banned automatically. Even in the absence of statutory prohibition of preservatives and other artificial ingredients in food, the prospects seemed bright for strict regulatory controls on their use, particularly since Harvey Wiley was adamant on their deleterious health effects.

Most of the canners who supported pure food legislation, however, were won over very late in the battle, and Harvey Wiley may have been responsible for their being politically active at all. On February 14, 1906, Wiley spoke to a large group of canners from several associations. "The canners were in a hostile mood," according to Anderson (1958:178), "for many blamed the pure-food agitation for a slump in demand and an accumulation of unsold inventories." Wiley ignored warnings that his speech might result in "physical injury" to himself, and talked to the canners about the ethical virtues of non-deceptive manufacturing and advertising practices. Under Wiley's magnetic influence, the mood changed from hostility to "enthusiastic applause," and Wiley had won for pure food the endorsement of the Western Packers' Canned Goods Association and the Atlantic States Packers' Association, representing scores of food processing plants (Anderson, 1958:178–179).

Many canners, on the other hand, depended upon artificial flavorings, colorings, preservatives, and other additives, not to mask inferior products, but to enhance their products' appeal to consumers. Green peas, for example, lost most of their color in pressure-retort canning; why not add a little green color to restore what had been lost? If natural vanilla was in short supply or extremely costly, why not use artificial vanillin instead to flavor candies and ice cream? If foodstuffs were to be shipped cross-country, why not use preservatives to extend their shelf lives and to reduce the risk of goods lost to spoilage? Some manufacturers engaged in interstate commerce sought federal acknowledgment that preserved food was healthier than putrid food. Prominent among these was the National Food Manufacturers Association, which represented 175 food manufacturers nationwide (Allen, 1906:58; Anderson, 1958; Potter 1959). They were concerned as well about attempts to control the use of glucose and corn syrup as inexpensive substitutes for cane sugar.

PUBLIC POLICY, SCIENCE, AND COMPETITIVE ADVANTAGE

Industrialization, technological advances, and the increasing diffusion of scientific knowledge to larger segments of the population promoted, as the trade wars clearly show, a redistribution of competitive advantage among food and drug companies in the Progressive Era. Modern scientific knowledge, particularly in chemistry and production techniques, could be put to use to produce foods, beverages, and medicines that were often functionally equivalent — and for some purposes superior — to "traditional" products, but that were much less costly.

Oleomargarine, "alum" baking powders, proprietary remedies, and "rectified" whiskey all relied upon some knowledge of chemistry for their composition and consumer appeal. Artificial preservatives, colorings, and flavorings also represented, from the perspectives of those who used them, the most up-to-date scientific techniques for feeding an increasingly urban and consumer-oriented population. Similarly, producers like Heinz and Pabst, first to see the advantages of production technology that required no preservatives, felt that the law should support the advantage promised them by the new technology.

The role of science and scientific knowledge in fostering this reallocation of competitive advantage should not be taken to indicate that the battles over a pure food law occurred because of some "misunderstanding" or general distrust of scientific matters. It is certain that some manufacturers, wholesalers, and retailers of foods and drugs were engaged in outright fraud, motivated by nothing other than greed. On the other hand, the arguments presented by various business interests during the prelegislative battles suggest that the spread of scientific knowledge and procedures gave rise to some unanticipated competitive pressures and thence to attempts to use the power of the federal government to gain (or regain) competitive advantage. It also produced new kinds of evidence — for example, chemistry-based evidence on baking powder residues, or Harvey Wiley's "clinical" experiments with food preservatives — that could be used by advocates to lend prestige and authority to their positions on pending legislation.

In that age of science, anyone could be a chemist. Anyone could produce foodstuffs or medicines in a small plant or laboratory and peddle them in local markets or by horse-drawn wagon. Start-up capital did not need to be large, but the potential rewards from a market success were enormous. On this basis one could construct some working hypotheses about the structure of industries and the nature of businesses' political participation within those industries.

In the cases of the drug and whiskey industries, for example, tentative evidence suggests that it was the larger, better-capitalized, well-established, more heavily industrialized firms in the industries (producing ethical drugs and bottled-in-bond liquors, respectively) that felt the threat of many small, aggressive competitors and sought to prevent erosion of their market positions by having these competitors' products legally declared adulterated, misbranded, or hazardous to human health. Interestingly, the entry of these established firms into the public policy process seems to have been *generated* by the new competitive threats; there is little evidence that these businesses were politically active (particularly at the federal level) prior to the emergence of small but potentially powerful competitors. The smaller firms representing competitive threats in both industries, however, seem to have sought to influence public policy in their favor actively and early, through their well-funded trade associations, the Proprietary Association of America and the National Wholesale Liquor Dealers Association.*

---

*Harvey Wiley (1929; 1930) claimed that patent medicine associations were critical in delaying the passage of a food and drug law. See also Representative Mann's comments after the House had approved the Conference Committee Report on S.88, the bill that became the Pure Food Act (*Congressional Record*, House. June 29, 1906).

In the case of the dairy industry, on the other hand, the established producers (local dairy farms and creameries) tended to be much smaller, less well capitalized, and less heavily industrialized than the oleomargarine companies who threatened to erode their market positions. The political activity of the dairy industry, however, preceded the new competitive threats. The dairymen had built strong political bridges long before the pure food controversy erupted; their supporters in Congress (and in various state legislatures as well) were able to secure special legislation protecting dairy interests, so that a federal pure food law would leave dairy products relatively unaffected (Wright, 1895; House Report 1854, 1900; *Congressional Record*, Senate. Feb. 21, 1906:2765; Allen, 1906; Riepma, 1970).

The oleomargarine manufacturers, despite their alleged backing by organized beef and cottonseed interests, seem not to have had as strong political connections as the dairymen, and thus were severely buffeted by legislative efforts sponsored by the dairy lobby to hinder the production and sale of their products. Indeed, if Clark (1929) is correct in stating that the meatpackers had gained control of most of the major creameries by the early 1900s, this would go a long way toward explaining the inability of the margarine manufacturers to gain a satisfactory hearing in Congress and the state legislatures. If the packers were playing both sides of the fence (as the Royal Baking Powder Company apparently did), they would be likely to place their heaviest political bets on the dairymen, who seemed to offer certain success, while hedging their future profit positions via quiet investments in margarine factories, just in case. The cottonseed interests, on the other hand, were represented by the Southern Democrats, who opposed any and all pure food bills on the grounds of states' rights, an argument that had already become ineffectual.

These tentative findings suggest that an early perception of *common interests* among business owners in an industry was critical to the development of well-organized, heavily funded, and strongly supported efforts to influence public policy to achieve (or retain) competitive advantage. In the cases of drugs and whiskey, these common interests represented *opportunities* to build highly profitable businesses by encroaching on the markets of less politically active businesses in the industry. In the case of butter, the common interests binding the dairy firms together were *threats* — not at first from margarine competition, although that become a later rationale for collective action, but from the supply and price uncertainties of agricultural production.

As we have seen, the strategic use of public policy by businesses is not a recent phenomenon. In some instances, as Chapter 4 showed, Progressive Era businesses sought to obtain laws and regulations that would help to protect the functioning of the free market. In other cases, such as the trade wars examined in this chapter, competitive threats and opportunities were used by food and drug businesses as incentives to seek competitive advantage through legislation and subsequent regulatory implementation. With their considerable success in using such a powerful strategic weapon as public policy, what could be expected of forward-looking capitalistic enterprises? The ideal of the free market, if it had ever truly guided business actions, was quietly abandoned.

Environment   Perception   Actions
_____   _____   _____

                    Pro-   New businesses
                    duc-   New product lines
Opportunity =>   tive   New products

                    Re-   "Better, Faster, Cheaper"
                    gu-
                    la-
Threat =>   tive   Court action based upon
                                laws

                    Lob-   Laws
                    by-   Interpretive Regulations
                    ing

six

Strategic Uses of "The Public Interest"

THE PURE FOOD ACT, SIGNED BY PRESIDENT THEODORE ROOSE-
velt on June 30, 1906 (Public Law No. 384), contains this general
statement of purpose in its preamble:

> . . . An Act for preventing the manufacture, sale, or transporta-
> tion of adulterated or misbranded or poisonous or deleterious
> foods, drugs, medicines, and liquors, and for regulating
> traffic therein. . . .

Congress had no authority to regulate manufacturing or transport within the states, nor could they interfere with intrastate commerce. Congress was authorized to control the manufacture and sale
of objectionable items within the Territories and the District of Columbia, and this they did before the Pure Food Act was passed. In
the face of concerted opposition from states' rights advocates and
those who complained about the inroads made by "sumptuary legislation" into personal freedom, Congress was faced with the task of
establishing their federal food and drug law on a solid legal foundation. The constitutionally guaranteed power of Congress to regulate

181

interstate and foreign commerce proved to be the desired foundation; it was on this power that the 1906 Pure Food Act rested.*

The Act described the formal process of examination, notification, hearings, appeals, judgments, penalties, and disposal of adulterated or misbranded goods. Important terms were defined, particularly "adulteration." Drugs were said to be adulterated if they were sold under a name recognized by the U.S. Pharmacopoeia or the National Formulary (the official repositories of standards for medicinal products) and failed to meet established standards of strength, quality, or purity; or if they were less strong or pure than their makers claimed them to be. Confectioneries were to be declared adulterated if they contained any poisonous ingredients. Food adulterations, occupying the lion's share of definitional attention in the act, were defined as follows (illustrations of the definition, drawn from the testimony presented in Chapter 3, are given in parentheses) (Allen, 1906; Brooks, 1906; Bureau of Chemistry, Bulletin 13, 1887–1902; Crampton, 1900; Ghent, 1906; *The Independent,* 1901, 1903, 1905; Mason, H. B., 1900; Mason, W. E., 1900; McCumber, 1905; *The Nation,* 1899, 1903, 1904; "Senatorial investigation," 1899; House Report No. 1426, 1900; Senate Document No. 141, 1901; Senate Document No. 447, 1900; Senate Report No. 516, 1899–1900; Wiley, 1929, 1930):

1. Reduction in "quality or strength" caused by the mixing or packing of food with some other substance (e.g., mixing terra alba — white earth — in flour).
2. Total or partial substitution of some other substance for the food itself (e.g., substituting oleomargarine for butter, or mixing the two together and selling the resulting product as butter).
3. Removal of "any valuable constituent of the article," in whole or in part (e.g., removing the butterfat from whole milk and replacing it with vegetable oil).
4. Mixing, coloring, powdering, coating, or staining food "in a man-

---

*Previous federal regulation of foods and drugs had been based for the most part on the Congressional power to tax and spend. For example, the Margarine Act of 1886, discussed in Chapter 5, was intended to limit the sale of oleomargarine — at the request of the dairy lobbyists — by taxing it into an uncompetitive price position. Consumers would not often choose oleomargarine if they could get fresh butter at about the same price.

ner whereby damage or inferiority is concealed" (e.g., using copper sulphate to color canned peas artificially, or covering canned meats with boracic acid to conceal decay).

5. The addition of "poisonous or other added deleterious ingredients," except for preservatives applied to the surface that could easily be removed by the consumer, and provided that directions for removal were printed on the label (e.g., a powdered preservative could be sprinkled over codfish if it was visible, if it could be washed off, and if the consumer could see instructions for doing so on the package).

6. "If it consists in whole or in part of a filthy, decomposed, or putrid animal or vegetable substance, or any portion of an animal unfit for food, whether manufactured or not, or if it is the product of a diseased animal, or one that has died otherwise than by slaughter" (e.g., ketchup made from rotting tomatoes, or potted meat made from tuberculous animals).

The term "misbranded" was defined generally by the act as follows:

> . . . all drugs, or articles of food, or articles which enter into the composition of food, the package or label of which shall bear any statement, design, or device regarding such article, or the ingredients or substances contained therein which shall be false or misleading in any particular, and to any food or drug product which is falsely branded as to the State, Territory, or country in which it is manufactured or produced.

Further specifications of misbranding included the sale of a product under a false name, failure to specify on the label the proportion of alcohol or narcotic content, incorrect statements of weight or measure (note that the law did not require weight or measure statements, only that they be accurate if they were made), and the sale of "compounds, imitations, or blends" without so stating on the label. The latter compromise opened the possibility that the rectifiers, such strong adversaries to a federal pure food law, could sell their products as "blended whiskey," instead of the abhorrent "imitation whiskey."

Retailers, wholesalers, and jobbers were guaranteed protection from prosecution under the law if they could obtain from the seller or manufacturer a written guarantee that the products purchased and resold were not adulterated and were properly labeled. Business enterprises and their officers, employees, and agents were held equally liable for compliance with the law. The entire act is five pages long and is reprinted, along with the initial budgetary enabling legislation, in Appendix B.

INTERESTS AND THEMES: A BRIEF SUMMARY

It would be easy to conclude that in the "good old days" of the Progressive Era, commercial, governmental, and consumer issues were so entangled as to be virtually inseparable. The wording of the pure food law indicates that many special and sectoral interests had been addressed in a fashion appropriate to the public policy-setting processes of a representative constitutional democracy. Although it is true that the interests of businesses, consumers, and government overlapped to a considerable extent, the development of the pure food issue suggests that some clear themes can be observed.

Consumer Interests Centered Upon the Need to Know.   As users and producers of foodstuffs and medicines became increasingly separated by layers of repackagers, distributors, and sellers, consumers found themselves with decreased ability to protect themselves from purchasing impure, hazardous, substituted, ineffective, or falsely advertised goods.

The need to know what was being purchased was a twofold need. The need for accurate labels — for appropriate information — was of course the most immediate and obvious need. If goods were honestly and fully labeled, consumers would know what they needed to know and could indeed judge for themselves the character of the goods they purchased. Market forces would work to regulate the quality of goods available *if* consumers had access to the information they needed to make informed choices. Underlying this demand, however, was another more fundamental aspect of the need to know. Consumers, becoming more and more distant (both geographically and organizationally) from producers, needed to know that the makers of foods and medicines could be trusted. Ironically, as the need for trust increased with the emergence of a nationwide production and distribution system, the foundation for that trust — a set of shared norms and values backed up by an observant community — declined.

There seemed to be no reasonable solution to this problem other than the intervention of the federal government. It alone had the power and authority to regulate interstate commerce and thus to exercise some control over the quality, content, and labeling of foods, beverages, and drugs.

Business Interests Focused on the Need to Survive. Reputable manufacturers, distributors, and retailers sought protection from those who stole their brands and regional distinctions, infringed on their markets, and undercut their prices by adulterating goods with cheap and hard-to-detect ingredients. Some industries and subindustries felt threatened with decline and sought to secure federally guaranteed competitive advantage over the rising industries and subindustries that apparently threatened them.

"Adulterators and misbranders"* sought the freedom offered by pure laissez-faire economic theory and the doctrine of caveat emptor to sell whatever would — or might — be bought by consumers. Some businesses, possessed of special competencies or locations or products, acted to use the power of the federal government to secure competitive advantage over other firms in their industries.

New and intense competitive conditions and the pressures of dramatically expanding interstate commerce made for more risky and yet potentially more rewarding environments for food, beverage, and drug companies. The federal government had the ability to provide some security to businesses threatened by new or stronger competitors. It could also solidify some of the competitive advantages possessed by some firms or industries. Why should businesses not try to use federal powers to gain some environmental stability and thus to enhance their chances of survival and growth?

---

*These terms are set in quotation marks because, as we have seen, their pejorative implications were neither clearly defined nor readily documented.

**Government Interests were Grounded in the Need to Pro-
tect.** But who or what needed protection, and how was it to be
granted? The United States Constitution stressed minimal federal in-
terference with the governmental affairs of the states, although the
focus of statutory and administrative law, as well as the outcomes of
the judicial review process, had already begun to shift toward more
centralized policy-setting in Washington (see Anderson, 1981). States'
rights advocates — primarily Southern Democrats — opposed pure
food legislation throughout the entire period of debate and voted
against the pure food law itself. On what basis could Congress intervene in the operations of the marketplace?

Overall, Congressional distaste for federal intervention in state
affairs, to the extent that it truly guided legislation, was overcome by
the Constitutional mandate "to secure the general welfare." It just so
happened that in the Progressive Era it was not only possible but
probable that "the general welfare" would be defined in terms that
could encompass the interests of almost all contesting parties. Pro-
tectionist activities and inclinations of the government clearly extended to businesses and industries as well as to consumers, and it
eventually became clear to the majority of Congressional members
that none of their constituencies could be protected adequately, given
the consequences of rapid industrialization, in the absence of a federal law.

These "sectoral" interests are in fact difficult to segregate, because together they form the tripartite foundation of interests in a
social system that is defined by capitalism and representative democracy. For the free market to operate effectively, businesses needed to
be free to allocate resources for activities that would meet existing or
potential consumer demand. Consumers needed accurate and adequate information to make market choices that would result in efficient resource allocation. Even at this relatively early stage in the
development of our industrialized economy, however, a truly efficient
market proved to be a theoretical construct with little connection to
the realities of the marketplace. Externalities — the costs of production and distribution that are borne by persons other than users of
the product or service — became visible in the system. Those who
perceived that their share of resources or their access to resources
was negatively affected sought redress, being the repository of the
legitimate use of coercive power. Congress held the power of redress,

and it was duty bound to protect "the public interest" by helping consumers to know and businesses to survive.

MORALITY, SCIENCE, AND INTERESTS

This mix of public and private interests becomes even more complicated when one introduces two conditions that influenced the nature of business–government–public relationships during the Progressive Era. One of these conditions was the moral overlay governing relations among people. The other was the set of epistemological and social structural changes wrought by the development of science and scientific knowledge.

Although morality was formally defined within the Judeo-Christian context, its behavioral prescriptions were in practice more Durkheimian than theological. That is, God might still be in his heaven, but all was not right with the world unless people could abide by social rules and conventions. These social rules, generated by the people themselves (and their forebears), were designed to ensure the smooth functioning of communities and to establish some minimum degree of trust among persons. One might have to answer to God in the next life, but on earth one had to answer to one's neighbors.

In the main, food and drug companies were not yet large, and most of them were still relatively independent of formal organizational ties with other companies. The merger wave in the food industry was looming in the near future, but it had not yet happened. Ownership and control still typically resided in a single person, a family unit, or some other small and readily identifiable group, not in an amorphous gaggle of stockholders and a coterie of hired professional managers.

We talk today of corporate actions, desires, objectives, and ethics, knowing full well that to do so is to anthropomorphize an abstract entity. But the "actions" of a food or drug company in the Progressive Era were much more clearly the actions of individuals, of flesh-and-blood people. These people were to be held accountable, under a communitarian model of morality, for the extent to which their actions contributed to the common good. That is, the rules for social behavior (including the economic or exchange behavior of persons) were set in the context of community life; deviations from the rules were to be dealt with by the community, and responsibility was still vested for the most part in the person, not in some abstract "complex organization."

Individuals were responsible for their actions and for the consequences of those actions. Parents had a duty to keep their children from ingesting poisons or other deleterious foods and medicines. Manufacturers and sellers were obligated to provide honest products with honest labels. In this moral context it was difficult to acknowledge fully the failure of traditional social rules to protect the rights of persons and to enforce their obligations as well. Within an industrialized, urban society, government had to assume some of the social control functions of the community. Government become obliged to set and enforce the formal rules under which both consumers and business owners could meet their own moral obligations without incurring undue economic loss.

Regarding the second theme — the development and use of science — constituencies and their interests once again become entangled. Scientific developments, both theoretical and applied, provided the technological means whereby America (as well as other nations, of course) could move toward undreamed-of standards of living for individuals and an incredible concentration of economic wealth and power for corporations. The ever-more-efficient mechanical harnessing of energy, and the ever-more-specialized division of labor, meant that more work could be done at less cost, more goods and services could become available to more people, and more workers could have the financial capability to purchase those goods and services.

Emergent technology also provided the rationale for some companies to attempt to use the power of government to secure competitive advantage. H.J. Heinz, for example, an industry leader in the development and application of pressure retort canning and bacteriological control techniques, found in this technology a distinctive competency that could serve a dual purpose. If the resulting products were accepted by consumers and could be priced at an appropriate level, the technology would dramatically improve the quality of Heinz canned goods, and could provide the edge that Heinz sought over the products of competitors. As policy analysts have since discovered, one way to secure consumer acceptance and appropriate price levels for an innovative product is to require product standards for an entire industry that can be met only with state-of-the-art technology. Heinz's prolegislation position in the pure food debate, although clearly articulated by him in terms of moral responsibilities, no doubt had an extra measure of emphasis because of the opportunity he had to make strategic use of public policy for the good of his company and his customers.

Beyond the technological base, the scientific method and its astonishing products provided an alternative way of knowing, an epistemology based upon rationality, linearity, predictability, natural laws, and above all, evidence that could be observed repeatedly by anyone who chose to replicate a procedure or an experiment. The development of science imposed a new set of rules on sensate and abstract knowing. Raw empiricism was on the way out; it was not enough any longer merely to observe phenomena and to understand them in the context of one's own sensory evidence. Instead, observations must be conducted with standardized procedures under controlled conditions, and the interpretation of findings must combine logical argument with replicable evidence. Similarly, knowledge based on faith, although it could certainly guide the actions of a believing person, was considerably less acceptable when presented as evidence in formal arguments or in policy-setting forums. Science promised to routinize the acquisition and organization of knowledge and to impose strict limits on what could and could not be defined as knowledge, but the societal values and behaviors of the time had not yet progressed quite so far.

Empiricism and the scientific method joined forces with moral themes in the pure food controversy. As an example, recall the opposition of the American Medical Association to secret medicinal formulas. First, since the therapeutic value of such preparations could not be determined in advance of use, the risks to patients were increased and physicians were prevented from exercising their moral obligation to enhance the well-being of their patients. Second, secret formulas stood in the way of science by making more difficult the process of creating, standardizing, disseminating, and utilizing medical knowledge. Physicians felt that the publication of formulas, processes, and therapeutic indications — done routinely by reputable pharmaceutical companies — contributed greatly to the advancement of medical and scientific knowledge. Secret formulas, however, were an affront to science and the *desire* to know, and an affront to ethics as well, since the doctrine of individual responsibility engendered a *need* to know. Congress, in passing a federal food and drug law, contributed to the establishment of the individual's *right* to know.

Physicians, pharmacists, agricultural chemists, city milk and food inspectors, and others engaged in scientific pursuits did not seem to distinguish consumer interests from commercial interests in any clear fashion. Harvey W. Wiley, for example, often described as the strongest of consumer advocates in the pure food controversy, was also responsible for the development of a viable domestic beet-sugar industry, and made many other contributions to industrial progress by conducting, supporting, and publishing technologically oriented research.

Science was not exclusively the domain of scientists, nor was its store of knowledge yet so technical and esoteric that it was reserved for a privileged few whose extensive training qualified them to work in highly specialized fields. Almost anyone could lay claim to scientific data and could attempt to establish scientific credibility. Further, science seemed to hold great promise of being the new salvation of humankind — workers, business owners, farmers alike — and thus was held in some considerable esteem. Science did not have a strong enough hold on the American consciousness, however, to dictate the terms of public policy. It proved to be a tool or a resource used by interest groups, just as any other tool or resource would be used, to win critical persons over to a position or to seize the opportunity to advance an interest.

This use of science as a tool was possible in part because, as a way of knowing, scientific methods proved to be as ambiguous and irritating as they were useful. For example, the inability of scientific researchers to make precise statements about what was and what was not harmful to the human body granted an extra measure of legitimacy to those who argued *against* a pure food law and to those who sought ad hoc exemptions from its provisions. Was boracic acid harmful to human health when used as a preservative? If so, was there a maximum quantity that could be consumed by humans without ill effects? Did this ceiling have any reasonable relation to the threshold below which boracic acid lost its preservative powers? Was it better for people to eat chemically preserved food that was otherwise wholesome than to eat rancid food masked with flavoring and coloring additives? Was this sort of choice inevitable in an age of mass-produced food, shipped impersonally across the large nation?

Needless to say, scientists could not answer these questions to the satisfaction of all. Indeed, as current experience with scientific testimony tells us, it would not have been possible for them to do so. Thus, one of the strongest arguments in favor of a federal food and drug law was made, not for prohibiting the use of certain items, but for stating the contents accurately and completely on the label so that consumers could make their own observations. So informed, consumers could then decide about the wholesomeness, desirability, and effectiveness of the foods and drugs they purchased.

Modern businesses are advised to scan and monitor "the environment," which is often characterized as having four "segments" — social, economic, political, and technological (see, e.g., Wilson, 1974). During the Progressive Era these four environmental segments were working together; it was a time when moral prescriptions and outrage, the technological state of the art, channels of political access, and an expansion of economic opportunity combined to push the development of a public policy "in the public interest," broadly defined.

For a moment, think of those "items" — moral outrage, economic opportunity, and so on — as resources that can serve as motivators, tools, or interests and that are distributed in some fashion (not randomly) through the population. Any actor or interest group will have a somewhat different configuration of access to these resources from that of any other actor or interest group. That is, some groups may be driven to act by moral outrage, and that resource may compensate for a lack of other resources. Other groups will be motivated by other interests and will have different combinations of resources available to them.

The science of mobilization would be to combine actors — that is, to build coalitions — until the "optimum" combination of moral, technological, political, and economic interests and resources exists within the coalition, and then to stop building and let the policy-making process proceed. The optimum combination would be expressed in terms of desirable outcomes, for example, the coalition of interest groups that achieves its legislative objective could be said to be "optimal." If excess energy is invested in unnecessary coalition building or unnecessary pressure on political players, the effort may be dissipated through the burnout of principal players, squabbling among coalition members, or a revolt against "too much" pressure on the part of policy makers. If too little coalition building is done, the combination of interests and demands cannot reach the threshold level necessary to push a bill through Congress.

The art of mobilization, on the other hand, is to permit the alignment of as many separate interests as possible so that a multitude of resources, motivations, and interests are brought to bear on decision makers. When a majority of Congressional members can say yes to some legislative proposal, it is not because they all agree with each other, but because the proposal meets one or more interests of theirs or of their constituents. Clearly, these interests need have little or nothing to do with each other, as long as they can be made to work together for a compromise position that satisfies some acceptable portion of numerous demands.

The environmental conditions of the Progressive Era were ripe for this sort of implacable, abstract mobilization of the interests and resources of a great many persons, groups, and organizations around the issue of pure food, and this indeed seems to be what occurred. Was "the public interest" well served by the outcome?

STRATEGIC USES OF "THE PUBLIC INTEREST"

Even though we have differentiated and examined separately the interests of consumers and businesses in the 1906 Food and Drug Act, the distinction is indeed somewhat arbitrary and artificial. Neither consumers nor manufacturers wanted to be cheated; accurate labeling was in the interests of most members of society, whether persons or organizations. A ban on fraudulent substitutions was clearly in the interests of consumers who wanted honest value for their dollars and in the interests of many business proprietors as well, especially those who did not like to defraud their friends and neighbors merely because the marketplace seemed to demand it in the abstract interplay of demand for certain goods at certain prices. "The public interest," then, may have been served well by a law protecting both consumers and businesspeople from false and fraudulent practices.

When the trade wars are considered, however, the concept of "the public interest" grows even fuzzier. On the basis of the evidence presented here, it seems that businesses in the food and drug industries were quick to understand that law and regulation could form a crucial part of any competitive strategy. In this case, at least, it seems that the federal government's power to regulate interstate commerce "in the public interest" was viewed by businesses as both threat and opportunity, and that the direction of the business response depended very much on the structure of the industry and the positioning of key firms within it.

It seems clear that relatively few food and drug companies during the Progressive Era were squarely against a pure food law, and many companies favored one, particularly if the wording, provisions, and implementation could provide them with some advantage over competitors. Threats from small, aggressive entrepreneurs; threats from cheaper substitutes; threats from fraudulently labeled items; threats from commercially adulterated products, all could be met by taking advantage of a single opportunity — the prospect of influencing federal legislation. The conditions of competition in interstate commerce, foreign trade, and within and between industries dictated that businesses take a position on pure food legislation that was consistent with their own interests.

Why, then, do we still hear the myth that the 1906 Pure Food Act represented one of the earliest examples of pure "social" or consumer protection legislation? Perhaps it is because the industries involved were not terribly powerful or large at the time, not as large, for example, as the oil companies, the steel companies, the railroads, and the banks. Perhaps it is because the consumer protection intent of the law seems so obvious to modern observers that further inquiry has been deemed unnecessary. Perhaps, too, we may relish the idea of a quieter, less cynical, less self-serving time when Congress actually seemed to have acted now and then "in the public interest" with sincerity and effectiveness. (Although this idea would be difficult to justify for anyone who has read the works of David Graham Phillips, Edward Bok, Upton Sinclair, Samuel Hopkins Adams, or other great muckraking novelists and journalists.) Perhaps the myth lives because it proves to be useful to those who wish to assert historical continuity (e.g., Congress responds to public pressure by enacting poorly thought-out consumer protection legislation), or historical discontinuity (e.g., Congress used to act in the public interest), or who claim certain rights regarding resource allocation (e.g., protecting "honest" businesses is always in the public interest).

In any case, when S.88 was finally reported out of the conference committee, accepted by both houses of Congress, and signed by President Roosevelt, Congressional leaders were confident that a great victory had been won. The law seemed to be a satisfying combination of many interests, public and private; those who voted "nay" did so mainly on grounds of states' rights.

In some ways the Pure Food Act was a resounding victory for consumers. It provided public, official notice that hazardous and fraudulent business practices would be punished; it promised adequate information for consumer choices; it reassured the people that Congress was not yet entirely captured by the trusts and that it could still establish policies promoting the general welfare. The law served as a powerful condensation symbol (Edelman, 1964), permitting public quiescence on a public policy issue that concerned them deeply but over which they had little effective control. Public concern over the quality and purity of foods and drugs did not emerge again until the early 1930s, when publication of such works as *100,000,000 Guinea Pigs* helped to initiate another long battle for new federal food and drug legislation (Kallett, 1932).

For businesses, with respect to interstate and foreign commerce, federal regulations promised to introduce greater certainty and efficiency into manufacturing and distribution. They would also provide protection for reputable manufacturers and retailers against dishonest competitors. The law allowed the possibility, however, that some firms could be protected from competition that may have been neither dishonest nor unfair. Oleomargarine manufacturers, for example, found themselves subject to long-standing legal discrimination in favor of butter, even when fraudulent substitutions and improper labeling had long since disappeared. The economic theory of regulation has found considerable support in this analysis, as has the strategic uses perspective, and yet this in no way negates the consumer protection aspects for which the 1906 Pure Food Act is so much better known.

Finally, the law's passage effectively removed the issue of food and drug adulteration and mislabeling from the public agenda for a number of years. Free from public scrutiny, manufacturers could cultivate access to administrative decision-making channels and attempt to secure ad hoc, unpublicized exemptions from the law or definitional and enforcement decisions that allowed them to proceed with their activities unhindered (Kolko, 1963; Wiley, 1929; 1930).

Whether or not the Bureau of Chemistry (and later the Food and Drug Administration) was partially or completely "captured" by the regulated industries has been a matter of considerable discussion over the years and is a topic that deserves further research. It is suggestive, however, that Dr. Harvey Wiley, pure food's principal crusader and from all accounts a scientist and administrator of the highest personal integrity, resigned in 1912 as Chief of the Bureau of Chemistry after a long series of bitter confrontations with his superiors over implementation of the 1906 Act (Wiley, 1929; 1930).

People of good will inevitably disagree, often over trivial matters, now and then over matters of great importance. A government "of the people" necessarily reflects these disagreements as well as the disparate underlying values that prompt them. When government is administered, as ours is, through a multitude of regulatory agencies that are incompletely linked to avenues for the expression of public interests, regulation will reflect many definitions of the "public interest," not just one.

As we know, in recent decades the concept of "the public interest" has come to be identified with the interests of consumers. Federal laws concerning equal employment opportunity, occupational safety and health, environmental protection, and product safety (institutionalized in the EEOC, OSHA, EPA, and CPSC) exemplify our current understanding of how the federal government fulfills its mandate to promote the general welfare. It has not always been the case, however, that "the public interest" represents a set of values and priorities that are believed to be directly counter to the interests of business. In the Progressive Era a much more complex definition of "the public interest" was prevalent than is true today. Economic and social ideology dictated that the interests of business, though of course not identical to the interests of workers, consumers, and other social groups, were certainly a valued and valid component of "the public interest," and in many cases were intermingled with those many other interests to constitute a social system that valued harmony and reciprocity, despite the many conflicts that characterized it. This state of affairs, combined with a growing federal presence in the affairs of the states and the nation, provided astute business leaders with new opportunities to seek competitive advantages from the state and federal legislatures. It also provided the opportunity for "the people" to feel themselves protected by laws such as the

Pure Food Act, which served as powerful symbols of government benevolence.

Flatly rejecting the validity of the regulatory capture versus public interest definitional context, Thomas K. McCraw (1975:180) has argued:

> Regulation is best understood as an institution capable of serving diverse, even contradictory ends, some economic, some political, some cultural. Regulatory experience over the last century suggests several major ends or functions.

Included among McCraw's list of regulatory functions are disclosure and publicity (of some undesirable state of affairs), cartelization, containing monopoly or oligopoly, economic harmony among industries, promotion or advocacy (of some industry, social value, or point of view), legitimizing parts of the capitalist order, and consumer protection. These functions recognize the inevitability and economic efficiency of very large business organizations, but they also acknowledge the possibilities of economic abuse and the need to protect the smaller, relatively voiceless and powerless components of the society. Clearly these functions are all protective of "the public interest," if one defines the public interest very broadly, to include the needs and desires of consumers, businesspeople, workers, children, government officials, and others.

McCraw reminds us that there is no reason to expect that regulatory philosophy or implementation will be internally consistent across time, across agencies, or even within the same agency. He argues that the definition of public interest changes, and so must the attention of the regulators shift:

> Despite the danger of internal inconsistency, regulators have identified whichever function they wished to emphasize at the moment with the "public interest." They could hardly have done otherwise. Almost nobody ever declares his hostility to the "public interest" (McCraw, 1975:181).

Internal consistency is a characteristic of formal models, not of living, complex social systems. The organic societal metaphor, suggesting that inconsistency (or conflict) is like an aberrant cell that becomes cancerous and rages through the body, fails to take into account the legitimacy of competing and conflicting values, norms, beliefs, desires, and goals. An ecosystem analogy works better, perhaps, in allowing for legitimate conflict within the context of an abstract harmony of interlocking chains of relationships and mutual dependence.

THE LEGITIMACY OF CORPORATE POLITICAL ACTION

In the United States, the legitimacy of capitalistic enterprise as a way of organizing economic activity is not truly in question, and never has been. What is still controversial, however, is the extent to which businesses can participate legitimately in political processes to attempt to gain resources (or access to resources) to further their own interests. If the interests of businesses are truly antithetical to the interests of consumers (and others), how much weight should be given to business's arguments for or against public policy proposals? If these interests are not antithetical, why should businesses not have a full voice in policy matters? The controversy thus centers around the extent to which business interests are opposed to, or compatible with, the interests of other persons, groups, and organizations, and the extent to which business's concentrated economic power can legitimately be brought to bear on a political system that emphasizes (at least in its theory) openness, participation, and "the people's" interests.

We have heard a great deal in recent years about the need of businesses to be "proactive," to plan and act in ways that will help them to achieve desirable futures. Proactivity is a difficult concept for analysts because its content depends very much upon the definition one gives to the outcome, "desirable futures." Desirable for whom, and under what framework? If profit maximization is the definition of a desirable future for businesses, then proactivity would consist of all those activities — including concentrated and well-planned political action — that would foster the maximizing of profit. On the other hand, if capitalistic legitimacy and corporate survival, growth, or success provides the definition of a desirable future, then the content of proactivity can be much broader and can include activities categorized as "corporate social responsibility." This is particularly true if corporate social responsibility is thought of in a forward-looking, op-portunity-seeking, positive way, and not the negative, proscriptive, rigidly moralistic way that has often seemed to characterize CSR thinking (see, for example, Drucker, 1984).

Corporate political action as it is currently being discussed in the scholarly and practitioner-oriented literature is a central feature of a proactive corporate posture toward the business environment. One might expect that corporations having a profit-maximizing orientation would tend to enter the political arena aggressively; that is, their ex-ecutives and lobbyists will talk about "playing hardball" and will ac-tually do so. Corporations with a more long-term or socially respon-sible orientation, on the other hand, should not hesitate to enter the public policy process, but they might be more likely to do so with a better-reasoned, less contentious set of arguments. Negotiations will often be possible (indeed, expected) with either orientation, but the socially responsible corporation should have a larger armament of ac-ceptable outcomes and possible strategies because it is able to see advantage to itself in many potential solutions that combine varying interests, including its own. The profit-maximizing corporation, fo-cusing primarily on the short-term profit and operating effects of pub-lic policy decisions, should have a smaller range of acceptable out-comes available to it, and thus a more rigid bargaining structure.

In the Progressive Era, as we have seen, neither corporate social responsibility nor corporate political action could be thought of as distinct concepts that had any real meaning for public policy process participants. Indeed, these concepts depend on the sectoral model of business-government-society relationships (see Figure 1.1), where the interests of each sector are examined separately to determine their compatibility with or hostility to the interests of the other sec-tors. If we look at the conditions of the Progressive Era in a different way, it becomes evident why neither corporate social responsibility nor corporate political action can truly be relevant concepts in seek-ing to explain business and government interactions during this period.

Figure 6.1 illustrates a way of visualizing the environment of Progressive Era businesses by focusing on three abstract sets of con-ditions that have real and specific outcomes: the economic, social structural, and ideological milieux of an historical period.

The items included in each of the overlapping circles do not by

FIGURE 6.1

An Interlocking Model of the Business Environment in the Progressive Era

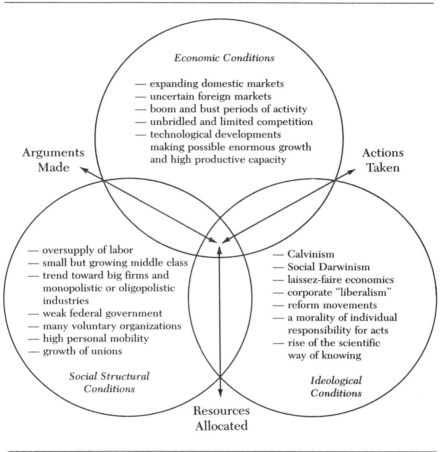

any means represent a comprehensive listing of conditions of the Progressive Era; they merely suggest the kinds of occurrences, trends, and characteristics that might be used to describe prevailing conditions. One of the great values of historical research is that it allows us to understand events of the present in relation to events of the past, and it permits this understanding to be built upon the unique configurations of an historical era that does not look like our own but that guided, informed, and set the pattern for the present.

Any culture or historical period can be understood in terms of the three environmental "sectors" that are mapped in Figure 6.1, although the specific patterns and outcomes will be different for each period. The model combines the structural realities of economic conditions and forms of social organization with the ideological and value-related factors that serve as motivators of human behavior and organizing frameworks for human interpretation and understanding. Only within the area of intersection of these three "subsets" of the social system can we comprehend the outcomes of human behavior (and in our specific case, the outcomes of human behavior in the context of the public policy process): the arguments that are made concerning public policy issues, the actions taken to influence policy formulation and implementation and to comply with policy directives, and the allocation of resources that results from these arguments and actions.

If one puts the "public interest" at the point of three-way intersection in Figure 6.1, it is easier to see how the definition of this concept continues to seem so vague and all-encompassing. The conditions of the Progressive Era dictated that the public interest be defined in terms of businesses, consumers, government, and others as well; perhaps another era — including our own — would display a very different configuration.

CONCLUSION

The Progressive Era stands as a regulatory watershed, a not-so-distant mirror (with apologies to Barbara Tuchman, 1978) that reflects many of our current concerns about business–government relations and especially their apparently adversarial nature (see McCraw, 1984). Increasing public involvement in processes of law and regulation, combined with population and geographic expansion and increasing competitive pressures within many industrial sectors, meant that a host of new needs and desires were placed upon local, state, and federal governments.

The emergence of the federal government as a real force in American economic development opened new opportunities to business leaders to gain competitive advantage. They began during this

period to see that the powers of government could be used as a tool
of strategic planning to reduce the uncertainties of competitive activity. Environmental threats and opportunities expanded from the marketplace to halls of government, and business's access to the policy-
making and policy-implementing processes began to be a critical
component of competitive strategies.

The Pure Food Act's visible significance was in its appeal to both
consumers and businesses as protection against the inefficiencies and
abuses of free-market competition, but it also addressed the needs of
businesses suffering from nothing more than competition itself. In
both symbolic and substantive ways, the law seems to have been a
victory for all except adulterators, misbranders, and, ironically, those
whose newer products threatened the market position of more established firms.

Opportunities for effective political action have not ceased to
present themselves. Businesses today can and do use their influence
in political affairs to bolster their economic positions, to hinder the
progress and the ability to compete of their domestic and foreign
competitors, and to exercise their right to a voice in the affairs of
government. Corporate political activity is not a new phenomenon,
nor can it necessarily be interpreted as a negative indication of societal alienation or organizational impropriety. The roots of business's
political activism are deep and strong, and perhaps that is as it should
be in a pluralistic democracy. Profit, political action, and questions of
legitimacy have been intertwined in this country for at least a century. The future of our democracy and of capitalistic enterprise itself,
however, may depend ultimately upon the degree to which businesses can exercise their right to a political voice in a manner that is
reasonably consistent with a socially responsible, long-term-oriented
view of their place in the larger social system.

appendix A

Census Data on Food, Drug, and Beverage Industries, 1870–1909

Note: The data in these tables were compiled and calculated from information provided in the *Census of Manufactures*, Department of Commerce, Washington, D.C.: U.S. Government Printing Office, 1870, 1880, 1890, 1900, 1904, and 1909.

TABLE A.1

All Industries

YEAR	NUMBER OF ESTABLISHMENTS	NUMBER OF EMPLOYEES		
		Adult Males	Adult Females	Children
1870	252,148	1,615,598	323,770	114,628
1880	253,852	2,019,035	531,639	181,921
1890	355,415	3,327,042	803,686	120,885
1900	512,254	4,110,527	1,029,296	168,583
1904*	216,180			
1909*	268,491			

	NUMBER OF EMPLOYEES			
	Proprietors	Salaried Employees	Wage Earners	TOTAL EMPLOYEES
1870				2,053,996
1880				2,732,595
1890		461,009	4,251,613	4,712,622
1900		396,759	5,308,406	5,705,165
1904	255,673	519,556	5,468,383	6,213,612
1909	273,265	790,267	6,615,046	7,678,578

	CAPITAL** (thousand $)	SALARIES (thousand $)	WAGES (thousand $)	COST OF MATERIALS (thousand $)	VALUE OF PRODUCTS (thousand $)
1870	2,118,209		775,584	2,488,427	4,232,325
1880	2,790,273		947,954	3,396,824	5,369,579
1890	6,525,156	391,988	1,891,228	5,793,269	9,372,437
1900	9,817,435	403,711	2,322,334	8,373,170	13,004,400
1904	12,675,581	574,439	2,610,445	8,500,208	14,793,903
1909	18,428,270	938,575	3,427,038	12,142,791	20,672,052

*The 1904 and 1909 Census data omit many industry classifications that were found in the 1870–1900 censuses. In most cases the omitted industries have been grouped with other industries; in a few cases, industry categories seem to have disappeared altogether.

**Financial data have been rounded to the nearest thousand.

TABLE A.2

*Baking and Yeast Powders**

| | | NUMBER OF EMPLOYEES | | |
| | NUMBER OF | Adult | Adult | |
YEAR	ESTABLISHMENTS	Males	Females	Children
1870	30	167	58	10
1880	110	660	326	56
1890	150	873	543	25
1900	191	959	946	33
1904	164			
1909	144			

NUMBER OF EMPLOYEES

	Proprietors	Salaried Employees	Wage Earners	TOTAL EMPLOYEES
1870				235
1880			1,042	1,042
1890		426	1,441	1,867
1900		749	1,938	2,687
1904	150	756	2,449	3,355
1909	110	1,266	2,155	3,531

	CAPITAL** (thousand $)	SALARIES (thousand $)	WAGES (thousand $)	COST OF MATERIALS (thousand $)	VALUE OF PRODUCTS (thousand $)
1870	249		88	601	895
1880	1,351		466	3,334	4,761
1890	3,588	427	574	4,980	7,407
1900	8,338	835	717	9,559	14,568
1904	13,233	939	1,042	8,940	19,043
1909	33,647	1,710	1,046	9,338	20,775

*Census categories are "baking powders" for 1870, "baking and yeast powders" for 1880 and beyond.

**Financial data have been rounded to the nearest thousand.

TABLE A.3

Bottling*

YEAR	NUMBER OF ESTABLISHMENTS	NUMBER OF EMPLOYEES		
		Adult Males	Adult Females	Children
1870	20	82	1	6
1880				
1890	716	2,904	58	82
1900	2,064	7,135	136	409
1904				
1909				

	NUMBER OF EMPLOYEES			TOTAL EMPLOYEES
	Proprietors	Salaried Employees	Wage Earners	
1870				89
1880				
1890		885	3,044	3,929
1900		987	7,680	8,667
1904				
1909				

	CAPITAL** (thousand $)	SALARIES (thousand $)	WAGES (thousand $)	COST OF MATERIALS (thousand $)	VALUE OF PRODUCTS (thousand $)
1870	473		28	56	157
1880					
1890	5,657	760	1,512	8,665	13,583
1900	16,620	917	3,589	30,551	41,641
1904					
1909					

*1870: "Bottling, malt liquors, and mineral waters"; 1880: no data; 1890, 1900: "Bottling"; 1904, 1909: no category.

**Financial data have been rounded to the nearest thousand.

TABLE A.4

Bread, Crackers, Bakery Goods

| | | NUMBER OF EMPLOYEES | | |
YEAR	NUMBER OF ESTABLISHMENTS	Adult Males	Adult Females	Children
1870	3,550	12,598	842	686
1880	6,396	18,925	2,210	1,353
1890	10,484	33,345	4,672	824
1900	14,917	47,926	10,452	1,893
1904	18,226			
1909	23,926			

| | NUMBER OF EMPLOYEES | | | |
	Proprietors	Salaried Employees	Wage Earners	TOTAL EMPLOYEES
1870				14,126
1880			22,488	22,488
1890		13,921	38,841	52,762
1900		9,177	60,271	69,448
1904	20,037	8,358	81,278	109,673
1909	26,982	17,124	100,216	144,322

	CAPITAL* (thousand $)	SALARIES (thousand $)	WAGES (thousand $)	COST OF MATERIALS (thousand $)	VALUE OF PRODUCTS (thousand $)
1870	10,026		5,353	22,212	36,908
1880	19,155		9,411	42,612	65,825
1890	45,758	9,669	19,120	78,896	128,422
1900	81,050	6,067	27,893	105,650	175,657
1904	122,353	6,273	43,172	155,989	269,583
1909	212,910	13,764	59,351	238,034	396,865

*Financial data have been rounded to the nearest thousand.

TABLE A.5

*Butter, Cheese**

		NUMBER OF EMPLOYEES		
		---	---	---
YEAR	NUMBER OF ESTABLISHMENTS	Adult Males	Adult Females	Children
1870	1,313	3,272	1,279	56
1880	3,932	6,419	1,330	154
1890	4,712	11,775	725	101
1900	9,355	11,694	1,049	122
1904	8,926			
1909	8,479			

	NUMBER OF EMPLOYEES			
	Proprietors	Salaried Employees	Wage Earners	TOTAL EMPLOYEES
1870				4,607
1880			9,724	9,724
1890		1,914	15,038	16,952
1900		2,123	19,054	21,177
1904	6,801	3,507	15,557	25,865
1909	8,019	5,056	18,431	31,506

	CAPITAL** (thousand $)	SALARIES (thousand $)	WAGES (thousand $)	COST OF MATERIALS (thousand $)	VALUE OF PRODUCTS (thousand $)
1870	3,690		707	14,089	16,772
1880	28,983		4,223	18,364	25,743
1890	55,032	2,383	7,308	51,365	62,686
1900	89,091	2,923	9,401	109,151	131,199
1904	47,256	1,376	8,413	142,920	168,183
1909	71,284	3,591	11,081	235,546	274,558

*1870: "Cheese"; 1880–1909: "Cheese, Butter, and Condensed Milk."
**Financial data have been rounded to the nearest thousand.

TABLE A.6

*Chocolate and Cocoa Products**

| | | NUMBER OF EMPLOYEES | | |
YEAR	NUMBER OF ESTABLISHMENTS	Adult Males	Adult Females	Children
1870	9	104	87	8
1880	7	110	113	
1890	11	544	343	6
1900	24	688	592	34
1904	25			
1909	27			

| | | NUMBER OF EMPLOYEES | | |
	Proprietors	Salaried Employees	Wage Earners	TOTAL EMPLOYEES
1870				199
1880			223	223
1890		70	893	963
1900		289	1,314	1,603
1904	15	291	2,090	2,396
1909	10	568	2,826	3,404

	CAPITAL** (thousand $)	SALARIES (thousand $)	WAGES (thousand $)	COST OF MATERIALS (thousand $)	VALUE OF PRODUCTS (thousand $)
1870	377		79	665	946
1880	531		82	812	1,302
1890	2,630	141	456	3,125	4,222
1900	6,891	371	526	7,650	9,666
1904	8,379	463	822	9,723	14,390
1909	13,685	970	1,269	15,523	22,390

*1870: "Chocolate."
**Financial data have been rounded to the nearest thousand.

TABLE A.7

*Canning and Preserving**

YEAR	NUMBER OF ESTABLISHMENTS	NUMBER OF EMPLOYEES		
		Adult Males	Adult Females	Children
1870	311	3,839	4,516	1,133
1880	520	11,501	15,775	5,962
1890	1,314	25,974	29,407	6,332
1900	2,839	29,887	15,974	4,883
1904	3,934			
1909	4,980			

	Proprietors	NUMBER OF EMPLOYEES		TOTAL EMPLOYEES
		Salaried Employees	Wage Earners	
1870				9,488
1880			33,238	33,238
1890		2,036	61,713	63,749
1900		3,950	50,744	54,694
1904	4,199	8,285	68,277	80,761
1909	5,375	12,626	74,936	92,937

	CAPITAL** (thousand $)	SALARIES (thousand $)	WAGES (thousand $)	COST OF MATERIALS (thousand $)	VALUE OF PRODUCTS (thousand $)
1870	4,629		1,689	7,214	12,112
1880	9,541		2,998	13,656	20,093
1890	26,325	1,376	6,630	36,127	54,200
1900	69,496	3,397	15,962	84,008	121,050
1904	131,030	8,230	20,734	120,815	191,646
1909	183,892	13,729	26,125	185,765	282,432

*Combines the following categories. 1870: fish, cured and packed, oysters; food preparations — animal, vegetable, vermicelli/macaroni; fruits and vegetables, canned and preserved; 1880–1900: fish, canning and preserving, food preparations, fruits and vegetables, canning and preserving; oysters, canning and preserving; 1904–1909: canning and preserving; food preparations.
**Financial data have been rounded to the nearest thousand.

TABLE A.8

Cider and Vinegar*

YEAR	NUMBER OF ESTABLISHMENTS	NUMBER OF EMPLOYEES		
		Adult Males	Adult Females	Children
1870	728	1,992	7	42
1880	306	1,160	44	53
1890	694	2,452	155	30
1900	1,152	1,643	136	22
1904	568			
1909	963			

	NUMBER OF EMPLOYEES			
	Proprietors	Salaried Employees	Wage Earners	TOTAL EMPLOYEES
1870				2,041
1880			1,257	1,257
1890		751	2,637	3,388
1900		456	1,801	2,257
1904	645	341	1,528	2,514
1909	1,050	481	1,542	3,073

	CAPITAL** (thousand $)	SALARIES (thousand $)	WAGES (thousand $)	COST OF MATERIALS (thousand $)	VALUE OF PRODUCTS (thousand $)
1870	1,845		319	1,020	3,472
1880	2,152		413	1,888	3,418
1890	5,858	428	721	3,624	6,649
1900	6,188	392	720	3,652	6,455
1904	7,520	359	725	3,852	7,265
1909	10,879	539	723	4,964	8,448

*Cider and Vinegar were separate categories in 1870 and were combined thereafter.

**Financial data have been rounded to the nearest thousand.

TABLE A.9

Coffee and Spices

		NUMBER OF EMPLOYEES		
YEAR	NUMBER OF ESTABLISHMENTS	Adult Males	Adult Females	Children
1870	156	1,054	100	66
1880	300	2,125	438	153
1890	358	2,751	941	74
1900	458	3,455	2,809	123
1904	421			
1909	607			

	NUMBER OF EMPLOYEES			
	Proprietors	Salaried Employees	Wage Earners	TOTAL EMPLOYEES
1870				1,220
1880			2,716	2,716
1890		1,356	3,766	5,122
1900		2,749	6,387	9,136
1904	442	2,844	5,959	9,245
1909	497	5,529	7,490	13,516

	CAPITAL* (thousand $)	SALARIES (thousand $)	WAGES (thousand $)	COST OF MATERIALS (thousand $)	VALUE OF PRODUCTS (thousand $)
1870	3,846		671	8,172	11,266
1880	6,366		1,371	18,201	22,925
1890	16,996	1,447	1,816	67,191	75,042
1900	28,437	2,951	2,487	58,547	69,527
1904	38,735	3,216	2,830	65,847	84,188
1909	46,042	6,596	3,676	83,205	110,533

*Financial data have been rounded to the nearest thousand.

TABLE A.10

Confectionery

YEAR	NUMBER OF ESTABLISHMENTS	NUMBER OF EMPLOYEES		
		Adult Males	Adult Females	Children
1870	949	4,151	1,225	449
1880	1,450	6,157	2,827	817
1890	2,921	11,882	9,254	588
1900	4,297	15,855	15,849	1,879
1904	1,348			
1909	1,944			

	NUMBER OF EMPLOYEES			
	Proprietors	Salaried Employees	Wage Earners	TOTAL EMPLOYEES
1870				5,825
1880			9,801	9,801
1890		5,487	21,724	27,211
1900		5,628	33,583	39,211
1904	1,366	5,124	36,239	42,729
1909	1,832	8,384	44,638	54,854

	CAPITAL* (thousand $)	SALARIES (thousand $)	WAGES (thousand $)	COST OF MATERIALS (thousand $)	VALUE OF PRODUCTS (thousand $)
1870	4,995		2,092	8,704	15,923
1880	8,487		3,243	17,126	25,637
1890	23,327	3,850	7,783	34,420	55,997
1900	35,155	4,171	10,868	51,546	81,291
1904	43,125	4,840	11,699	48,810	87,087
1909	68,326	9,137	15,615	81,151	134,796

*Financial data have been rounded to the nearest thousand.

TABLE A.11

Cordials and Syrups

		NUMBER OF EMPLOYEES		
YEAR	NUMBER OF ESTABLISHMENTS	Adult Males	Adult Females	Children
1870	33	185	51	22
1880	16	81		
1890	40	202	58	21
1900	39	228	130	4
1904	63			
1909	117			

	NUMBER OF EMPLOYEES			
	Proprietors	Salaried Employees	Wage Earners	TOTAL EMPLOYEES
1870				258
1880			81	81
1890		106	281	387
1900		112	362	474
1904	68	171	660	899
1909	94	449	1,095	1,638

	CAPITAL* (thousand $)	SALARIES (thousand $)	WAGES (thousand $)	COST OF MATERIALS (thousand $)	VALUE OF PRODUCTS (thousand $)
1870	527		119	505	955
1880	128		43	211	331
1890	784	122	111	1,352	1,903
1900	1,153	121	117	1,663	2,107
1904	1,666	242	235	2,149	3,510
1909	4,804	627	503	5,341	9,662

*Financial data have been rounded to the nearest thousand.

TABLE A.12

Drugs* (All Categories)

YEAR	NUMBER OF ESTABLISHMENTS	NUMBER OF EMPLOYEES		
		Adult Males	Adult Females	Children
1870	611	5,693	1,083	389
1880**	563	2,504	1,186	335
1890	2,932	6,004	2,879	206
1900	2,276	8,198	9,111	266
1904	2,777			
1909	3,642			

	NUMBER OF EMPLOYEES			
	Proprietors	Salaried Employees	Wage Earners	TOTAL EMPLOYEES
1870				7,165
1880			4,025	4,025
1890		4,241	9,089	13,330
1900		7,465	17,575	25,040
1904	2,293	9,483	20,472	32,248
1909	2,802	15,404	22,895	41,101

	CAPITAL*** (thousand \$)	SALARIES (thousand \$)	WAGES (thousand \$)	COST OF MATERIALS (thousand \$)	VALUE OF PRODUCTS (thousand \$)
1870	19,419		3,159	19,001	35,675
1880	10,621		1,652	6,705	14,682
1890	23,222	3,238	3,795	21,170	39,280
1900	53,530	7,605	6,449	50,596	82,804
1904	75,607	9,975	7,913	39,494	117,436
1909	99,942	17,007	9,897	50,376	141,942

*Includes, 1870: Drugs and chemicals, Patent medicines and compounds; 1880–1900: Druggists' preparations, Patent medicines and compounds; 1904–1909: Patent medicines and compounds, Druggists' preparations.

**Chemicals are excluded from 1880 on. No data were available on "Druggists' preparations" for 1880.

***Financial data have been rounded to the nearest thousand.

TABLE A.13

Patent Medicines

		NUMBER OF EMPLOYEES		
YEAR	NUMBER OF ESTABLISHMENTS	Adult Males	Adult Females	Children
1870	319	1,667	631	138
1880	563	2,504	1,186	335
1890	1,127	4,231	2,670	157
1900	2,026	5,598	6,001	210
1904	2,777			
1909	3,642			

	NUMBER OF EMPLOYEES			
	Proprietors	Salaried Employees	Wage Earners	TOTAL EMPLOYEES
1870				2,436
1880			4,025	4,025
1890		2,332	7,058	9,390
1900		5,419	11,809	17,228
1904	2,293	9,483	20,472	32,248
1909	2,802	15,404	22,895	41,101

	CAPITAL* (thousand $)	SALARIES (thousand $)	WAGES (thousand $)	COST OF MATERIALS (thousand $)	VALUE OF PRODUCTS (thousand $)
1870	6,668		1,018	7,320	16,258
1880	10,621		1,652	6,705	14,682
1890	18,597	2,139	2,955	18,094	32,620
1900	37,210	5,330	4,408	36,214	59,611
1904	75,607	9,975	7,913	39,494	117,436
1909	99,942	17,007	9,897	50,376	141,942

*Financial data have been rounded to the nearest thousand.

TABLE A.14

Dyewoods, Stuffs, Extracts

YEAR	NUMBER OF ESTABLISHMENTS	NUMBER OF EMPLOYEES		
		Adult Males	Adult Females	Children
1870	19	517	5	26
1880	41	976	10	6
1890	62	2,099	4	8
1900	71	1,607	35	5
1904	98			
1909	107			

	NUMBER OF EMPLOYEES			TOTAL EMPLOYEES
	Proprietors	Salaried Employees	Wage Earners	
1870				548
1880			992	992
1890		191	2,111	2,302
1900		229	1,647	1,876
1904	82	361	2,707	3,150
1909	65	553	2,397	3,015

	CAPITAL* (thousand $)	SALARIES (thousand $)	WAGES (thousand $)	COST OF MATERIALS (thousand $)	VALUE OF PRODUCTS (thousand $)
1870	1,228		301	1,275	2,053
1880	2,364		512	3,919	5,253
1890	8,645	252	1,038	6,881	9,293
1900	7,839	312	788	5,204	7,351
1904	14,904	609	1,264	6,829	10,893
1909	17,935	942	1,291	9,684	15,955

*Financial data have been rounded to the nearest thousand.

TABLE A.15

Flour and Grist Mill Products

		NUMBER OF EMPLOYEES		
YEAR	NUMBER OF ESTABLISHMENTS	Adult Males	Adult Females	Children
1870	22,573	57,795	91	562
1880	24,338	38,239	42	126
1890	18,470	47,889	308	206
1900	25,258	36,419	497	157
1904	10,051			
1909	11,691			

	NUMBER OF EMPLOYEES			
	Proprietors	Salaried Employees	Wage Earners	TOTAL EMPLOYEES
1870				58,448
1880			58,407	58,407
1890		16,078	47,403	63,481
1900		5,790	37,073	42,863
1904	13,098	7,415	39,110	59,623
1909	14,570	12,031	39,453	66,054

	CAPITAL* (thousand $)	SALARIES (thousand $)	WAGES (thousand $)	COST OF MATERIALS (thousand $)	VALUE OF PRODUCTS (thousand $)
1870	151,565		14,578	367,392	444,985
1880	177,362		17,422	441,545	505,186
1890	208,474	8,897	18,138	447,354	513,917
1900	218,714	5,405	17,703	486,152	560,719
1904	265,117	7,352	19,822	619,971	713,033
1909	349,152	12,517	21,464	767,576	883,584

*Financial data have been rounded to the nearest thousand.

TABLE A.16

Flavoring Extracts

| YEAR | NUMBER OF ESTABLISHMENTS | NUMBER OF EMPLOYEES | | |
		Adult Males	Adult Females	Children
1870				
1880	58	238	104	32
1890	148	341	150	16
1900	352	653	573	28
1904	377			
1909	420			

| | NUMBER OF EMPLOYEES | | | |
	Proprietors	Salaried Employees	Wage Earners	TOTAL EMPLOYEES
1870				
1880			374	374
1890		262	507	769
1900		594	1,254	1,848
1904	384	672	1,543	2,599
1909	377	1,028	1,229	2,634

	CAPITAL* (thousand $)	SALARIES (thousand $)	WAGES (thousand $)	COST OF MATERIALS (thousand $)	VALUE OF PRODUCTS (thousand $)
1870					
1880	405		129	796	1,196
1890	1,362	233	209	1,584	2,615
1900	3,320	654	479	3,756	6,315
1904	4,405	698	653	3,936	7,772
1909	5,341	1,082	558	4,458	8,828

*Financial data have been rounded to the nearest thousand.

TABLE A.17

Glucose

YEAR	NUMBER OF ESTABLISHMENTS	NUMBER OF EMPLOYEES		
		Adult Males	Adult Females	Children
1870				
1880	7	1,167	5	20
1890	7	1,719	5	
1900	8	3,266	22	
1904*				
1909*				

	NUMBER OF EMPLOYEES			
	Proprietors	Salaried Employees	Wage Earners	TOTAL EMPLOYEES
1870				
1880			1,192	1,192
1890		35	1,724	1,759
1900		147	3,288	3,435
1904				
1909				

	CAPITAL** (thousand $)	SALARIES (thousand $)	WAGES (thousand $)	COST OF MATERIALS (thousand $)	VALUE OF PRODUCTS (thousand $)
1870					
1880	2,255		606	3,044	4,551
1890	5,991	72	902	5,953	7,757
1900	41,011	280	1,755	16,419	21,694
1904					
1909					

*Glucose and starch are combined in 1904 and 1909; no reliable data are available for glucose only for these years.

**Financial data have been rounded to the nearest thousand.

TABLE A.18

Lard*

YEAR	NUMBER OF ESTABLISHMENTS	NUMBER OF EMPLOYEES		
		Adult Males	Adult Females	Children
1870				
1880	26	1,030	46	105
1890	17	686	141	61
1900	19	438	20	41
1904	9			
1909	7			

	NUMBER OF EMPLOYEES			
	Proprietors	Salaried Employees	Wage Earners	TOTAL EMPLOYEES
1870				
1880			1,181	1,181
1890		130	888	1,018
1900		54	499	553
1904	10	77	441	528
1909	6	110	399	515

	CAPITAL** (thousand $)	SALARIES (thousand $)	WAGES (thousand $)	COST OF MATERIALS (thousand $)	VALUE OF PRODUCTS (thousand $)
1870					
1880	2,513		546	21,949	23,196
1890	3,899	188	460	13,499	15,475
1900	1,336	80	238	7,924	8,631
1904	1,163	108	219	5,640	6,129
1909	1,434	108	180	9,631	10,326

*For 1904 and 1909 the category is qualified by "not made in slaughtering and meatpacking establishments." Data for 1899 under this category are identical to data for 1900 under the previous category, "Lard, refined."

**Financial data have been rounded to the nearest thousand.

TABLE A.19

Malt

YEAR	NUMBER OF ESTABLISHMENTS	NUMBER OF EMPLOYEES		
		Adult Males	Adult Females	Children
1870	208	1,634	0	6
1880	216	2,320	8	4
1890	202	3,328	0	0
1900	146	1,986	4	0
1904	141			
1909	114			

	NUMBER OF EMPLOYEES			TOTAL EMPLOYEES
	Proprietors	Salaried Employees	Wage Earners	
1870				1,640
1880			2,332	2,332
1890		366	3,328	3,694
1900		290	1,990	2,280
1904	96	444	2,054	2,594
1909	52	425	1,760	2,237

	CAPITAL** (thousand $)	SALARIES (thousand $)	WAGES (thousand $)	COST OF MATERIALS (thousand $)	VALUE OF PRODUCTS (thousand $)
1870	8,017		701	9,002	12,017
1880	14,390		1,005	14,321	18,273
1890	24,294	513	1,590	18,405	23,443
1900	39,288	471	1,183	15,734	19,374
1904	47,934	747	1,457	23,621	30,289
1909	60,286	884	1,348	30,646	38,252

*Financial data have been rounded to the nearest thousand.

TABLE A.20

Liquors, Distilled

| | | NUMBER OF EMPLOYEES | | |
| | | Adult | Adult | |
YEAR	NUMBER OF ESTABLISHMENTS	Males	Females	Children
1870	719	5,068	6	57
1880	844	6,452	10	40
1890	440	4,753	3	6
1900	967	3,623	81	18
1904	805			
1909	613			

| | | NUMBER OF EMPLOYEES | | |
	Proprietors	Salaried Employees	Wage Earners	TOTAL EMPLOYEES
1870				5,131
1880			6,502	6,502
1890		581	4,762	5,343
1900		661	3,722	4,383
1904	794	1,080	5,355	7,229
1909	563	1,335	6,430	8,328

	CAPITAL* (thousand $)	SALARIES (thousand $)	WAGES (thousand $)	COST OF MATERIALS (thousand $)	VALUE OF PRODUCTS (thousand $)
1870	15,545		2,020	19,729	36,191
1880	24,248		2,664	27,744	41,064
1890	31,006	569	2,246	80,089	104,198
1900	32,552	890	1,733	88,366	96,798
1904	50,101	1,393	2,657	25,626	131,270
1909	72,450	1,988	3,074	35,977	204,699

*Financial data have been rounded to the nearest thousand.

TABLE A.21

Liquors, Malt

| YEAR | NUMBER OF ESTABLISHMENTS | NUMBER OF EMPLOYEES | | |
		Adult Males	Adult Females	Children
1870	1,972	12,320	29	94
1880	2,191	26,001	29	190
1890	1,248	29,491	250	516
1900	1,509	38,385	504	643
1904	1,530			
1909	1,414			

| | NUMBER OF EMPLOYEES | | | TOTAL EMPLOYEES |
	Proprietors	Salaried Employees	Wage Earners	
1870				12,443
1880			26,220	26,220
1890		4,543	30,257	34,800
1900		7,153	39,532	41,953
1904	876	9,055	48,137	58,068
1909	639	11,507	54,579	66,725

	CAPITAL* (thousand $)	SALARIES (thousand $)	WAGES (thousand $)	COST OF MATERIALS (thousand $)	VALUE OF PRODUCTS (thousand $)
1870	48,779		6,759	28,178	55,707
1880	91,208		12,198	56,837	101,058
1890	232,471	7,669	20,713	112,280	182,732
1900	415,284	13,047	25,826	161,004	237,270
1904	515,630	17,316	34,541	74,907	298,346
1909	671,158	22,804	41,206	96,596	374,730

*Financial data have been rounded to the nearest thousand.

TABLE A.22

Liquors, Vinous

		NUMBER OF EMPLOYEES		
YEAR	NUMBER OF ESTABLISHMENTS	Adult Males	Adult Females	Children
1870	398	1,426	32	28
1880	117	781	57	129
1890	236	1,016	26	6
1900	359	1,099	61	3
1904	435			
1909	290			

	NUMBER OF EMPLOYEES			
	Proprietors	Salaried Employees	Wage Earners	TOTAL EMPLOYEES
1870				1,486
1880			967	967
1890		234	1,048	1,282
1900		344	1,163	1,507
1904	396	492	1,913	2,801
1909	236	579	1,911	2,726

	CAPITAL* (thousand $)	SALARIES (thousand $)	WAGES (thousand $)	COST OF MATERIALS (thousand $)	VALUE OF PRODUCTS (thousand $)
1870	2,334		231	1,203	2,225
1880	2,582		217	1,341	2,169
1890	5,793	181	299	1,588	2,846
1900	9,838	365	446	4,242	6,547
1904	17,775	573	1,002	5,693	11,098
1909	27,908	863	972	6,626	13,121

*Financial data have been rounded to the nearest thousand.

TABLE A.23

*Meat, Cured and Packed**

		NUMBER OF EMPLOYEES		
YEAR	NUMBER OF ESTABLISHMENTS	Adult Males	Adult Females	Children
1870	259	6,055	191	239
1880	872	26,113	0	1,184
1890	1,367	43,097	1,011	704
1900	1,134	64,810	2,960	1,671
1904	1,221			
1909	1,641			

	NUMBER OF EMPLOYEES		
	Proprietors	Salaried Employees	Wage Earners	TOTAL EMPLOYEES
---	---	---	---	---
1870				6,485
1880			27,297	27,297
1890		4,240	44,812	49,052
1900		10,290	69,441	79,731
1904	1,324	12,096	75,399	88,819
1909	1,659	17,329	89,728	108,716

	CAPITAL** (thousand $)	SALARIES (thousand $)	WAGES (thousand $)	COST OF MATERIALS (thousand $)	VALUE OF PRODUCTS (thousand $)
1870	22,125		2,007	50,634	62,140
1880	49,419		10,509	267,739	303,562
1890	118,016	4,735	24,668	498,730	564,667
1900	190,707	10,179	33,923	711,061	790,253
1904	240,419	13,453	41,067	811,426	922,038
1909	383,429	20,054	51,645	1,202,828	1,370,568

*For 1870 three subcategories are combined here — "unspecified," "beef," and "pork." For 1880–1900 the census category is "slaughtering and meatpacking, excluding retail butchers." The qualifying phrase is dropped for 1904–1909.

**Financial data have been rounded to the nearest thousand.

TABLE A.24

Mineral and Soda Waters

| | | NUMBER OF EMPLOYEES | | |
| | | Adult | Adult | |
YEAR	NUMBER OF ESTABLISHMENTS	Males	Females	Children
1870	387	2,128	16	239
1880	512	2,480	27	219
1890	1,377	5,642	100	177
1900	2,816	8,380	309	296
1904	3,468			
1909	4,916			

NUMBER OF EMPLOYEES

	Proprietors	Salaried Employees	Wage Earners	TOTAL EMPLOYEES
1870				2,383
1880			2,726	2,726
1890		1,798	5,919	7,717
1900		1,464	8,985	10,449
1904	4,099	1,576	10,879	16,544
1909	5,743	3,170	13,147	22,060

	CAPITAL* (thousand $)	SALARIES (thousand $)	WAGES (thousand $)	COST OF MATERIALS (thousand $)	VALUE OF PRODUCTS (thousand $)
1870	3,642		924	1,688	4,222
1880	2,570		1,066	2,118	4,742
1890	10,782	1,427	2,780	4,563	14,354
1900	20,519	1,203	4,169	8,801	23,874
1904	28,098	1,393	5,488	10,002	30,251
1909	42,305	2,846	6,902	16,466	43,508

*Financial data have been rounded to the nearest thousand.

TABLE A.25

Oil, Cottonseed

		NUMBER OF EMPLOYEES		
YEAR	NUMBER OF ESTABLISHMENTS	Adult Males	Adult Females	Children
1870	26	639	10	15
1880	45	3,114	53	172
1890	119	5,814	55	87
1900	369	10,936	54	17
1904	715			
1909	817			

	NUMBER OF EMPLOYEES			
	Proprietors	Salaried Employees	Wage Earners	TOTAL EMPLOYEES
1870				664
1880			3,339	3,339
1890		395	5,906	6,301
1900		1,569	11,007	12,576
1904	63	3,229	15,540	18,832
1909	110	4,092	17,071	21,273

	CAPITAL* (thousand $)	SALARIES (thousand $)	WAGES (thousand $)	COST OF MATERIALS (thousand $)	VALUE OF PRODUCTS (thousand $)
1870	1,225		292	1,334	2,206
1880	3,862		881	5,091	7,691
1890	12,809	414	1,494	15,527	19,336
1900	34,451	1,579	3,143	47,600	58,727
1904	73,770	3,062	4,838	80,030	96,408
1909	91,086	4,295	5,835	119,833	147,868

*Financial data have been rounded to the nearest thousand.

TABLE A.26

Oleomargarine

		NUMBER OF EMPLOYEES		
YEAR	NUMBER OF ESTABLISHMENTS	Adult Males	Adult Females	Children
1870				
1880	15	561	18	20
1890	12	252	11	1
1900	24	1,007	65	12
1904	14			
1909	12			

		NUMBER OF EMPLOYEES		
	Proprietors	Salaried Employees	Wage Earners	TOTAL EMPLOYEES
1870				
1880			599	599
1890		64	264	328
1900		394	1,084	1,478
1904	2	206	522	730
1909	1	166	606	773

	CAPITAL* (thousand $)	SALARIES (thousand $)	WAGES (thousand $)	COST OF MATERIALS (thousand $)	VALUE OF PRODUCTS (thousand $)
1870					
1880	1,680		213	5,486	6,893
1890	635	92	154	2,561	2,989
1900	3,024	412	534	10,129	12,500
1904	1,551	253	316	4,398	5,574
1909	3,558	276	413	6,497	8,148

*Financial data have been rounded to the nearest thousand.

TABLE A.27

Pickles, Preserves, and Sauces*

YEAR	NUMBER OF ESTABLISHMENTS	NUMBER OF EMPLOYEES		
		Adult Males	Adult Females	Children
1870	30	195	121	19
1880	109	592	230	108
1890	316	1,964	1,585	28
1900	474	3,606	3,081	125
1904				
1909				

	NUMBER OF EMPLOYEES			
	Proprietors	Salaried Employees	Wage Earners	TOTAL EMPLOYEES
1870				335
1880			930	930
1890		675	3,577	4,252
1900		1,845	6,812	8,657
1904				
1909				

	CAPITAL** (thousand $)	SALARIES (thousand $)	WAGES (thousand $)	COST OF MATERIALS (thousand $)	VALUE OF PRODUCTS (thousand $)
1870	411		113	845	1,243
1880	841		259	1,473	2,407
1890	4,913	608	1,159	5,857	9,791
1900	10,657	1,652	2,162	14,677	21,507
1904					
1909					

*1870: "Preserves and sauces"; 1880–1900: "Pickles, preserves, and sauces"; 1904–1909: no category.

**Financial data have been rounded to the nearest thousand.

TABLE A.28

Rice, Cleaning and Polishing

| | | NUMBER OF EMPLOYEES | | |
YEAR	NUMBER OF ESTABLISHMENTS	Adult Males	Adult Females	Children
1870				
1880	22	376	94	46
1890	32	630	9	8
1900	80	639		12
1904	74			
1909	71			

| | | NUMBER OF EMPLOYEES | | |
	Proprietors	Salaried Employees	Wage Earners	TOTAL EMPLOYEES
1870				
1880			516	516
1890		96	647	743
1900		169	651	820
1904	33	436	1,492	1,961
1909	38	500	1,239	1,777

	CAPITAL* (thousand $)	SALARIES (thousand $)	WAGES (thousand $)	COST OF MATERIALS (thousand $)	VALUE OF PRODUCTS (thousand $)
1870					
1880	562		110	2,666	3,133
1890	2,074	96	223	5,749	6,693
1900	2,601	182	266	7,806	8,724
1904	8,821	549	641	13,315	16,297
1909	13,347	613	564	19,501	22,371

*Financial data have been rounded to the nearest thousand.

TABLE A.29

Sugar and Molasses, Beet

| | | NUMBER OF EMPLOYEES | | |
YEAR	NUMBER OF ESTABLISHMENTS	Adult Males	Adult Females	Children
1870	2	66	25	25
1880	4	350	0	0
1890				
1900	30	1,951	4	15
1904	51			
1909	58			

| | NUMBER OF EMPLOYEES | | | |
	Proprietors	Salaried Employees	Wage Earners	TOTAL EMPLOYEES
1870				116
1880			350	350
1890				
1900		350	1,970	2,320
1904		763	3,963	4,726
1909	1	1,184	7,204	8,389

	CAPITAL* (thousand $)	SALARIES (thousand $)	WAGES (thousand $)	COST OF MATERIALS (thousand $)	VALUE OF PRODUCTS (thousand $)
1870	67		8	91	120
1880	365		62	186	283
1890					
1900	20,142	357	1,092	5,245	7,324
1904	55,923	1,005	2,487	14,487	24,394
1909	129,629	1,769	4,808	27,265	48,122

*Financial data have been rounded to the nearest thousand.

TABLE A.30

Sugar and Molasses, Cane

| | | NUMBER OF EMPLOYEES | | |
| | NUMBER OF | Adult | Adult | |
YEAR	ESTABLISHMENTS	Males	Females	Children
1870	1,089	21,255	3,868	1,942
1880	49	5,832	0	25
1890	393	6,697	246	100
1900	832	13,644	422	196
1904	344			
1909	233			

| | | NUMBER OF EMPLOYEES | | |
	Proprietors	Salaried Employees	Wage Earners	TOTAL EMPLOYEES
1870				27,065
1880			5,857	5,857
1890		486	7,043	7,529
1900		1,881	14,262	16,143
1904	364	1,886	13,549	15,799
1909	204	1,928	13,526	15,658

	CAPITAL* (thousand $)	SALARIES (thousand $)	WAGES (thousand $)	COST OF MATERIALS (thousand $)	VALUE OF PRODUCTS (thousand $)
1870	30,937		3,225	97,152	119,669
1880	27,433		2,875	144,698	155,485
1890	24,013	430	2,386	113,680	123,118
1900	184,246	1,697	6,946	229,539	240,970
1904	165,468	2,154	7,576	244,753	277,285
1909	153,167	2,392	7,484	247,583	279,249

*Financial data have been rounded to the nearest thousand.

The Pure Food Act: Public Law No. 384, June 30, 1906; and Pure Food Act, Expenses: Public Law No. 2, December 19, 1906

The Pure Food Act:
Public Law No. 384, June 30, 1906

CHAP. 3915.-- An Act for preventing the manufacture, sale, or transportation of adulterated or misbranded or poisonous or deleterious foods, drugs, medicines, and liquors, and for regulating traffic therein, and for other purposes.

Be it enacted by the Senate and House of Representatives of the United States of America in Congress assembled, That it shall be unlawful for any person to manufacture within any Territory or the District of Columbia any article of food or drug which is adulterated or misbranded, within the meaning of this Act; and any person who shall violate any of the provisions of this section shall be guilty of a misdemeanor, and for each offense shall, upon conviction thereof, be fined not to exceed five hundred dollars or shall be sentenced to one year's imprisonment, or both such fine and imprisonment, in the discretion of the court, and for each subsequent offense and conviction thereof shall be fined not less than one thousand dollars or sentenced to one year's imprisonment, or both such fine and imprisonment, in the discretion of the court.

SEC. 2.   That the introduction into any State or Territory or the District of Columbia from any other State or Territory or the District of Columbia, or from any foreign country, or shipment to any foreign country of any article of food or drug which is adulterated or misbranded, within the meaning of this Act, is hereby prohibited; and any person who shall ship or deliver for shipment from a State or Territory or the District of Columbia to any other State or Territory or the District of Columbia, or to a foreign country, or who shall receive in any State or Territory or the District of Columbia from any other State or Territory or the District of Columbia, or foreign country, and having so received, shall deliver, in original unbroken packages, for pay or otherwise, or offer to deliver to any other person, any such article so adulterated or misbranded within the meaning of this Act, or any person who shall sell or offer for sale in the District of Columbia or the Territories of the United States any such adulterated or misbranded foods or drugs, or export or offer to export the same to any foreign country, shall be guilty of a misdemeanor, and for such offense be fined not exceeding two hundred dollars for the first offense, and upon conviction for each subsequent offense not exceeding three hundred dollars or be imprisoned not exceeding one year, or both, in the discretion of the court: *Provided,* That no article shall be deemed misbranded or adulterated within the provisions of this Act when intended for export to any foreign country and prepared or packed according to the specifications or directions of the foreign purchaser when no substance is used in the preparation or packing thereof in conflict with the laws of the foreign country to which said article is intended to be shipped; but if said article shall be in fact sold or offered for sale for domestic use or consumption, then this proviso shall not exempt said article from the operation of any of the other provisions of this Act.

SEC. 3.   That the Secretary of the Treasury, the Secretary of Agriculture, and the Secretary of Commerce and Labor shall make uniform rules and regulations for carrying out the provisions of this Act, including the collection and examination of specimens of foods and drugs manufactured or offered for sale in the District of Columbia, or in any

Territory of the United States, or which shall be offered for sale in unbroken packages in any State other than that in which they shall have been respectively manufactured or produced, or which shall be received from any foreign country, or intended for shipment to any foreign country, or which may be submitted for examination by the chief health, food, or drug officer of any State, Territory, or the District of Columbia, or at any domestic or foreign port through which such product is offered for interstate commerce, or for export or import between the United States and any foreign port or country.

SEC. 4. That the examinations of specimens of food and drugs shall be made in the Bureau of Chemistry of the Department of Agriculture, or under the direction and supervision of such Bureau, for the purpose of determining from such examinations whether such articles are adulterated or misbranded within the meaning of this Act; and if it shall appear from any such examination that any of such specimens is adulterated or misbranded within the meaning of this Act, the Secretary of Agriculture shall cause notice thereof to be given to the party from whom such sample was obtained. Any party so notified shall be given an opportunity to be heard, under such rules and regulations as may be prescribed as aforesaid, and if it appears that any of the provisions of this Act have been violated by such party, then the Secretary of Agriculture shall at once certify the facts to the proper United States district attorney, with a copy of the results of the analysis or the examination of such article duly authenticated by the analyst or officer making such examination, under the oath of such officer. After judgment of the court, notice shall be given by publication in such manner as may be prescribed by the rules and regulations aforesaid.

SEC. 5. That it shall be the duty of each district attorney to whom the Secretary of Agriculture shall report any violation of this Act, or, to whom any health or food or drug officer of any State, Territory, or the District of Columbia shall present satisfactory evidence of any such violation, to cause appropriate proceedings to be commenced and prosecuted in the proper courts of the United States, without delay, for the enforcement of the penalties as in such case herein provided.

SEC. 6. That the term "drug," as used in this Act, shall include all medicines and preparations recognized in the United States Pharmacopoeia or National Formulary for internal or external use, and any substance or mixture of substances intended to be used for the cure, mitigation, or prevention of disease of either man or other animals. The term "food," as used herein, shall include all articles used for food, drink, confectionery, or condiment by man or other animals, whether simple, mixed, or compound.

SEC. 7. That for the purposes of this Act an article shall be deemed to be adulterated:
In the case of drugs:
First. If, when a drug is sold under or by a name recognized in the United States Pharmacopoeia or National Formulary, it differs from the standard of strength, quality, or purity, as determined by the test laid down in the United States Pharmacopoeia or National Formulary official at the time of investigation: *Provided*, That no drug defined in the United States Pharmacopoeia or National Formulary shall be deemed to be adulterated under this provision if the standard of strength, quality, or purity be plainly stated upon the bottle, box, or other container thereof although the standard may differ from that determined by the test laid down in the United States Pharmacopoeia or National Formulary.
Second. If its strength or purity fall below the professed standard or quality under which it is sold.
In the case of confectionery:
If it contain terra alba, barytes, talc, chrome yellow, or other mineral substance or poisonous color or flavor, or other ingredient deleterious or detrimental to health, or any

vinous, malt or spirituous liquor or compound or narcotic drug.

In the case of food:

First. If any substance has been mixed or packed with it so as to reduce or lower or injuriously affect its quality or strength.

Second. If any substance has been substituted wholly or in part for the article.

Third. If any valuable constituent of the article has been wholly or in part abstracted.

Fourth. If it be mixed, colored, powdered, coated, or stained in a manner whereby damage or inferiority is concealed.

Fifth. If it contain any added poisonous or other added deleterious ingredient which may render such article injurious to health: *Provided,* That when in the preparation of food products for shipment they are preserved by any external application applied in such manner that the preservative is necessarily removed mechanically, or by maceration in water, or otherwise, and directions for the removal of said preservative shall be printed on the covering of the package, the provisions of this Act shall be construed as applying only when said products are ready for consumption.

Sixth. If it consists in whole or in part of a filthy, decomposed, or putrid animal or vegetable substance, or any portion of an animal unfit for food, whether manufactured or not, or if it is the product of a diseased animal, or one that has died otherwise than by slaughter.

SEC. 8. That the term "misbranded," as used herein, shall apply to all drugs, or articles of food, or articles which enter into the composition of food, the package or label of which shall bear any statement, design, or device regarding such article, or the ingredients or substances contained therein which shall be false or misleading in any particular, and to any food or drug product which is falsely branded as to the State, Territory, or country in which it is manufactured or produced.

That for the purposes of this Act an article shall be deemed to be misbranded:

In the case of drugs:

First. If it be an imitation of or offered for sale under the name of another article.

Second. If the contents of the package as originally put up shall have been removed, in whole or in part, and other contents shall have been placed in such package, or if the package fail to bear a statement on the label of the quantity or proportion of any alcohol, morphine, opium, cocaine, heroin, alpha or beta eucaine, chloroform, cannabis indica, chloral hydrate, or acetanilide, or any derivative or preparation of any such substances contained therein.

In the case of food:

First. If it be an imitation of or offered for sale under the distinctive name of another article.

Second. If it be labeled or branded so as to deceive or mislead the purchaser, or purport to be a foreign product when not so, or if the contents of the package as originally put up shall have been removed in whole or in part and other contents shall have been placed in such package, or if it fail to bear a statement on the label of the quantity or proportion of any alcohol, morphine, opium, cocaine, heroin, alpha or beta eucaine, chloroform, cannabis indica, chloral hydrate, or acetanilide, or any derivative or preparation of any such substances contained therein.

Third. If in package form, and the contents are stated in terms of weight or measure, they are not plainly and correctly stated on the outside of the package.

Fourth. If the package containing it or its label shall bear any statement, design, or device regarding the ingredients or the substances contained therein, which statement, design, or device shall be false or misleading in any particular: *Provided,* That an article of food which does not contain any added poisonous or deleterious ingredients shall not be deemed to be adulterated or misbranded in the following cases:

First. In the case of mixtures or compounds which may be now or from time to time hereafter known as articles of food, under their own distinctive names, and not an imitation of or offered for sale under the distinctive name of another article, if the name be accompanied on the same label or brand with a statement of the place where said article has been manufactured or produced.

Second. In the case of articles labeled, branded, or tagged so as to plainly indicate that they are compounds, imitations, or blends, and the world "compound," "imitation," or "blend," as the case may be, is plainly stated on the package in which it is offered for sale: *Provided,* That the term blend as used herein shall be construed to mean a mixture of like substances, not excluding harmless coloring or flavoring ingredients used for the purpose of coloring and flavoring only: *And provided further,* That nothing in this Act shall be construed as requiring or compelling proprietors or manufacturers of proprietary foods which contain no unwholesome added ingredient to disclose their trade formulas, except in so far as the provisions of this Act may require to secure freedom from adulteration or misbranding.

SEC. 9. That no dealer shall be prosecuted under the provisions of this Act when he can establish a guaranty signed by the wholesaler, jobber, manufacturer, or other party residing in the United States, from whom he purchases such articles, to the effect that the same is not adulterated or misbranded within the meaning of this Act, designating it. Said guaranty, to afford protection, shall contain the name and address of the party or parties making the sale of such articles to such dealer, and in such case said party or parties shall be amenable to the prosecutions, fines, and other penalties which would attach, in due course, to the dealer under the provisions of this Act.

SEC. 10. That any article of food, drug, or liquor that is adulterated or misbranded within the meaning of this Act, and is being transported from one State, Territory, District, or insular possession to another for sale, or, having been transported, remains unloaded, unsold, or in original unbroken packages, or if it be sold or offered for sale in the District of Columbia or the Territories, or insular possessions of the United States, or if it be imported from a foreign country, shall be liable to be proceeded against in any district court of the United States within the district where the same is found, and seized for confiscation by a process of libel for condemnation. And if such article is condemned as being adulterated or misbranded, or of a poisonous or deleterious character, within the meaning of this Act, the same shall be disposed of by destruction or sale, as the said court may direct, and the proceeds thereof, if sold, less the legal costs and charges, shall be paid into the Treasury of the United States, but such goods shall not be sold in any jurisdiction contrary to the provisions of this Act or the laws of that jurisdiction: *Provided, however,* That upon the payment of the costs of such libel proceedings and the execution and delivery of a good and sufficient bond to the effect that such articles shall not be sold or otherwise disposed of contrary to the provisions of this Act, or the laws of any State, Territory, District, or insular possession, the court may by order direct that such articles be delivered to the owner thereof. The proceedings of such libel cases shall conform, as near as may be, to the proceedings in admiralty, except that either party may demand trial by jury of any issue of fact joined in any such case, and all such proceedings shall be at the suit of and in the name of the United States.

SEC. 11. The Secretary of the Treasury shall deliver to the Secretary of Agriculture, upon his request from time to time, samples of foods and drugs which are being imported into the United States or offered for import, giving notice thereof to the owner or consignee, who may appear before the Secretary of Agriculture, and have the right to introduce testimony, and if it appear from the examination of such samples that any article of food or drug offered to be imported into the United States is adulterated or misbranded within the meaning of this Act, or is otherwise dangerous to the health of the people of the United States, or is of a kind forbidden entry into, or forbidden to be sold or restricted in sale in the country in which it is made or from which it is exported, or is otherwise falsely labeled in any respect, the said article shall be refused admission, and the Secretary of the Treasury shall refuse delivery to the consignee and shall cause the destruction of any goods refused delivery which shall not be exported by the consignee within three months from the date of notice of such refusal under such regulations as the Secretary of the Treasury may prescribe: *Provided,* That the Secretary of the Treasury may deliver to the consignee such goods pending examination and decision in the matter on execution of a penal bond for the amount of the full invoice value of such goods, together with the duty thereon, and on refusal to return such goods for any cause to the custody of the Secretary of the Treasury, when demanded, for the purpose of excluding them from the country, or for any other purpose, said consignee shall forfeit the full amount of the bond: *And provided further:* That all charges for storage, cartage, and labor on goods which are refused admission or delivery shall be paid by the owner or consignee, and in default of such payment shall constitute a lien against any future importation made by such owner or consignee.

SEC. 12.   That the term "Territory" as used in this Act shall include the insular possessions of the United States.   The word "person" as used in this Act shall be construed to import both the plural and the singular, as the case demands, and shall include corporations, companies, societies and associations.   When construing and enforcing the provisions of this Act, the act, omission, or failure of any officer, agent, or other person acting for or employed by such corporation, company, society, or association, within the scope of his employment or office, shall in every case be also deemed to be the act, omission, or failure of such corporation, company, society, or association as well as that of the person.

SEC. 13.   That this Act shall be in force and effect from and after the first day of January, nineteen hundred and seven.

Pure Food Act: Expenses
Public Law No. 2, December 19, 1906

CHAP. 2--An Act Making appropriations to supply urgent deficiencies in the appropriations for the fiscal year ending June thirtieth, nineteen hundred and seven, and for other purposes.

Be it enacted by the Senate and House of Representatives of the United States of America in Congress assembled, That the following sums be, and the same are hereby, appropriated, out of any money in the Treasury not otherwise appropriated, to supply urgent deficiencies in the appropriations for the fiscal year nineteen hundred and seven, and for other objects hereinafter stated, namely:

DEPARTMENT OF AGRICULTURE.

To carry out, during the fiscal year nineteen hundred and seven, the provisions of the Act of Congress of June thirtieth, nineteen hundred and six, entitled "An Act for preventing the manufacture, sale, or transportation of adulterated, or misbranded, or poisonous, or deleterious foods, drugs, medicines, and liquors, and for other purposes," to be expended under the direction of the Secretary of Agriculture for all expenses necessary to carry into effect the provisions of the said Act, including rent and the employment of labor in Washington and elsewhere, two hundred and fifty thousand dollars, or so much thereof as may be necessary.

References

Adams, Roger. "Drugs made by man: The duplication of natural products." Pp. 122–141 in J.C. Krantz (ed.), *Fighting Disease with Drugs: The Story of Pharmacy.* Baltimore: National Conference of Pharmaceutical Research, Williams & Wilkins, 1931.

Adams, Samuel Hopkins. "The great American fraud." *Collier's* (Oct. 7, 1905):14–15, 29.

Adams, Samuel Hopkins. "The great American fraud: II — Peruna and the 'bracers.' " *Collier's* (Oct. 28, 1905):17–19.

Adams, Samuel Hopkins. "The great American fraud: III — Liquozone." *Collier's* (Nov. 18, 1905):20–21.

Adams, Samuel Hopkins. "The great American fraud: IV — The subtle poisons." *Collier's* (Dec. 2, 1905):16–18.

Adams, Samuel Hopkins. "The great American fraud: V — Preying on the incurables." *Collier's* (Jan. 13, 1906):18–20.

Adams, Samuel Hopkins. "The great American fraud: VI — The fundamental fakes." *Collier's* (Feb. 17, 1906):22–24, 26, 28.

Adams, Samuel Hopkins. "The great American fraud: VII — Warranted harmless." *Collier's* (April 28, 1906):16–18, 30.

A Golden Day. Pittsburgh, Pa.: The H.J. Heinz Company, 1929.

Alberts, Robert C. *The Good Provider: H.J. Heinz and His 57 Varieties.* Boston: Houghton Mifflin, 1973.

Allen, Robert McD. "Pure food legislation." *Popular Science Monthly* (July, 1906):52–64.

American Medicine. "Lay manufacturers and physicians," (July 6, 1901):2; "The sale of 'patent medicines,' " (Aug. 3, 1901):162; "A medicine selling scheme," (Aug. 10, 1901):203; "The taxation of nostrum advertisements," (Nov. 2, 1901):677; "Success in advertising quackery," (Nov. 23, 1901):804; "Caveat emptor," (Dec. 21, 1901):974; "The market price of patent medicine testimonials," (May 31, 1902):894; "The dating of canned foods," (July 12, 1902):44; "Bad physiology and bad temperance," (July 12, 1902):44; "A scientific test of food preservatives, etc.," (Sept. 20, 1902):441; "Governmental encouragement of intemperance," (Nov. 8, 1902):719; "The sale of poisons and narcotics," (Nov. 8, 1902):719; " 'Drug-habits' and some of their 'cures,' " (Nov. 8, 1902):719–720; "Why do not the temperance people fight the patent medicine enemy?" (Nov. 8, 1902):720; "International standard for patent remedies," (Nov. 8, 1902):721; "The W.C.T.U. and real temperance," (Nov. 29, 1902):840; "The W.C.T.U. and 'patent medicines,' " (Dec. 13, 1902):917; "What the Women's Christian Temperance Union is doing to fight the 'patent medicine enemy,' " (Dec. 13, 1902):925.

Anderson, Oscar E., Jr. *The Health of a Nation: Harvey W. Wiley and the Fight for Pure Food*. Chicago: University of Chicago Press, 1958.

Anderson, Ronald A. *Government and Business*, 4th ed. Cincinnati: South-Western, 1981.

Bailey, Elizabeth E. "Deregulation, competition, and economic survival: What is happening to the airlines?" University of Chicago, Seminar on the Analysis of Security Prices, November 17–18, 1983.

Bailey, Thomas A. "Congressional opposition to pure food legislation." *American Journal of Sociology* 36:1 (July, 1930):52–64.

Banfield, Maud. "The Journal's trained nurse: About patent medicines." *Ladies Home Journal* (May, 1903):26.

Beal, James H. "Introduction." Pp. xiii-xix in J.C. Krantz (ed.), *Fighting Disease with Drugs: The Story of Pharmacy*. Baltimore: National Conference of Pharmaceutical Research, Williams & Wilkins, 1931.

Benson, Lee. *Merchants, Farmers, and Railroads: Railroad Regulation and New York Politics, 1850-1877.* Cambridge: Harvard University Press, 1955.

Bernstein, Marvur H. *Regulating Business by Independent Commission.* Westport, Ct.: Greenwood Press, 1955.

Bevirt, Joseph L. "The cost impact of federal government regulation on the Dow Chemical Company." *Proceedings of the American Statistical Association* (1978):354–358.

Bok, Edward. "The 'patent medicine' curse." *Ladies' Home Journal* (May, 1904):18.

Bok, Edward. "How the private confidences of women are laughed at." *Ladies' Home Journal* (Nov., 1904):18.

Bok, Edward. "Why 'patent medicines' are dangerous." *Ladies' Home Journal* (March, 1905):18.

Bok, Edward. "Pictures that tell their own stories." *Ladies' Home Journal* (Sept., 1905):15.

Bok, Edward. "To you: A personal word." *Ladies' Home Journal* (Feb. 1906):20.

Bowen, Howard. *Social Responsibilities of the Businessman.* New York: Harper & Row, 1955.

Brooks, R.O. "Food science and the pure-food question." *The American Monthly Review of Reviews* (April, 1906):452–457.

Bureau of Chemistry, U.S. Department of Agriculture. "Bulletin 13: Foods and food adulterants." Washington, D.C.: U.S. Government Printing Office, 1887–1902. The parts of Bulletin 13 and their issue dates are as follows: Part 1, "Dairy products," 1887; Part 2, "Spices and condiments," 1887; Part 3, "Fermented alcoholic beverages, malt liquors, wine and cider," 1887; Part 4, "Lard and lard adulterations," 1887; Part 5, "Baking powders," 1889; Part 6, "Sugar, molasses and sirup, confections, honey, and beeswax," 1892; Part 7, "Tea, coffee, and cocoa preparations," 1892; Part 8, "Canned vegetables," 1893; Part 9, "Cereals and cereal products," 1898; Part 10, "Preserved meats," 1902.

Bureau of the Census, U.S. Department of Commerce. "Apparent civilian per capita consumption of foods: 1849 to 1970," Series G-881-915, and "Exports and imports of farm products, 1901 to 1970," Series K-251-255, in *Historical Statistics of the United States.* Washington, D.C.: U.S. Government Printing Office, 1975.

Busey, Samuel C., M.D. "Address: The code of ethics." *Journal of the American Medical Association* 34:4(Feb. 3, 1900):255–259.

Buss, Dale D. "To dairymen's dismay, imitation cheeses win growing market share." *The Wall Street Journal* (July 20, 1981).

Carosso, Vincent P. *The California Wine Industry: A Study of the Formative Years.* Berkeley, Ca.: University of California Press, 1951.

Carson, Gerald H. "Who put the borax in Dr. Wiley's butter?" *American Heritage* 7:5(1956):58–63.

Carson, Gerald. *The Social History of Bourbon.* New York: Dodd, Mead, 1963.

Cavers, David F. "The Food, Drug and Cosmetic Act of 1938: Its legislative history and its substantive provisions." *Law and Contemporary Problems* (Winter, 1939):2–42.

Chandler, Alfred Dupont, Jr. "The beginnings of big business in American industry." Pp. 277–306 in R.L. Andreano (ed.), *New Views on American Economic Development: A Selective Anthology of Recent Work.* Cambridge, Ma.: Schenkman, 1965.

Clark, Victor S. *History of Manufactures in the United States, Vol. 3, 1893–1928.* New York: McGraw-Hill, 1929.

Clough, Shepard B., and Theodore F. Marburg. *The Economic Basis of American Civilization.* New York: Thomas Y. Crowell Co., 1968.

Cobb, Roger W., and Charles D. Elder. *Participation in American Politics: The Dynamics of Agenda-Building.* Baltimore: Johns Hopkins University Press, 1972.

Cochran, Thomas C. *The Pabst Brewing Company: The History of an American Business.* New York: New York University Press, 1948.

Congressional Record, House of Representatives. "Pure-food bill." Floor debate (June 23, 1906): 9048–9077; (June 29, 1906):9655.

Congressional Record, Senate. "Pure-food bill." Floor debate (Jan. 10, 1906):894–898; (Jan. 16, 1906):1129–1135; (Jan. 18, 1906):1173, 1216–1221; (Jan. 23, 1906):1414–1417; (Feb. 19, 1906):2643–2666; (Feb. 20, 1906):2719; (Feb. 21, 1906):2747–2773.

Crampton, Charles A. "Food preservation and food adulteration." *The Independent* (April 10, 1900):942–944.

Darrah, Juanita E. *Modern Baking Powder: An Effective, Healthful*

Leavening Agent. Chicago: Calumet Baking Powder Company and Commonwealth Press, 1927.

Davis, Keith, and William C. Frederick. *Business and Society: Management, Public Policy, Ethics,* 5th ed. New York: McGraw-Hill, 1984.

De Fina, Robert. "Public and private expenditures for federal regulation of business." Working Paper No. 22; Center for the Study of American Business, Washington University, St. Louis, November, 1977.

Dohme, A.R.L. "What drug standardization means for the physician." *Journal of the American Medical Association* (April 13, 1901):1021–1023.

Drucker, Peter. "Converting social problems into business opportunities: The new meaning of corporate social responsibility." *California Management Review* 26:2(Winter, 1984):53–63.

Durkheim, Emile. *The Division of Labor in Society.* Glencoe, Ill.: The Free Press, 1947.

Edelman, Murray. *The Symbolic Uses of Politics.* Urbana: University of Illinois Press, 1964.

Edelman, Murray. *Politics as Symbolic Action: Mass Arousal and Quiescence.* New York: Academic Press, 1971.

Emshoff, James R., and R. Edward Freeman. "Who's butting into your business?" *The Wharton Magazine* (Fall, 1979): 44–59.

Fabricant, Solomon. *The Output of Manufacturing Industries, 1899–1937.* New York: National Bureau of Economic Research, 1940.

Fahey, Liam, and Richard E. Wokutch. "Business and society exchanges: A framework for analysis." *California Management Review* 25:4(Summer, 1983):128–142.

Federal Trade Commission. Finding of Fact: Federal Trade Commission vs. Royal Baking Powder Company, Docket No. 539.

"Food legislation." *The Encyclopedia Americana* (1963):452–453.

Frasure, William Wayne. "Longevity of manufacturing concerns in Allegheny County. 1856–1873 (with special reference to those surviving the 1873–1947 period)." Pittsburgh: Doctoral Dissertation, University of Pittsburgh, 1949.

Freeman, R. Edward. *Strategic Management: A Stakeholder Approach.* Boston: Pitman Publishing, 1984.

Ghent, W.J. "The cure of graft." *The Independent* (May 24, 1906):1189–1195.

"Going public." *Wall Street Journal* (May 30, 1978):22.

Goldberg, Victor J. "Regulation and administered contracts." *Bell Journal of Economics and Management Science* 7:2(Autumn, 1976):426–448.

Goldman, Eric F. *Rendezvous with Destiny: A History of Modern American Reform.* New York: Vintage Books, 1952.

Gould, Lewis L. *Reform and Regulation: American Politics, 1900–1916.* New York: Wiley, 1978.

Grabowski, Henry G. "The determinants of industrial research and development: A study of the chemical, drug, and petroleum industries." *Journal of Political Economy* (March/April, 1968):292–305.

Grabowski, Henry G. *Drug Regulation and Innovation.* Washington, D.C.: American Enterprise Institute, 1976.

Grabowski, Henry G., and John M. Vernon. *The Regulation of Pharmaceuticals: Balancing the Benefits and Risks.* Washington, D.C.: American Enterprise Institute, 1983.

Hacker, Louis M. *The Course of American Economic Growth and Development.* New York: Wiley, 1970.

Hampe, Edward C., and Merle Wittenberg. *The Lifeline of America: Development of the Food Industry.* New York: McGraw-Hill, 1964.

Harbeson, Robert W. "Railroads and regulation, 1877–1916: Conspiracy or public interest?" *Journal of Economic History* 27:2(June, 1967):230–242.

Harris, Richard. *The Real Voice.* New York: Macmillan, 1964.

Hays, Samuel P. *The Response to Industrialism, 1885–1914.* Chicago: University of Chicago Press, 1957.

Hays, Samuel P. "The social analysis of American political history: 1880–1920." *Political Science Quarterly* 70(Sept., 1965):373–394.

Hilton, George W. "The consistency of the Interstate Commerce Act." *Journal of Law and Economics* 9(October, 1966):87–113.

Hinich, Melvin J., and Richard Staelin. *Consumer Protection Legislation and the U.S. Food Industry.* New York: Pergamon Press, 1980.

The Independent. "Editorial: Food adulteration scares," (May 16, 1901):1148–1150; "Editorial: Pure food laws for private purposes," (May 21, 1903):1224; "Editorial: The exaggeration of food adulteration," (Jan. 5, 1905):49–51.

Insight Team, Sunday Times of London. *Suffer the Children: The Story of Thalidomide* New York: Viking Press, 1979.

Josephson, Matthew. *The Robber Barons: The Great American Capitalists, 1861–1901*. New York: Harcourt, Brace, 1935.

Journal of the American Medical Association. "Alcohol as a food," (Feb. 3, 1900):302–303; "Endorsed by physicians," (Feb. 3, 1900):304–305; "Food adulteration," (March 3, 1900):564–565; "What shall we class as ethical preparations?," and "Shall alcohol be recognized as a food?," (March 31, 1900):818–819; "Tablet-triturates and ready-made prescriptions," (April 14, 1900):944–945; "Relations of pharmacy to the medical profession," Part 1 (April 21, 1900):986–988, Part 2 (April 28, 1900):1049–1051, Part 3 (May 5, 1900):1114–1116, Part 4 (May 12, 1900):1178–1179, Part 5 (May 26, 1900):1327–1329, Part 6 (June 2, 1900):1405–1407, Part 7 (July 7, 1900):27–29, Part 8 (July 14, 1900):89–91; "Secret nostrums and the Journal," (June 2, 1900):1420; "Dangers from the use of proprietary remedies," (July 21, 1900):166–167; "Testimonials and patent medicines," (July 13, 1901): 126.

Julien, Claude. *America's Empire*. New York: Pantheon Books, 1971.

Kallett, Arthur. *100,000,000 Guinea Pigs: Dangers in Everyday Foods, Drugs, and Cosmetics*. New York: Vanguard, 1932.

Koch, Charles. "Business can have free enterprise — if it dares." *Business and Society Review* (Winter, 1978–79):54–56.

Kogan, Herman. *The Long White Line: The Story of Abbott Laboratories*. New York: Random House, 1963.

Kolko, Gabriel. *The Triumph of Conservatism: A Reinterpretation of American History, 1900–1916*. Glencoe, Il.: Free Press, 1963.

Kolko, Gabriel. *Railroads and Regulation, 1877–1916*. Princeton, N.J.: Princeton University Press, 1965.

Krantz, John Christian, Jr. (ed.). *Fighting Disease with Drugs: The Story of Pharmacy*. Baltimore: National Conference of Pharmaceutical Research, Williams & Wilkins, 1931.

Ladies' Home Journal. "A diabolical patent medicine story" (April, 1905):20.

Langdon, H.H. "Correspondence: The crusade against borax." *The Nation* (Jan. 5, 1905):9.

Leone, Robert A. "The real costs of regulation." *Harvard Business Review* (Nov./Dec., 1977):57–66.

Lindblom, Charles E. "Why government must cater to business." *Business and Society Review* 27(Fall, 1978):4–6.

Magaziner, Ira C., and Robert B. Reich. *Minding America's Business: The Decline and Rise of the American Economy.* New York: Harcourt Brace Jovanovich, 1982.

Mahon, John F. "Corporate political strategies: An empirical study of chemical firm responses to Superfund legislation." Pp. 143–182 in Lee E. Preston (ed.), *Research in Corporate Social Performance and Policy,* Vol. 5, Greenwich, Ct: JAI Press, 1983.

Mahon, John F., and Edwin A. Murray. "Deregulation and strategic transformation." *Journal of Contemporary Business* 9:2(1980):123–138.

Mahoney, Tom. *The Merchants of Life.* New York: Harper & Brothers, 1959.

Maitland, Ian. "House divided: Business lobbying and the 1981 budget." Pp. 1–26 in Lee E. Preston (ed.), *Research in Corporate Social Performance and Policy,* Vol. 5. Greenwich, Ct: JAI Press, 1983.

Mason, Harry B. "The vital question of pure food." *The American Monthly Review of Reviews* (Jan. 1900):67–70.

Mason, W.E. "Food adulteration." *Current Literature* (June, 1900):306.

McCraw, Thomas K. "Regulation in America: A review article." *Business History Review* 59:2(Summer, 1975):159–183.

McCraw, Thomas K. "Business and government: The origins of the adversary relationship." *California Management Review* 26:2(Winter, 1984):33–52.

McCumber, Porter J. "The alarming adulteration of food and drugs." *The Independent* (Jan. 5, 1905):28–33.

Mendelow, Aubrey L. "Environmental scanning — the impact of the stakeholder concept." Presented at the Second Annual International Conference on Information Systems, Dec. 7–9, 1981, Boston.

Mendelow, Aubrey L. "The stakeholder approach to organizational effectiveness." Presented at the Joint National Meeting of the Canadian Operations Research Society, The Institute of Management Sciences, and the Operations Research Society of America, 1982.

Miles, Robert H. *Coffin Nails and Corporate Strategies.* Englewood Cliffs, N.J.: Prentice-Hall, 1982.

Mills, C. Wright. *The Sociological Imagination*. London: Oxford University Press, 1959.

Mitnick, Barry M. "Deregulation as a process of organizational reduction." *Public Administration Review* (July/August, 1978):350–357.

Mitnick, Barry M. "Myths of creation and fables of administration: Explanation and the strategic use of regulation." *Public Administration Review* (May/June, 1980):275–286.

Mitnick, Barry M. *The Political Economy of Regulation: Creating, Designing, and Removing Regulatory Forms*. New York: Columbia University Press, 1980.

Mitnick, Barry M. "The strategic uses of regulation — and deregulation." *Business Horizons* (March, 1981):71–83.

Moffitt, Donald. "The Idaho potato people tell us this is an extremely serious matter." *The Wall Street Journal* (Feb. 17, 1982):27.

Molander, Earl C. *Responsive Capitalism: Case Studies in Corporate Social Conduct*. New York: McGraw-Hill, 1980.

Moore, Wilbert F. *The Conduct of the Corporation*. New York: Random House, 1962.

Mott, Frank L. *A History of American Magazines, 1850–1865*, Vol. 1. Cambridge, Mass.: Harvard University Press, 1938.

Mowry, George E., and Judson A. Grenier. "Introduction." Pp. 9–46 in David Graham Phillips, *The Treason of the Senate*. Chicago: Quadrangle Books, 1964 (reissue of the 1906 original).

Myers, Gustavus. *History of the Great American Fortunes*. New York: Modern Library. 1936.

The Nation. "Editorial: The poison in our food" 68:1769(May 25, 1899):390–391; "Editorial: Our chaotic food laws" 77:1987(July 30, 1903):88; "Editorial: The pursuit of pure food" 79:2059(Dec. 15, 1904):472–473.

Nelson, Ralph L. *Merger Movements in American Industry, 1895–1956*. Princeton, N.J.: Princeton University Press, 1959.

Nordhauser, Norman. "Origins of federal oil regulation in the 1920s." *Business History Review* 47:1(Spring, 1973):53–71.

"Our Food Products." *Current Literature* 28(June 1900):306–308.

Peltzman, Sam. *Regulation of Pharmaceutical Innovation*. Washington, D.C.: American Enterprise Institute, 1974.

Phillips, David Graham. *The Treason of the Senate*. Chicago: Quadrangle Books, 1964 (reissue of 1906 original).

Posner, Richard A. "Theories of Economic Regulation." *Bell Journal of Economics and Management Science* 5:2(Autumn, 1974):335–358.

Potter, Stephen. *The Magic Number: The Story of '57.* London: Max Reinhardt, 1959.

Pressman, Jeffrey L., and Aaron Wildavsky. *Implementation.* Berkeley: University of California Press, 1972.

Public Law No. 384. "Pure Food Act." *Congressional Record,* 59th Congress, First Session (June 30, 1906):770.

Purcell, Edward A., Jr. "Ideas and interests: Businessmen and the Interstate Commerce Act." *Journal of American History* 54(Dec. 1967):561–578.

Regier, C.C. "The struggle for federal food and drugs legislation." *Law and Contemporary Problems* (Dec. 1933):3–15.

Remington, Joseph P. "The United States Pharmacopoeia of 1900." *Journal of the American Medical Association* (March 16, 1901):729–731.

"Report of the Pure Food Committee of the General Federation of Women's Clubs." *Annals of the American Academy of Political and Social Sciences* 28(Sept. 1906):296–301.

Riepma, S.F. *The Story of Margarine.* Washington, D.C.: National Association of Margarine Manufacturers, Public Affairs Press, 1970.

"Salad bar hazard." *Better Homes and Gardens* (February 1985):74.

Schultze, Charles L. *The Public Use of Private Interest.* Washington, D.C.: The Brookings Institution, 1977.

Seligman, Ben B. *The Potentates: Business and Businessmen in American History.* New York: Dial Press, 1971.

"Senatorial investigation of food adulteration." *Science* 9:232(June 9, 1899):793–795.

Shaw, William Howard. *Value of Commodity Output Since 1869.* New York: National Bureau of Economic Research, 1947.

Sinclair, Upton. *The Jungle.* Cambridge, Mass.: Robert Bentley, 1971. Originally published by Doubleday, Page and Co., 1906.

Stigler, George J. "The theory of economic regulation." *The Bell Journal of Economics and Management Science* 2:1(Spring, 1971):3–21.

Sturdivant, Frederick D. "Executives and activists: A test of stakeholder management." *California Management Review* 22:1(Fall, 1979):53–59.

Sullivan, Mark. "The inside story of a sham." *Ladies' Home Journal* (Jan. 1906):14.

Sullivan, Mark. "Did Mr. Bok tell the truth?" *Ladies' Home Journal* (Jan. 1906):18.

Sullivan, Mark. "How the game of free medical advice is worked, as told in two or three actual instances." *Ladies Home Journal* (Feb. 1906):23.

Sullivan, Mark. *Our Times: The United States, 1900–1925.* Volume II: *America Finding Herself.* New York: Scribner's, 1946.

Taylor, Robert E. "U.S. plans to deregulate alcohol industry, but suppliers and retailers oppose move." *The Wall Street Journal* (Feb. 12, 1982):18.

Temin, Peter. *Taking Your Medicine: Drug Regulation in the United States.* Cambridge, Mass.: Harvard University Press, 1980.

Toennies, Ferdinand. *Community and Society* (also translated as *Fundamental Concepts of Sociology*). New York: American Book, 1940.

Tuchman, Barbara J. *A Distant Mirror: The Calamitous 14th Century.* New York: Ballantine Books, 1978. ·

United States Department of Commerce, Bureau of the Census. *Historical Statistics of the United States, Colonial Times to 1970,* Parts 1 and 2. Washington, D.C.: U.S. Government Printing Office, 1975.

United States Department of Commerce, Bureau of the Census. *Statistical Abstract of the United States, 1981.* Washington, D.C.: U.S. Government Printing Office, 1981.

United States House of Representatives. "The adulteration, misbranding, and imitation of foods, etc., in the District of Columbia, etc." House Report No. 1426, Serial Set 4025, 56th Congress, First Session, May 10, 1900.

United States House of Representatives. "Oleo margarine." House Report No. 1854, Serial Set 4027, 56th Congress, First Session, May 31, 1900.

United States Senate. "Adulteration of food products." Senate Document No. 141, Serial Set 4039, 56th Congress, Second Session, February 6, 1901.

United States Senate. "Memorial of the American Baking Powder Association in the matter of Bill S.3618." Senate Document No. 303, Serial Set 3868, 56th Congress, Second Session, April 20, 1900.

United States Senate. "Investigation of adulteration of food and drink products." Senate Report No. 516, Serial Set 3888, 56th Congress, First Session, Dec. 4, 1899–June 7, 1900.

Veblen, Thorstein. *The Theory of the Leisure Class*. New York: New American Library, 1953.

Vietor, Richard H.K. "Businessmen and the political economy: The railroad rate controversy of 1905." *Journal of American History* 64:1(June, 1977):47–66.

Vogel, David. "The 'new' social regulation in historical and comparative perspective." Pp. 155–186 in Thomas K. McCraw (ed.), *Regulation in Perspective: Historical Essays*. Cambridge, Mass.: Harvard University Press, 1981.

Walton, Clarence C. *Corporate Social Responsibilities*. Belmont, Cal.: Wadsworth, 1967.

Weber, Gustavus Adolphus. *The Food, Drug, and Insecticide Administration: Its History, Activities, and Organization*. Baltimore, Md: Johns Hopkins University Press, 1928.

Weber, Max. *The Protestant Ethic and the Spirit of Capitalism*. New York: Scribner's, 1958.

Weidenbaum, Murray L. *Business, Government and the Public*. Englewood Cliffs, N.J.: Prentice-Hall, 1977.

Weinstein, James. *The Corporate Ideal in the Liberal State: 1900–1918*. Boston: Beacon Press, 1968.

Wiebe, Robert H. *Businessmen and Reform: A Study of the Progressive Movement*. Cambridge, Mass.: Harvard University Press, 1962.

Wilcox, Clair. *Public Policies Toward Business*, 4th ed. Homewood, Ill.: Richard D. Irwin, 1971.

Wiley, Harvey Washington. *The History of a Crime Against the Food Law*. Washington, D.C.: by the author, 1929.

Wiley, Harvey Washington. *An Autobiography*. Indianapolis: Bobbs-Merrill, 1930.

Wilson, Ian H. "Socio-political forecasting: A new dimension to strategic planning." *Michigan Business Review* 26(July, 1974):15–25.

Wilson, James Q. "The politics of regulation." Pp. 135–168 in James W. McKie (ed.), *Social Responsibility and the Business Predic-*

ament. Washington, D.C.: Brookings Institution, 1974.

Witherspoon, J.A. "Oration on medicine: A protest against some of the evils in the profession of medicine." *Journal of the American Medical Association* 34:25(June 23, 1900):1589–1592.

Wood, Donna J. "Business and public policy in the Progressive Era: The Food and Drug Act of 1906." Pp. 213–252 in Lee E. Preston (ed.), *Research in Corporate Social Performance and Policy,* Vol. 6. Greenwich, Ct: JAI Press, 1984.

Wood, Horatio C., Jr. "Facts about nostrums." *Popular Science Monthly* (June 1906):531–536.

Wright, Carroll D. *The Industrial Evolution of the United States.* New York: Russell & Russell, 1895 (reissued 1967).

Young, James Harvey. *The Toadstool Millionaires.* Princeton, N.J.: Princeton University Press, 1961.

Name Index

253

Subject Index